D0166659

Discover
Barcelona

Experience the best of Barcelona

MAR 1 2 2015

This edition written and researched by
Regis St Louis,
Sally Davies, Andy Symington

Discover Barcelona

La Rambla & Barri Gòtic (p47)

Stroll Barcelona's famous boulevard, then lose yourself in the Gothic quarter.

Don't Miss: La Rambla, La Catedral

El Raval (p71)

A once-seedy quarter that's home to cutting-edge museums and bohemian bars and eateries.

La Ribera (p87)

The trendiest part of the Ciutat Vella, with first-rate tapas bars and restaurants, medieval architecture and a stunning Modernista concert hall.

Don't Miss: Museu Picasso

Barceloneta & the Waterfront (p107)

Bountiful plates of seafood, a long waterfront promenade and pretty beaches make for a memorable day on the Mediterranean.

La Sagrada Família & L'Eixample (p125)

Modernisme rules in Barcelona's 19th-century 'extension', crowned by masterpieces by Gaudí and others.

Don't Miss: La Sagrada Família

Montjuïc, Poble Sec & Sant Antoni (p155)

Home to manicured parks and gardens, excellent museums and cinematic views over the city.

Don't Miss: Museu Nacional d'Art de Catalunya

Park Güell, Camp Nou & La Zona Alta (p173)

Take in Gaudí's fairy-tale woodlands, a medieval monastery and lofty Tibidabo – followed by football excitement at hallowed Camp Nou.

Don't Miss: Park Güell

Day Trips (p193)

Frolic on scenic beaches, see Roman ruins and explore monastic shrines just outside Barcelona.

Contents

This Is Barcelona

A city of fabled architecture, inspiring museums and a world-class dining scene, Barcelona has long enchanted visitors. This is a city of narrow medieval lanes, elegant boulevards lined with sculpted buildings and sun-kissed beaches fronting the deep-blue Mediterranean. Galleries showcase Catalonia's renowned artistic heritage, while inventive chefs carve a name for themselves in colour-ful dining rooms all across town. Barcelona is no less enchanting by nightfall, with its vintage 19th-century bars, historic concert halls and buzzing nightclubs and lounges.

Barcelona's architectural heritage dates back more than 700 years. At its

core lies one of Europe's best-preserved medieval centres. Centuries later, that heritage lent Gaudí and his Modernista contemporaries the historical foundation and inspiration for some of their wildest architectural creations. Their adventurousness is in the city's DNA, and local and inter-national architects continue to unleash their fantasies here.

Architecture is just one manifestation of Catalan creativity. The heady mix of Gothic

monuments and contemporary skyscrapers is accompa-nied by a bevy of world-class museums that take you from the wonders of giant Romanesque frescos to the playful-ness of Joan Miró, from pre-Columbian South American gold to early Picasso.

Barcelonins are passionate about their cooking. Thousands of restaurants offer an incred-

ible palette for the palate, from traditional Catalan cuisine to the last word in 21st-century *nueva cocina española*. A plethora of tippling establishments and dance clubs also spreads in a hedonistic arc across the city – drop into century-old taverns or glam it up in bright seaside bars.

Shoppers, meanwhile, may never make it to a museum. L'Eixample is filled with

avenues lined with top boutiques and shopping galler-ies, while the meandering streets of the Ciutat Vella hide all manner of unique finds from vintage boutiques and record stores to wine sellers and handicraft shops.

> **This is a city of medieval lanes, elegant boulevards and sun-kissed beaches**

Park Güell (p178)

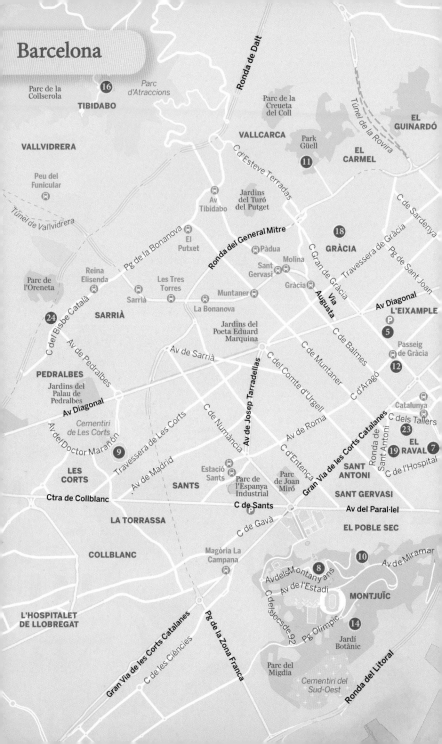

25
Top Experiences

25 Barcelona's Top Experiences

La Sagrada Família (p130)

One of Barcelona's icons, this Modernista masterpiece remains a work in progress more than 80 years after the death of its creator, Antoni Gaudí. Fanciful, profound, inspired by nature and barely restrained by a Gothic style, Barcelona's quirky temple soars skyward with an almost playful majesty. Stepping through its sculpted portals is like walking into a fairy tale, where a forest of columns branch toward the ceiling and light shimmers through brilliant stained-glass windows. Rich with beautifully wrought detail and packed with symbols, the basilica invites hours of contemplation. Below: Nativity Facade

2

La Rambla (p52)

Sure, it's the most touristy spot in town. But you can't come to Barcelona and not stroll down this famous pedestrian boulevard. It's sensory overload – with a parade of people amid open-air cafes, fragrant flower stands, a much-overlooked mosaic by Joan Miró and rather surreal human sculptures. Key venues line both sides of the street, including the elegant Gran Teatre del Liceu (p59), the sprawling La Boqueria market (p82) and some intriguing galleries.

Museu Picasso (p92)

For a portrait of the artist as a young man, head to Museu Picasso, which showcases perhaps the world's best collection of the master's early work. Picasso lived in Barcelona between the ages of 15 and 23, and elements of the city undoubtedly influenced his work, from the dramatic, wide-eyed frescoes hanging in the Museu Nacional d'Art de Catalunya to the imaginative *trencadís*-style mosaics (pre-Cubist some say) of Gaudí. The museum's setting inside five contiguous medieval mansions adds to the appeal.

The Best...
Museums

MUSEU PICASSO
Finest collection of early works by the legendary Spanish artist. (p92)

MACBA
Proof of Barcelona's place at the cutting edge of contemporary art. (p81)

FUNDACIÓ JOAN MIRÓ
World's biggest Miró collection, in the city of his birth. (p167)

MUSEU NACIONAL D'ART DE CATALUNYA
Fine Romanesque art collection in a striking neo-baroque palace. (p160)

The Best...
Modernista Buildings

LA PEDRERA
Gaudí's famous head-turner on busy Passeig de Gràcia. (p142)

LA SAGRADA FAMÍLIA
Spain's most popular visitor attraction – come and see why. (p130)

PALAU DE LA MÚSICA CATALANA
Music turned to glass and stone. (p102)

CASA AMATLLER
The dark horse of the Manzana de la Discordia. (p134)

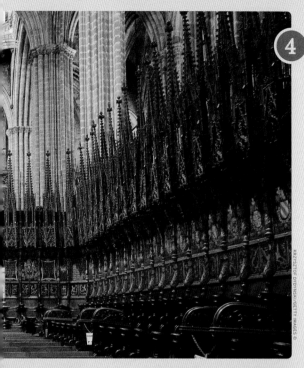

La Catedral
(p56)

La Catedral is a master-piece of Catalan Gothic architecture. Wander wide-eyed through the shadow-filled interior, which houses a dozen well-concealed chapels, an eerie crypt and a curious garden-style cloister, which has 13 geese connected to Barcelona's co-patron saint, Santa Eulàlia. Outside, there's always entertainment afoot, from *sardana* dancing on weekends to periodic processions and open-air markets.

La Pedrera
(p142)

Astonishing architec-tural works dominate L'Eixample. The area was a blank canvas for some of Spain's finest build-ings, erected in the late 19th and early 20th cen-turies. At La Pedrera, one of Gaudí's masterpieces, you'll find classic Gaudí flourishes: an undulating cliff-like facade, wildly sculpted wrought-iron balconies and cavern-like parabolic arches. On the rooftop, you can clamber beneath much-photographed chimney pots.

Basílica de Santa Maria del Mar (p99)

Blessed in 1384, this church is one of the purest examples of Catalan Gothic. It was raised in record time with stones painstakingly carried down from a quarry on Montjuïc. The church is remarkable for its architectural harmony and managed to survive a devastating 11-day fire during the civil war. Live concerts and recitals are regularly staged inside.

Mercat de la Boqueria (p82)

This temple of temptation is one of Europe's greatest permanent produce fairs. Restaurant chefs, homemakers, office workers and tourists all stroll amid the seemingly endless bounty of glistening fruits and vegetables, gleaming fish counters, dangling rolls of smoked meats, pyramids of pungent cheeses, barrels full of olives and marinated peppers, and chocolate truffles and other sweets. A handful of popular tapas bars serve up delectable morsels so you won't have to walk away empty-handed. There's always a line, but it's well worth the wait.

Museu Nacional d'Art de Catalunya (p160)

For many Catalans, Catalonia is not Spain but a country unto its own, with a unique and proud history. The Museu Nacional d'Art de Catalunya proves the point with an impressive collection that delves into the riches of 1000 years of Catalan art. Its Romanesque frescoes, altarpieces and wood carvings, rescued from decaying churches in the Pyrenees, are truly staggering, and its collection of Gothic art gives a meaningful context to the Barri Gòtic down below.

The Best... Live-Music Spots

HARLEM JAZZ CLUB
Small, atmospheric spot in the old town that's great for hearing jazz. (p67)

JAZZ SÍ CLUB
Intimate space in El Raval that hosts a wide range of sounds, including flamenco. (p84)

SALA APOLO
Photogenic old theatre where you can catch top local bands followed by DJs working a dance-loving crowd. (p171)

SIDECAR FACTORY CLUB
Young festive space on Plaça Reial that's known for its indie bands. (p68)

Camp Nou (p182)

For the sports-minded, little can compete with the spectacle of a match at FC Barcelona's massive football stadium. With a loyal fan base and an incredibly gifted team led by the likes of Lionel Messi, Camp Nou always hosts a good show. If you can't make it to a game, it's still worth visiting. The 'Camp Nou Experience' is an interactive museum and stadium tour that takes you through the locker rooms and out onto the pitch, which is hallowed ground for many Catalans.

The Best...
Parks

PARC DE LA CIUTADELLA
The manicured gardens make a serene setting for a stroll after spending time in the narrow lanes of the Ciutat Vella. (p94)

PARC DE COLLSEROLA
Find your own private space in Europe's largest municipal park. (p190)

MONTJUÏC
Parks and gardens lace the lofty vantage points around the Castell de Montjuïc. (p162)

PARK GÜELL
Here Gaudí turned his hand to landscape gardening. (p178)

Fundació Joan Miró (p167)

Picasso was born in Málaga and Dalí hailed from Figueres, but surrealist visionary Joan Miró was a true dyed-in-the-wool *barcelonin*. As a revolutionary artist and proud Catalan, Miró etched much of his legacy on the city. The Fundació Joan Miró contains a treasure trove of his work, spanning a long and illustrious career. Footage of Miró and works by contemporaries provide an illuminating portrait of the artist and his time. The spacious gallery is set up on Montjuïc and is flanked by sculpture gardens. Left: *Pair of lovers playing with almond blossoms. Model for the sculptural group at La Défense, Paris, 1975*

Park Güell (p178)

What a fine flop! It started in 1900 as the dream of *barcelonin* magnate Eusebi Güell for an English-style 'garden city' for the hoity-toity and ended up as an enchanting park for the hoi polloi designed by Antoni Gaudí. Dazzling mosaic-covered architectural details, curious Hansel-and-Gretel-style gatehouses and a museum packed with Gaudían intrigue are but a few of the park's many captivating features. Don't miss the splendid view over the city from the cross-topped Turó del Calvari.

MATT MUNRO/LONELY PLANET ©

Casa Batlló (p147)

Yet another of Gaudí's stunning Modernista masterpieces, Casa Batlló has astonishing details. Shimmering blue and green tiles, wildly sculpted balconies and bone-like columns adorn its facade, while the roof undulates like the scaly backside of a dragon. Inside, you glimpse the artistry that left nothing to chance, from curved and sinuous walls to corridors o parabolic arches: the brilliant use of organic forms coupled with the masterful use of natural light and colour showcase Gaudí's talents at the height of his career.

Barceloneta Seafood (p115)

Barcelona's gastronomy com bines regional cuisine, experi-mentalism and artistic chefs. Then there's the simplicity of Barceloneta restaurateurs who have been knocking out uncomplicated but mag-nificent seafood dishes for decades. Whether stopping by a tapas bar for anchovies and *cava* (Catalan sparkling wine) or lingering over an afternoon long lunch of *suquet* (hearty seafood stew), seafood lovers should not miss Barceloneta.
Left: Potato and cuttlefish stew

FELIPE RODRIGUEZ FERNANDEZ/GETTY IMAGES ©

Gardens of Montjuïc (p168)

After a few days of exploring the narrow lanes of the Ciutat Vella and the bustling boulevards of L'Eixample, you may need a dose of greenery and fresh air. The scenic gardens of Montjuïc provide the perfect antidote. Here you'll find elegant manicured gardens complete with fountains and sculptures, all overlooking the restless city below. You can take scenic walks through greenery, enjoy a picnic with views of the sea or delve into the world of Mediterranean flora at the Jardí Botànic (p163).

14

The Best...
Catalan Restaurants

PLA
Mouth-watering dishes that blend Catalan traditions with accents from the east. (p65)

CINC SENTITS
A showcase of world-class cooking featuring top-notch, regionally sourced ingredients.(p148)

CAFÈ DE L'ACADÈMIA
High-quality dishes served in a medieval-style dining room. (p64)

The Best...
Gothic
Masterpieces

LA CATEDRAL
Contemplate the incredible decoration on the northwest facade. (p56)

BASÍLICA DE SANTA MARIA DEL MAR
Catalan Gothic at its purest and most refined. (p99)

MUSEU MARÍTIM
One of the largest shipyards in Europe once lay under these Gothic arches. (p114)

ESGLÉSIA DE SANTS JUST I PASTOR
Often neglected example of early Gothic ecclesial architecture. (p59)

15

Museu Marítim (p114)

Venice had its Arsenal and Barcelona the Reials Drassanes (Royal Shipyards), from which Don Juan of Austria's flagship galley was launched to lead a joint Spanish-Venetian fleet into the momentous Battle of Lepanto against the Turks in 1571. This site has been a museum since the 1940s and it's a fascinating place to explore Barcelona's fabled maritime legacy. On display are vessels and models of all types, representing all epochs from sail to steam. The highlight is a life-sized replica of Don Juan of Austria's 16th-century galley.

Left: A tall ship in Port Vell; Above: A display at Museu Marítim

JEAN-PIERRE LESCOURRET/GETTY IMAGES ©

RICHARD CUMMINS/GETTY IMAGES ©

Tibidabo (p190)

Come to the mountain. The trip to the city's highest peak, Tibidabo, is an old-style family outing that bursts with nostalgia. The panoramic vistas are themselves a fine reward and the amusement-park rides are a retro trip to fun parks of yore. One of the best parts of the experience is getting here. Take the old tram that rattles along an avenue lined with Modernista mansions. Then hop aboard the funicular for a speedy ascent to the top, where the city and sea spread out beneath you.

Right: Stone apostle at Temple del Sagrat Cor (p190)

Palau de la Música Catalana (p102)

Finished in 1908, this Modernista gem remains an enchanting concert setting. The exterior and foyer are opulent, but these are nothing compared with the auditorium interior. Stepping inside is like entering a nether world, with a magnificent stained glass skylight and wonderfully baroque carvings adorning the stage area.

GETTY IMAGES ©

Cafe Culture in Gràcia (p183)

Gràcia bubbles with life. A separate town until 1897, its warren of straight, narrow streets and lanes opens here and there onto a series of peaceful squares, each dotted with outdoor cafes and bars that invite lingering. Spend the day window-shopping amid cutting-edge boutiques, vintage shops and tiny food markets, then join the bohemian crowd over a few drinks. For something a little different, pull up a chair at picture-perfect La Nena (p183), famed for its thick rich hot chocolate.

The Best...
Viewpoints

TIBIDABO
Ascend the old church or the new tower for an even better view. (p190)

CASTELL DE MONTJUÏC
Strategically positioned fortress atop Montjuïc. (p162)

LA SAGRADA FAMÍLIA
Head up one of the towers for bird's-eye rooftop views. (p130)

TRANSBORDADOR AERI
Grab the cable car over the restored Port Vell up to Montjuïc. (p113)

The Best...
Bars with a View

MIRABLAU
Gaze out over the city from this magnificently sited bar in Tibidabo. (p189)

OPIUM MAR
Popular bar and dance club perched right on the waterfront. (p121)

LA CASETA DEL MIGDIA
Gaze through the pine-scented surrounds to the sea beyond at this well-hidden Montjuïc gem. (p170)

Bars in El Raval (p82)

Of the old town districts, El Raval is the grittiest and perhaps the sexiest. Long a slum and still edgy in parts, it's perfect for a night of bar-crawling. You'll find a mix of 19th-century drinking dens, jazz-filled absinthe bars, tiny DJ clubs and sleek modern lounges all vying for attention. The crowd is no less diverse: bohemians and out-of-towners, tourists and touts, artists and characters who might have just stepped from the pages of a Carlos Ruiz Zafón novel are all here.

19

LOOK DIE BILDAGENTUR DER FOTOGRAFEN GMBH/ALAMY ©

㉒ Shopping in El Born (p104)

As reinventions go, once-decrepit El Born is up there with New York's Lower East Side as the ghetto that made good. A time traveller from the 1980s would have trouble recognising this compact pocket of La Ribera, with its cool bars, trendy restaurants and – for haters of modern chain stores – chic indie boutiques. In addition to hip little fashion boutiques, these medieval lanes hide a fascinating collection of shops, from magic stores and early-20th-century coffee roasters to hallowed wine cellars and picture-perfect patisseries.

DIEGO LEZAMA/GETTY IMAGES ©

Municipal Beaches (p114)

An afterthought until the 1980s, Barcelona's beaches are now one of the city's finest selling points, luring recreationists who might otherwise have headed to the Costa del Sol or the Caribbean. In summer, crowds pack the sands for volleyball, football and frolicking in the waves. *Chiringuitos* (beachside bars) dole out snacks and cold drinks. During the weekends, the beach party continues long after sundown. Right: Barceloneta beach

Gran Teatre del Liceu (p59)

The splendiferous Gran Teatre del Liceu has been knocking out Puccini arias longer than – well – Puccini. If you can't make a performance, come for a guided tour, where you'll get a peak at the grand foyer, with its thick pillars and sumptuous chandeliers. Head up the marble staircase to the fresco-filled Saló dels Miralls (Hall of Mirrors) before heading into the gilded theatre itself.

MACBA (p81)

The ever-expanding contemporary art collection of the dynamic MACBA starts in the Gothic chapel of the Convent dels Àngels and continues into the main gleaming-white building across the square. It's a stage for the best of Catalan, Spanish and international contemporary art. Artists frequently on show include Antoni Tàpies, Miquel Barceló and a host of very-now installation artists. The ultramodern white building, designed by North American architect Richard Meier, was one of a series of art and cultural institutions that helped revitalise El Raval. Below: MACBA; architect: Richard Meier & Partners

23

The Best...
Outdoor Activities

BEACH PROMENADE
Go for a walk, a bike ride or a jog along the lovely 4.6km-long seaside path. (p110)

BOAT TOURS
Go for a sunset cruise for a picturesque view of Barcelona and its sparkling waterfront. (p239)

PICNIC ON MONTJUÏC
Buy goodies at Mercat de la Boqueria, then head up to Montjuïc for a picnic with fantastic views. (p158)

PARC D'ATRACCIONS
Take in hyperfast rides, 3D movies and 19th-century puppetry at this lively amusement park. (p190)

CONTEMPORANI DE BARCELONA

Museu-Monestir de Pedralbes (p181)

Founded in the 14th century by Queen Elisenda of Montcada for the Poor Clares, this peaceful convent feels like a world removed from the bustling 21st-century city beyond its gates. The three-storey cloister is an exquisite work of Catalan Gothic architecture. Enter the medieval building and wander through the refectory, kitchens, stables and reconstructed infirmary – all of which give a good idea of convent life. Upstairs a small collection of monastery art completes the time travel with works by Catalan artists dating back to the Middle Ages.

The Best...
Unexpected Spots

OBSERVATORI FABRA
Book for dinner under the stars in this Zona Alta observatory. (p181)

COSMOCAIXA
Wander through a lush piece of the Amazon rainforest without leaving Europe. (p180)

EL REY DE LA MAGIA
Century-old magic shop that materialises like something out of a Carlos Ruiz Zafón novel. (p98)

SINAGOGA MAJOR
Inspect Roman and medieval ruins in a synagogue reclaimed for posterity in the 1990s. (p62)

25

Waterfront Promenade (p110)

Barcelona's waterfront is abuzz these days, not just with fit *barcelonins* jogging, biking, blading and bantering their way through the afternoon siesta, but also with a slew of ambitious architectural projects that have created a new Barcelona apart from the Gothic city of lore. The best way to see it all is to hire a bike and cycle up the promenade (safely separated from traffic) from Barceloneta to the supermodern El Fòrum. You'll pass lovely beaches, intriguing public art and plenty of places to refuel along the way.

Top Days in Barcelona

Barcelona's Must-Sees

On your first day in Barcelona, visit the city's major highlights: stroll La Rambla, explore the atmospheric lanes of the Barri Gòtic and linger over the stunning artistry of La Sagrada Família. History, great architecture and a celebrated food market are all part of this sensory-rich experience.

❶ La Rambla (p52)

Start with La Rambla. Don't miss the human statues, the Miró mosaic and key buildings facing La Rambla, including the 18th-century Palau de la Virreina.

LA RAMBLA ➲ MERCAT DE LA BOQUERIA

🚶 Find the market's entrance on La Rambla's west side.

❷ Mercat de la Boqueria (p82)

Packed with culinary riches, this staggering market is a stomping ground for chefs and conjurers, weekend cooks and hungry-looking tourists. Don't leave without having a few snacks – perhaps from one of the delectable tapas bars in the back.

MERCAT DE LA BOQUERIA ➲ BARRI GÒTIC

🚶 Turn left into Plaça Reial after passing Carrer de Ferran.

❸ Barri Gòtic (p47)

Delve into Barcelona's old city. Cross the picturesque Plaça Reial (p59) before wandering narrow lanes that date back to at least the Middle Ages. Make your way to the magnificent Catedral (p56), then visit the Temple Romà d'August (p63).

Plaça Reial (p59)
MATT MUNRO/LONELY PLANET ©

BARRI GÒTIC ➲ CAFÈ DE L'ACADÈMIA

🚶 Cross Plaça de Sant Jaume, walk along Carrer de la Ciutat and take the first left.

❹ Lunch at Cafè de l'Acadèmia (p64)

Arrive early to get a seat at this small atmospheric restaurant serving excellent Catalan cuisine. The multicourse lunch special is fantastic value.

CAFÈ DE L'ACADÈMIA ➲ LA SAGRADA FAMÍLIA

Ⓜ Take Line 4 north from Jaume I; transfer at Passeig de Gràcia for Line 2 to Sagrada Família.

❺ La Sagrada Família (p130)

Roll the drums, turn on the stage lights and get ready for Spain's most visited church. This one-of-a-kind religious monument is as unique as the Giza pyramids and as beautiful as the Taj Mahal.

LA SAGRADA FAMÍLIA ➲ ALKIMIA

🚶 Walk three blocks northwest along Carrer de Sardenya and turn left on Carrer de l'Indústria.

❻ Dinner at Alkimia (p143)

This much-lauded restaurant serves daring new Catalan cuisine. For pure decadence, opt for the 10-course tasting menu, a great chance to experience culinary magic.

DAY
2

Mar i Muntanya (Sea & Mountain)

This itinerary takes you along the promenade that skirts the Mediterranean, then into the old fishing quarter of Barceloneta before whisking you up to the heights of Montjuïc for fine views, fragrant gardens and superb art galleries – including two of the city's top museums.

① Barceloneta Beach (p111)

Start the morning with a stroll along the waterfront. Take in the scenic views of this once derelict area that experienced a dramatic makeover in days before and after the 1992 Olympics. Look north and you'll see Frank Gehry's shimmering fish sculpture while to the south rises the spinnaker-shaped tower of the W Hotel.

BARCELONETA BEACH ◆ CAN MAJÓ

🏃 Look for the restaurant just north of the rectangular beach sculpture, off Carrer del Almirall Aixada.

② Lunch at Can Majó (p118)

You'll find more great views at Can Majó, a seafood restaurant with outdoor tables overlooking the seaside. Top picks include the hearty seafood platter or the *suquets* (fish stews).

CAN MAJÓ ◆ TRANSBORDADOR AERI

🏃 Walk to the southern end of Barceloneta and you'll see the cable car to your right.

③ Transbordador Aeri (p113)

After lunch take a scenic ride on this aerial cable car, which affords fantastic views over the port and the dazzling city beyond. At the top, you'll arrive in Montjuïc, a mini-mountain that's packed with gardens – both sculptural and floral – as well as a few first-rate museums.

TRANSBORDADOR AERI ◆ FUNDACIÓ JOAN MIRÓ

🚡 Take the cable car up to Montjuïc, disembark and follow the main road 800m west.

④ Fundació Joan Miró (p167)

You can see a full range of works by one of the giants of the art world at this impressive museum. Paintings, sculptures and drawings by the prolific Catalan artist are displayed along with photos and other media elucidating Miró's life. Outside is a peaceful sculpture garden with views over Poble Sec.

FUNDACIÓ JOAN MIRÓ ◆ MUSEU NACIONAL D'ART DE CATALUNYA

🏃 Follow the path through the sculpture gardens east, take the steps up to main road and continue east to the museum.

⑤ Museu Nacional d'Art de Catalunya (p160)

Not to be missed is the incomparable collection of artwork inside the enormous Museu Nacional d'Art de Catalunya. The highlight is the impressive Romanesque collection – rescued from 900-year-old churches in the Pyrenees. Other halls showcase Catalan works from the Middle Ages up to the early 20th century. Out front, you can take in the view over Placa d'Espanya to the distant peak of Tibidabo.

MUSEU NACIONAL D'ART DE CATALUNYA ◆ TICKETS

🏃 Descend toward Plaça d'Espanya. Turn right before the fountain, left on Carrer de Leida and right on Avinguda del Paral·lel.

⑥ Dinner at Tickets (p170)

You'll need to book weeks in advance, but it's well worth the effort if you can score a table at Tickets, one of Barcelona's hottest attractions. The celebrated restaurant is run by the Adrià brothers and showcases an ever-changing menu of molecular gastronomy.

View from Montjuïc (p158)
JOHN HARPER/GETTY IMAGES©

La Ribera

Like Barri Gòtic to the west, La Ribera has narrow cobblestone streets and medieval architecture galore. Yet it is also home to high-end shopping, a brilliant Modernista concert hall and a treasure trove of artwork by Picasso. Great restaurants and a fanciful green space complete the Ribera ramble.

DAY
3

1 Museu Picasso (p92)

Picasso spent his formative years in Barcelona and you can see his early masterpieces inside this inspiring museum, which contains some 3500 of his works. Perhaps just as impressive as the artwork are the galleries themselves – set in a series of merchant houses dating back to the 1300s.

MUSEU PICASSO ◯ EL BORN

🏃 Stroll southeast along Carrer de Montcada.

2 Window Shopping in El Born (p104)

The medieval streets of El Born hide an abundance of shopping intrigue, from magic shops to purveyors of fine wines to eye-catching fashion boutiques. For unique, beautifully made men's and women's designs, stop in the Barcelona-born boutique Custo Barcelona (p105).

EL BORN ◯ CAL PEP

🏃 Walk across Plaça de les Olles.

3 Lunch at Cal Pep (p102)

For lunch, belly up to the bar at this bustling eatery for some of the city's tastiest seafood tapas. Set on a tiny square, this place is always packed – and for good reason.

CAL PEP ◯ BASÍLICA DE SANTA MARIA DEL MAR

🏃 Walk northwest along Carrer de la Vidrieria and turn left on Carrer de Santa Maria.

4 Basílica de Santa Maria del Mar (p99)

A few blocks away is one of the most captivating Catalan Gothic churches. The 14th-century masterpiece soars above the medina-like streets surrounding it.

BASÍLICA DE SANTA MARIA DEL MAR ◯ PARC DE LA CIUTADELLA

🏃 Walk northeast on Carrer de Santa Maria and continue around the former Mercat del Born site to the park.

5 Parc de la Ciutadella (p94)

Just east of the compact streets of La Ribera, you can catch your breath strolling through the open green expanse of this manicured park. You'll find sculptures, a small zoo, the Parlament de Catalunya and the centerpiece, a dramatic if utterly artificial waterfall dating from the 19th century.

PARC DE LA CIUTADELLA ◯ PALAU DE LA MÚSICA CATALANA

🏃 Take Carrer de la Princesa back into El Born and turn right after 200m, making your way northwest.

6 Palau de la Música Catalana (p102)

Designed by Domènech i Montaner in the early 1900s, this intimate concert hall is a Modernista masterpiece, with luminescent stained glass and elaborately sculpted details throughout. Come for a concert, but it's also worth returning by day for a guided tour.

PALAU DE LA MÚSICA CATALANA ◯ EL XAMPANYET

🏃 Make your way back (southeast) to Carrer de Montcada.

7 El Xampanyet (p104)

Just up the road, El Xampanyet is a festive spot to end the night. You can sample mouth-watering bites and let your cup runneth over with ever-flowing *cava* (Catalan sparkling wine). It's usually crowded but friendly, just politely elbow your way in for a bit of refreshment.

Palau de la Música Catalana (p102)
MATT MUNRO/LONELY PLANET ©

Art & Architecture

This tour takes you up to the enchanting (if accidental) park Gaudí designed overlooking the city, down the elegant architectural showpiece avenue of Passeig de Gràcia and into El Raval. There you'll find the city's top contemporary art museum anchoring Barcelona's most bohemian neighbourhood.

1 Park Güell (p178)

Go early to Park Güell to beat the crowds and see the early morning rays over Barcelona and the Mediterranean beyond. Stroll the expanse of the park, taking in the mosaic-covered Banc de Trencadís, the fairy-tale-like columns of Sala Hipóstila and the view from Turó del Calvari. End your visit at Casa Museu Gaudí, where you can learn more about the life and work of the great Catalan architect.

PARK GÜELL ⟶ GRÀCIA
M Take Line 3 from Vallcarca to Fontana.

2 Gràcia (p180)

The village-like feel of Gràcia makes for some great exploring. Stroll from plaza to plaza along the narrow shop-lined lanes, stopping perhaps at open-air cafes along the way. Good streets for browsing include Carre de Verdi, Travessera de Gràcia and Carrer de Torrijos.

GRÀCIA ⟶ LES TRES A LA CUINA
🏃 Walk northeast along Carrer d'Astúries, right on Carrer de Verdi and left on Carrer de Sant Lluis.

3 Lunch at Les Tres a la Cuina (p183)

Join the neighbourhood crowd at this imaginative eatery that serves market fresh fare at unbeatable prices. There are only a handful of tables, so try to get there early.

LES TRES A LA CUINA ⟶ PASSEIG DE GRÀCIA
🏃 Walk southeast toward Carrer Gran de Gràcia and turn left. This turns into Passeig de Gràcia after 400m.

4 Passeig de Gràcia (p125)

After taking in the bohemian charm of Gràcia, head over to L'Eixample for a look at high-concept architecture. Passeig de Gràcia is a busy but elegant boulevard lined with exquisite Modernista buildings and fanciful boutiques. You'll see incredible designs by Gaudí, including La Pedrera (p142) and Casa Batlló (p147).

PASSEIG DE GRÀCIA ⟶ MACBA
🏃 Continue along Passeig de Gràcia, cross Plaça de Catalunya to La Rambla and turn right on Carrer del Bonsuccés.

5 MACBA (p81)

A few streets away from Placa d'Espanya you'll reach the city's top contemporary art gallery, MACBA. It houses an excellent range of Catalan and European works from WWII to the present.

MACBA ⟶ EL RAVAL
🏃 Walk along Carrer dels Àngels and turn left on Carrer del Carme.

6 El Raval (p71)

Spend the early evening strolling the lively multicultural street scene of El Raval. You'll find record stores, vintage fashion and curious bric-a-brac throughout. Stop for a breather in the pretty courtyard of the Antic Hospital de la Santa Creu (p76) and check out another Gaudí masterpiece at the Palau Güell.

EL RAVAL ⟶ KOY SHUNKA
M Take Line 3 from Paral·lel to Catalunya.

7 Dinner at Koy Shunka (p65)

Top off your night with a multicourse feast at Koy Shunka. This zenlike den of haute cuisine features a magnificent marriage of Catalan creativity with Japanese tradition. The 11-course *menú degustacion gastronómico* is worth the hefty price tag.

La Pedrera (p142)

Month by Month

January

 Festes dels Tres Tombs

In addition to live music and *gegants* (papier maché giants worn over the shoulders of processionists), the festival dedicated to Sant Antoni features a parade of horse-drawn carts in L'Eixample near the Mercat de Sant Antoni every 17 January.

February

Carnestoltes/ Carnaval

Celebrated in February or March, this festival involves several days of fancy-dress parades and merrymaking, ending on the Tuesday before Ash Wednesday. The *Gran Rua* (Grand Parade) takes place on the Saturday evening from 5.30pm.

Festes de Santa Eulàlia

Around 12 February, this big winter fest celebrates Barcelona's first patron saint with a week of cultural events, from concerts to *castellers* (human-castle builders). See www.bcn. cat/santaeulalia for more details.

April

 Día de Sant Jordi

Catalonia honours its patron saint, Sant Jordi (St George), on 23 April. Traditionally, men give women a rose and women give men a book – and La Rambla and Plaça de Sant Jaume fill with book and flower stalls.

May

L'Ou Com Balla

On Corpus Christi (late May or June), L'Ou com Balla ('the Dancing Egg') bobs on top of flower-festooned fountains around the city. There's also an early evening procession from La Catedral and *sardanes* (traditional Catalan folk dance) is danced out front at 7pm.

⭐ **Primavera Sound**

For three days in late May (or early June), the Auditori Fòrum and other locations around town welcome a host of international DJs and musicians (www. primaverasound.com).

Ciutat Flamenco

One of the best occasions to see great flamenco in Barcelona, this concentrated festival (ciutatflamenco. com) is held over four days in May at the Teatre Mercat de les Flors on Montjuïc.

June

 Festival Piknic Electronik

Every Sunday from June through September, you

can enjoy a day of electronic music at an outdoor space on Montjuïc (piknice-lectronik.es/en). It attracts a mix of young families and party people.

 July

Festival del Grec

The major cultural event of the year is a month-long fest with dozens of theatre, dance and music performances held around town including at the Teatre Grec amphitheatre on Montjuïc, from which the festival takes its name (grec.bcn.cat).

La Revetlla de Sant Joan/Verbenas de Sant Joan

The night before the Día de San Juan Bautista (Feast of St John the Baptist, 24 June), the people of Barcelona hit the streets or hold parties at home to celebrate the Revetlla de Sant Joan (St John's Night), which involves drinking, dancing, bonfires and fireworks.

Pride Barcelona

The Barcelona Gay Pride festival is a week of celebrations held towards the end of June with a crammed program of culture and concerts,

along with the traditional Gay Pride march on the last Sunday of the month (www.pridebarcelona.org, in Catalan).

Sónar

Usually in mid-June, Sónar is Barcelona's celebration of electronic music and is said to be Europe's biggest such event. Locations change each year (www.sonar.es).

 August

Festa Major de Gràcia

Locals compete for the most elaborately decorated street in this popular week-long Gràcia festival held around 15 August. People pour in to listen to bands in the streets and squares, fuel on snacks and drink at countless street stands (www.festamajordegracia.org, in Catalan).

Festa Major de Sants

The district of Sants launches its own week-long version of decorated mayhem, held around 24 August, hot on the heels of Gràcia's (www.festamajordesants.net, in Catalan).

Festes de Sant Roc

For four days in mid-August, Plaça Nova in the Barri Gòtic becomes the

scene of parades, the *correfoc* (fire race), a market, traditional music and magic shows for kids.

 September

Festes de la Mercè

Barcelona's co-patron saint is celebrated with fervour in this massive four-day fest. The city stages sporting events, free concerts, human towers of *castellers*, folksy *sardanes*, parades of *gegants* and *capgrossos* (big heads), and a huge *correfoc* (www.bcn.cat/merce).

Festa Major de la Barceloneta

Barcelona's other big September celebration honours the local patron saint, Sant Miquel, on 29 September. It lasts about a week and involves plenty of dancing and drinking, especially on the beach.

 December

Fira de Santa Llúcia

Held from early December to Christmas, this holiday market has hundreds of stalls selling all manner of Christmas decorations and gifts – including the infamous Catalan Nativity scene character, the *caganer* (the crapper).

What's New

For this new edition of Discover Barcelona, our authors hunted down the fresh, the transformed, the hot and the happening. Here are a few of our favourites. For up-to-the-minute recommendations, see lonelyplanet.com/Barcelona.

1 ADRIÀ'S GROWING EMPIRE
Celebrated chef Albert Adrià shows no sign of stopping. Bodega 1900, one of his latest restaurant openings, is dedicated to vermouth and high-end pub fare. Plans for other Adrià eateries are in the works. (p169)

2 DRINK OF THE GODS
The fashionable drink of choice these days is *vermut* (vermouth), which has enjoyed a strong resurgence in recent years. The anytime drink goes nicely with tapas, particularly at Bormuth. (p100)

3 BELLESGUARD
Another of Gaudí's masterpieces has opened to the public. The neo-Gothic Bellesguard has an imposing stone facade modelled on the medieval castle that once stood here. Join a guided tour to see inside. (p181)

4 MUSEU DEL DISSENY DE BARCELONA
Barcelona's newest museum was on the verge of opening at press time. Dedicated to design of all sorts, exhibitions cover decorative arts, ceramics, fashion and graphic arts. (p114)

5 BORN CENTRE CULTURAL
Recently unveiled excavations, set inside a 19th-century marketplace, reveal what life was like for Catalans in the early 1700s in the Born Centre Cultural. Also on-site is an excellent new restaurant. (p98)

6 CAUSE FOR CELEBRATION
Several new festivals have entered Barcelona's summer calendar in the last few years. Festival Piknic Electronik (http://piknicelectronik.es/en/) features DJs and outdoor revelry on Montjuïc; Festival Pedralbes (http://www.festivalpedralbes.com/en/) stages big-name concerts in a lush garden.

7 DINE IN SOMEONE'S HOME
Locals with culinary skills are hosting dinner parties on EatWith (www.eatwith.com). For about what you'd pay in a restaurant, you can get in on the action. There are hundreds of offerings in Barcelona.

8 BOUTIQUE BEAUTIES
A crop of new boutique hotels has opened in the Barri Gòtic, bringing an ample dose of style. The beautifully designed DO has lovely rooms, a roof terrace and superb restaurants. (p230)

9 MODERNISTA MAKEOVER
At long last, several architectural treasures in L'Eixample have opened their doors to visitors: Casa Amatller (p134) and Casa Lleó Morera (p135), essential parts of the so-called Manzana de la Discordia.

10 REINVENTING CATALAN CUISINE
Culinary maestro Carles Abellan (of Tapas 24 and Comerç 24 fame) continues to add to the city's roster of great restaurants with Suculent, one of his latest successes. (p80)

Get Inspired

 ## Books

° **The Shadow of the Wind** (Carlos Ruiz Zafón) With a twisting, turning plot that uses post-civil-war Barcelona as a vivid backdrop, Catalan-native Zafón's classic has sold millions.

° **Homage to Catalonia** (George Orwell) Orwell's reportorial masterpiece provides on-the-spot commentary of the city at one of the most volatile moments of its history during the civil war.

° **Cathedral of the Sea** (Ildefonso Falcones) Historical novel set in 14th-century Barcelona against a backdrop of the Inquisition and grand building projects.

° **Homage to Barcelona** (Colm Tóibín) Easy-to-digest travelogue of the city by the noted Irish writer.

 ## Films

° **All About My Mother** One of Pedro Almodovar's best-loved films is full of plot twists and dark humour, complete with trans-sexual prostitutes and doe-eyed nuns.

° **L'Auberge Espagnole** This warmly told coming-of-age story shows what happens when a mishmash of young students are thrown together on their first trip abroad.

° **Barcelona** Whit Stillman's smart romantic comedy revolves around two American expats living in Barcelona in the late '80s.

 ## Music

° **Joan Manuel Serrat** Acclaimed troubadour and king of Nueva Canción; key track 'Mediterráneo'.

° **The Pinker Tones** Electronic alternative pop band; key track 'The Whistling Song'.

° **Sopa de Cabra** Ultimate Catalan rock band; key track 'Si et Quedes amb Mi'.

° **Luís Llach** Hugely popular Catalan-language singer; key song 'Laura'.

Websites

° **Barcelona Tourism** (www.barcelonaturisme. cat) Official Barcelona tourism website.

° **Lonely Planet** (www. lonelyplanet.com) Up-to-date hotel and restaurant reviews plus Thorn Tree travel forum.

° **Spotted by Locals** (www.spottedbylocals. com) Insider tips.

Short on time?

This list will give you an instant insight into the city.

Read Celebrated art critic Robert Hughes pays homage to a city of burgeoning creativity in *Barcelona, the Great Enchantress*.

Watch In *Vicky Cristina Barcelona*, Woody Allen gives Barcelona the Manhattan treatment, showing its mix of beauty and neuroticism.

Listen Ojo de Brujo's *Bari* is a superb album that blends flamenco with hip-hop and electronica.

Log on Barcelona's Mini-guide (www.miniguide.es) keeps you up to date on art, fashion, food and nightlife.

Casa Batlló (p147)
MATT MUNRO/LONELY PLANET ©

Need to Know

Currency
The euro (€)

Language
Spanish and Catalan

Visas
Not required for US, Canadian, Australian, New Zealand or South African visitors for up to 90 days. European Union nationals can stay indefinitely.

Money
ATMs widely available. Credit cards accepted in most hotels, shops and restaurants.

Mobile Phones
Local SIM cards can be used in unlocked European and Australian phones. Set other phones to roaming.

Time
Central European Time (GMT/UTC plus one hour)

Wi-Fi
Common in midrange and top-end hotels, hostels and some cafes. Usually free.

Tipping
A service charge is usually included. For top-end places, it's common to tip 5% to 10%.

For more information, see Survival Guide (p227).

When to Go

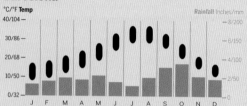

Barcelona

Spring (Mar–May) For pleasant weather, come in late spring.

Summer (Jun–Aug) Peak tourist season. Crowds swarm the city.

Autumn (Sep–Nov) Warm but pleasant. October can be rainy.

Winter (Dec–Feb) Expect cool blue skies. Snowfall is very rare.

Advance Planning

Two months before Reserve a table at a top restaurant. Buy tickets for important football matches.

One month before Check out reviews for theatre and live music and book tickets.

One week before Browse the latest nightlife listings, art exhibitions and other events to attend while in town. Reserve spa visits and organised tours.

A few days before Check the forecast on weather.com.

Your Daily Budget

Budget Under €50
- Dorm beds €15–€25
- Set lunches from €9
- Free museums on Sundays

Midrange €50–€200
- Standard double room €80–€120
- Two-course dinner with wine for two €50
- Walking and guided tours €15–€25

Top end Over €200
- Boutique and luxury hotels €200 and up
- Multi-course meal at top restaurants €80 per person
- Tickets to a top show at the Gran Teatre del Liceu around €50.

Arriving in Barcelona

El Prat Airport Frequent Aerobuses make the 35-minute run into town (€5.90) from 6am to 1am. Taxis cost around €25. Train operator Renfe runs the R2 Nord line every half hour from the airport to Estació Sants and Passeig de Gràcia in central Barcelona.

Estació Sants Long-distance trains arrive at this big station near the centre of town, which is linked by metro to other parts of the city.

Estació del Nord The long-haul bus station is in L'Eixample, about 1.5km northeast of Plaça de Catalunya. It's a short walk from several metro stations.

Getting Around

Metro The most convenient way to get around. Runs from 5am to midnight Sunday through Thursday, to 2am on Friday and 24 hours on Saturday. Targeta T-10 (10-ride passes) are the best value at €10.30. Otherwise it's €2.15 per ride.

Bus The hop-on, hop-off Bus Turístic, which leaves from Plaça de Catalunya, is handy for those wanting to see the city's highlights in one or two days.

Walking For exploring the old town, all you need is a good pair of walking shoes.

Sleeping

Barcelona has a wide range of sleeping options from inexpensive hostels hidden in the old quarter to luxury hotels overlooking the waterfront. Good-value options include small-scale B&B-style apartment rentals scattered around the city. Typical prices for a midrange room for two people runs from about €80 to €120 per night. Wherever you stay it's wise to book well ahead. If you plan to travel around holidays like Christmas, New Year's Eve, Easter or in the summer months, reserve a room three or four months ahead of time.

Useful Websites

○ **Airbnb** (www.airbnb.com) The global network has hundreds of rooms and apartments listed for Barcelona.

○ **Oh-Barcelona** (www.oh-barcelona.com) Selection of good-value hotels, hostels and apartment rentals.

○ **Barcelona 30** (www.barcelona30.com) Economical options for staying on a budget.

What to Bring

○ **An appetite** For fresh seafood and excellent, inexpensive wines.

○ **A Catalan phrasebook** Although you can get by in Spanish (and English in many parts), Catalans really appreciate the effort.

○ **A rain jacket** Especially if you come in early spring or in the autumn.

Be Forewarned

○ **Theft** Petty theft is a major problem in the city centre. Be vigilant and keep a close guard on your possessions.

○ **Areas to avoid** El Raval can be a little sketchy late at night, particularly in the southern part of the neighbourhood.

○ **Seasons** Locals disappear in August, with many restaurants and shops closing or keeping limited hours.

○ **Crowds** Prepare for heavy tourist crowds if coming in the summer.

La Rambla & Barri Gòtic

Packed with historic treasures, Barri Gòtic is one of Europe's most atmospheric neighbourhoods. Its tangle of narrow lanes and tranquil plazas lie amid Roman ruins, medieval churches and converted palaces, with history lurking around every lamplit corner. There are swarms of tourists afoot, but these cobbled streets have plenty of local character, with first-rate restaurants, creative boutiques and a vibrant nightlife keeping things buzzing until early in the morning.

Nearby, La Rambla is Spain's most talked-about boulevard. It certainly packs a lot of colour into a short walk, with flower stands, historic buildings, a sensory-rich food market, overpriced beers, tourist tat and a ceaselessly changing parade of people from all corners of the globe. Once a river and sewage ditch on the edge of medieval Barcelona, it still marks the southwest flank of Barri Gòtic.

Plaça Reial (p59)
ALAN COPSON/GETTY IMAGES ©

La Rambla & Barri Gòtic Highlights

Strolling La Rambla (p52)

Snaking its way through the Ciutat Vella (Old City), this 1.2km-long boulevard is always awhirl with activity. There are street performers, food and drink stalls, souvenir stands and a pastiche of architectural intrigue lining both sides of the street. Come early in the morning to see La Rambla at its most serene, then return later to the people-packed lane to see it in all its carnivalesque glory.

Plaça Reial (p59)

The elegant Plaça Reial is wonderfully recuperative after wandering the narrow, sometimes pungent streets of the medieval quarter. Outdoor cafes and restaurants set beneath the arcades draw a relaxed crowd by day, while after dark the plaza becomes a hidden hive of candlelit restaurants and clubs. A trickling fountain, intricately sculpted street lamps and occasional live music sets the scene. Left: A restaurant on Plaça Reial

JEAN-PIERRE LESCOURRET/GETTY IMAGES ©

Museu d'Història de Barcelona (p67) ③

More subterranean adventure trail than stash of dusty exhibits, this museum takes visitors on a journey through time. Start in ancient Roman-era Barcino and stroll past fragments of old bathhouses, laundrettes and wine-making stores. Then wind your way up through the centuries past Visigothic ruins, picture-perfect Gothic halls and medieval chapels.

④ La Catedral (p52)

La Catedral de la Santa Creu i Santa Eulàlia is a riot of Gothic and gargoyles, high altars and murky crypts, Catalan legends and 13 resident geese. Like many Spanish churches, it is a hybrid – the 14th-century shell has been overlaid by a 19th-century neo-Gothic facade – a factor that makes it all the more fascinating and enigmatic. Don't miss the superb view from the rooftop.

⑤ Plaça de Sant Jaume (p58)

The epicentre of the historic Ciutat Vella (Old City), this plaza has been an essential part of civic life since the Romans erected a forum here 2000 years ago. Several key government buildings continue to play a role in political affairs, including the Ajuntament, where Barcelona's first ruling council met in the 1300s. By day, the buzzing plaza brings a mishmash of bureaucrats, protestors and gawking tourists.

Above: Plaça de Sant Jaume during Festes de la Mercè (p41)

La Rambla & Barri Gòtic Walk

This scenic walk through the Barri Gòtic will take you back in time to the early days of Roman-era Barcino. Amid architectural treasures from previous centuries, you'll pass picturesque plazas, looming Gothic churches and an atmospheric quarter once the centre of a medieval Jewish quarter.

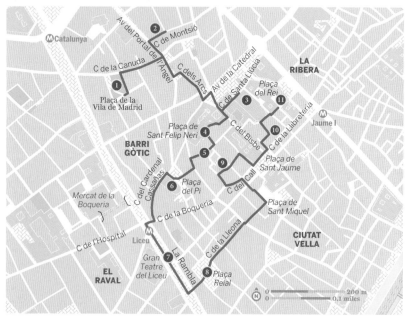

WALK FACTS

- **Start** Plaça de la Vila de Madrid
- **Finish** Plaça del Rei
- **Distance** 2.5km
- **Duration** Two hours

1 Roman Tombs

On Plaça de la Vila de Madrid is a sunken garden with various **Roman tombs** (p63). It was customary to line highways leading out of cities with tombs and it's believed this road connected Roman Barcino with the Via Augusta, which linked Rome and Cádiz.

2 Els Quatre Gats

Next, head over to one of the few Modernista buildings in the Gothic quarter. **'The Four Cats'** restaurant, started life as Casa Martí. From 1897 to 1903, it was the hang-out for bohemians and artists, including Picasso.

3 La Catedral

Head down Avinguda del Portal de l'Angel to the magnificent **cathedral** (p56). Before entering, look at the three Picasso friezes on the building facing the square.

4 Plaça de Sant Felip Neri

Enter the former gates of the ancient fortified city and turn right into **Plaça de Sant**

Felip Neri. Note the shrapnel-scarred walls of the **old church**, damaged by pro-Francist bombers in 1939.

5 Santa Eulàlia

Head out of the square and turn right. On this narrow lane, you'll spot a small **statue** of Santa Eulàlia (p205), one of Barcelona's patron saints. Martyred by the Romans, she allegedly suffered numerous tortures.

6 Església de Santa Maria del Pi

Make your way west to the 14th-century **Església de Santa Maria del Pi**, which is famed for its magnificent rose window. Adjacent to the church are two serene plazas with outdoor cafes.

7 La Rambla

Continue west to Barcelona's liveliest **pedestrian boulevard** (p52). As you stroll south, you'll walk over a striking **Miró mural** and pass the **Gran Teatre del Liceu**, Barcelona's famous opera house.

8 Plaça Reial

Turn down the small lane leading into **Plaça Reial** (p59), one of Barcelona's prettiest squares.

9 Sinagoga Major

Make your way northeast to the atmospheric, narrow lanes of **El Call**, the medieval Jewish quarter until a bloody pogrom of 1391. The **Sinagoga Major** (p62), one of Europe's oldest, was discovered in 1996.

10 Roman Temple

Head across Plaça de Sant Jaume and turn left after Carrer del Bisbe. You'll soon pass the remnants of a **Roman temple**, with four columns hidden in a small courtyard.

11 Plaça del Rei

The final stop is **Plaça del Rei**. The former palace houses a superb **history museum** (p67), which boasts significant Roman ruins underground.

The Best…

PLACES TO EAT

Pla Mouth-watering fusion fare in a spacious medieval dining room. (p65)

La Vinateria del Call An atmospheric setting for classic Catalan and Mediterranean cooking in El Call. (p64)

Koy Shunka Artfully prepared Japanese cuisine is worth a splurge – especially the 11-course *menú degustación*. (p65)

PLACES TO DRINK

Salterio Medieval ambience in the picturesque quarter of El Call. (p66)

Ocaña Stylish spot with a beautifully designed interior. (p65)

Sor Rita Join festive crowds in a whimsical Almodovar-esque world. (p65)

HISTORICAL TREASURES

Temple Romà d'August Mighty columns from a once great empire. (p63)

Via Sepulcral Romana Funereal markers from the days of Barcino. (p63)

Sinagoga Major A tiny medieval synagogue attests to a once flourishing Jewish quarter. (p62)

Don't Miss
La Rambla

Flanked by narrow traffic lanes and plane trees, the middle of La Rambla is a broad pedestrian boulevard, crowded every day until the wee hours with a cross-section of *barcelonins* (people of Barcelona) and out-of-towners. Dotted with cafes, restaurants, kiosks and news stands, and enlivened by buskers, pavement artists, mimes and living statues, La Rambla rarely allows a dull moment.

Map p58

Ⓜ Catalunya, Liceu or Drassanes

La Rambla de Canaletes

The stretch from Plaça de Catalunya is La Rambla de Canaletes, named after an inconspicuous turn-of-the-20th-century **drinking fountain**, the water of which supposedly emerges from what were once known as the springs of Canaletes. It used to be said that *barcelonins* 'drank the waters of Les Canaletes'. People claim that anyone who drinks from the fountain will return to Barcelona. Delirious football fans gather here to celebrate whenever the main home side, FC Barcelona, wins a cup or the league premiership.

Església de Betlem

Just north of Carrer del Carme, this **church** was constructed in baroque style for the Jesuits in the late 17th and early 18th centuries to replace an earlier church destroyed by fire in 1671. Fire was a bit of a theme for this site: the church was once considered the most splendid of Barcelona's few baroque offerings, but leftist arsonists torched it in 1936.

Palau Moia

Looming over the eastern side of La Rambla, **Palau Moja** is a rare pure neo-classical pile. Its classical lines are best appreciated from across La Rambla.

Palau de la Virreina

The **Palau de la Virreina** is a grand 18th-century rococo mansion (with some neoclassical elements) that houses a municipal arts-and-entertainment information and ticket office. It's home to the **Centre de la Imatge**, which has rotating photography exhibits. Admission prices and opening hours vary.

Mosaïc de Miró

At Plaça de la Boqueria, where four side streets meet just north of Liceu Metro station, you can walk all over a Miró – the colourful **mosaic** in the pavement. Miró chose this site since it's near the house where he was born on the Passatge del Crèdit. The mosaic's bold colors and vivid swirling forms are instantly recognisable to Miró fans, but plenty of tourists stroll right over it without noticing it. Near the bottom of the work, there's one tile signed by the artist.

La Rambla dels Caputxins

Named after a now nonexistent monastery, this stretch of La Rambla runs from Plaça de la Boqueria to Carrer dels Escudellers. The latter street is named after the potters' guild, founded in the 13th century, whose members lived and worked here. On the western side of La Rambla is the Gran Teatre del Liceu (p59). Further south on the eastern side is the entrance to the palm-shaded Plaça Reial (p59).

La Rambla de Santa Mònica

The final stretch of La Rambla widens out to approach the Mirador de Colom overlooking Port Vell. La Rambla here is named after the Convent de Santa Mònica, which once stood on the western flank of the street. It has since been converted into an art gallery and cultural centre, the **Centre d'Art Santa Mònica**, which tends to exhibit modern, multimedia installations; admission is free.

Civil War & La Rambla

La Rambla saw action during the Civil War. In *Homage to Catalonia*, George Orwell described the avenue gripped by revolutionary fervour in the early days of the war: 'Down the Ramblas, the wide central artery of the town where crowds of people streamed constantly to and fro, the loudspeakers were bellowing revolutionary songs all day and far into the night... There was much in it that I did not understand, in some ways I did not even like it, but I recognised it immediately as a state of affairs worth fighting for.' Later in the war, heavy street fighting took place on La Rambla. Anarchists shot at Orwell as he dashed across La Rambla.

La Rambla

A TIMELINE

Look beyond the human statues and tourist-swarmed restaurants, and you'll find a fascinating piece of Barcelona history dating back many centuries.

13th century A serpentine seasonal stream (called ramla in Arabic) runs outside the city walls. As Barcelona grows, the stream will eventually become an open sewer until it's later paved over.

1500–1800 During this early period, La Rambla was dotted with convents and monasteries, including the baroque **Església de Betlem ❶**, completed in the early 1700s.

1835 The city erupts in anticlericism, with riots and the burning of convents. Along La Rambla, many religious assets are destroyed or seized by the state. This paves the way for new developments, including the **Mercat de la Boqueria ❷** in 1840, **Gran Teatre del Liceu ❸** in 1847 and **Plaça Reial ❹** in 1848.

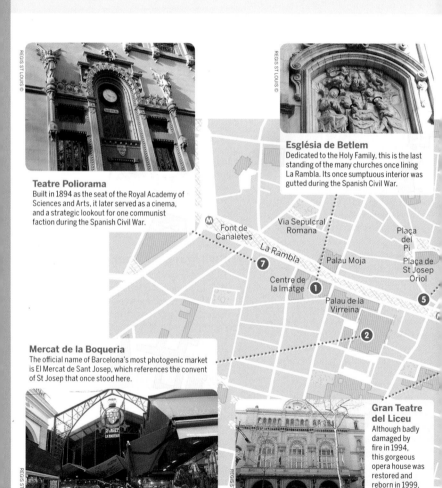

Teatre Poliorama
Built in 1894 as the seat of the Royal Academy of Sciences and Arts, it later served as a cinema, and a strategic lookout for one communist faction during the Spanish Civil War.

Església de Betlem
Dedicated to the Holy Family, this is the last standing of the many churches once lining La Rambla. Its once sumptuous interior was gutted during the Spanish Civil War.

Font de Canaletes

Via Sepulcral Romana

Plaça del Pi

La Rambla

Palau Moja

Plaça de St Josep Oriol

Centre de la Imatge ❶

Palau de la Virreina

❷

Mercat de la Boqueria
The official name of Barcelona's most photogenic market is El Mercat de Sant Josep, which references the convent of St Josep that once stood here.

Gran Teatre del Liceu
Although badly damaged by fire in 1994, this gorgeous opera house was restored and reborn in 1999, and remains one of Europe's finest theatres.

1883 Architect Josep Vilaseca refurbishes the **Casa Bruno Cuadros** ❺. As Modernisme is sweeping across the city, Vilaseca creates an eclectic work using stained glass, wrought iron, Egyptian imagery and Japanese prints.

1888 Barcelona hosts the Universal Exhibition. The city sees massive urban renewal projects, with the first electric lights coming to La Rambla, and the building of the **Mirador de Colom** ❻.

1936–39 La Rambla becomes the site of bloody street fighting during the Spanish Civil War. British journalist and author George Orwell, who spends three days holed up in the **Teatre Poliorama** ❼ during street battles, later describes the tumultuous days in his excellent book, *Homage to Catalonia*.

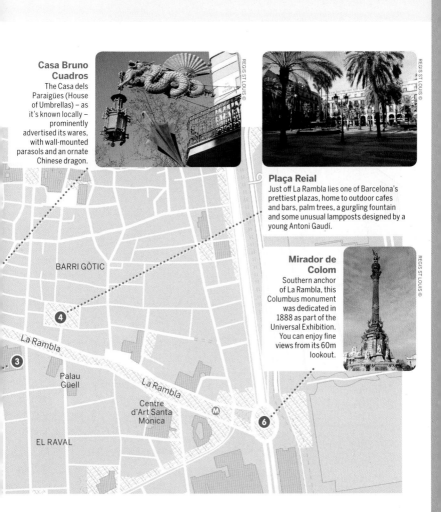

Casa Bruno Cuadros
The Casa dels Paraigües (House of Umbrellas) – as it's known locally – prominently advertised its wares, with wall-mounted parasols and an ornate Chinese dragon.

Plaça Reial
Just off La Rambla lies one of Barcelona's prettiest plazas, home to outdoor cafes and bars, palm trees, a gurgling fountain and some unusual lampposts designed by a young Antoni Gaudí.

Mirador de Colom
Southern anchor of La Rambla, this Columbus monument was dedicated in 1888 as part of the Universal Exhibition. You can enjoy fine views from its 60m lookout.

BARRI GÒTIC

La Rambla

Palau Güell

La Rambla

Centre d'Art Santa Monica

EL RAVAL

REGIS ST LOUIS ©

Don't Miss
La Catedral

Approached from the broad Avinguda de la Catedral, Barcelona's central place of worship presents a magnificent image. The richly decorated main (northwest) facade, laced with gargoyles and the stone intricacies you would expect of northern European Gothic, sets it quite apart from other churches in Barcelona. The facade was actually added in 1870, but it's based on a 1408 design. The rest of the building was built between 1298 and 1460. The other facades are sparse in decoration, and the octagonal, flat-roofed towers are a clear reminder that, even here, Catalan Gothic architectural principles prevailed.

Map p58

☎ 93 342 82 60

www.website.es/catedralbcn

Plaça de la Seu

admission free, special visit €5, coro admission €2.20

🕑 8am-12.45pm & 5.15-8pm Mon-Sat, special visit 1-5pm Mon-Sat, 2-5pm Sun & holidays

Ⓜ Jaume I

Choir

In the middle of the central nave is the late-14th-century exquisitely sculpted timber *coro* (choir stalls). The coats of arms on the stalls belong to members of the Barcelona chapter of the Order of the Golden Fleece. Emperor Carlos V presided over the order's meeting here in 1519. Take the time to look at the craft up close; the Virgin Mary and Child depicted on the pulpit are especially fine.

Rooftop View

With so much going on inside, it's easy to forget the outside. The roof is notable not just for the views of medieval Barcelona but also for the opportunity to evaluate the cathedral's huge footprint from above. Access to the higher echelons is gained via a lift from the Capella de les Animes del Purgatori near the northeast transept.

Geese

The Tower of London has ravens; Barcelona's Catedral has geese. The 13 birds in the leafy *claustre* (cloister) supposedly represent the age of Santa Eulàlia at the time of her martyrdom and have, generation after generation, been squawking here since medieval days. They make fine watchdogs!

Crypt

Here lies the hallowed tomb of Santa Eulàlia, one of Barcelona's two patron saints, more affectionately known as Laia. The reliefs on the alabaster sarcophagus, executed by Pisan artisans, recount some of her tortures and, along the top strip, the removal of her body to its present resting place.

Baptismal Font

Columbus purportedly kidnapped two dozen North American Indians from the Caribbean island of Hispaniola after his first voyage and brought them back to Spain. Only six survived the journey and, according to legend, they were bathed in holy water at this font just left from the main entrance.

Don't Miss List

BY GORKA REGIDOR, TOUR GUIDE AND FOUNDER OF RUNNER BEAN TOURS

1 CRYPT OF SANTA EULÀLIA

References to the patron saint of Barcelona can be found all over the cathedral but nowhere is as striking as in the crypt. In the centre, an Italian 15th-century alabaster sarcophagus stands where Eulàlia's remains supposedly still lie within. The crypt only opens on the 12 February, Saint Eulàlia's Day, but you can take a peek from the outside. Add 50 céntimos to the box and let the place light up for a more intimate experience.

2 MAIN NAVE

If there is an organ concert going on, sit down on one of the benches, relax and wonder at the magnificence of this Catalan Gothic stone masterpiece. The sounds from the 15th-century carved wooden organ surround the whole place with magic and mystery.

3 THE CHOIR

In 1519, the Order of the Golden Fleece, the elite of Europe's nobility, were invited to Barcelona by the king of Spain, Charles I. A visit to the cloister is a voyage to old times with the coat of arms of each participant painted on the back of the chairs. Try to find Henry VIII of England!

4 CLOISTER

A glimpse of Paradise where the 13 geese in honour of Saint Eulàlia live. While you walk around, look at the tombstones on the floor and find shoes, scissors and the different symbols of the medieval guilds (including shoemakers, tailors and carpenters). If you are here during the Corpus Christi, marvel at one of Barcelona's most popular traditions: the *Ou Com Balla* (dancing egg).

5 EXTERIOR GARGOYLES

There are 160 different gargoyles in the cathedral. Always a good excuse to lift your eyes to the sky and discover not only the obvious dragons and mythological beasts, but also elephants, unicorns and medieval warriors. Great for the young ones and for the not so young.

Discover La Rambla & Barri Gòtic

Getting There & Away

○ **Metro** Key stops near or on La Rambla include Catalunya, Liceu and Drassanes. For Barri Gòtic's east side, Jaume I and Urquinaona are handiest.

○ **Bus** Airport and night buses arrive and depart from Plaça Catalunya.

○ **Taxi** Easiest to catch on La Rambla or Plaça Catalunya.

Carrer dels Comtes, Barri Gòtic
MANFRED GOTTSCHALK/GETTY IMAGES ©

◉ Sights

La Rambla Street
See p52

La Catedral Church
See p56

Palau del Lloctinent Historic Site
Map p60 (Carrer dels Comtes; ☺10am-7pm; Ⓜ Jaume I) **FREE** This converted 16th-century palace has a peaceful courtyard worth wandering through. Look upwards from the main staircase to admire the extraordinary timber *artesonado*, a sculpted ceiling made to seem like the upturned hull of a boat. Temporary exhibitions, usually related in some way to the archives, are often held here.

Museu Diocesà Museum
Map p60 (Casa de la Pia Almoina; ☎93 315 22 13; www.arqbcn.org; Avinguda de la Catedral 4; adult/child €6/3; ☺10am-2pm & 5-8pm Tue-Sat, 11am-2pm Sun; Ⓜ Jaume I) Next to the cathedral, the Diocesan Museum has a handful of exhibits on Gaudí (including a fascinating documentary on his life and philosophy) on the upper floors. There's also a sparse collection of medieval and romanesque religious art usually supplemented by a temporary exhibition or two.

Plaça de Sant Jaume Square
Map p60 (Ⓜ Liceu or Jaume I) In the 2000 or so years since the Romans settled here, the area around this square (often remodelled), which started life as the forum, has been the focus of Barcelona's civic life. This is still the central staging area for Barcelona's traditonal festivals. Facing each other across the square are the Palau de la Generalitat

(seat of Catalonia's regional government) on the north side and the *ajuntament* (town hall) to the south.

Ajuntament
Architecture

Map p60 (📞93 402 70 00; www.bcn.cat; Plaça de Sant Jaume; 🕐10.30am-1.30pm Sun; Ⓜ Liceu, Jaume I) **FREE** The *ajuntament,* also known as the Casa de la Ciutat, has been the seat of power for centuries. The Consell de Cent (the city's ruling council) first sat here in the 14th century, but the building has lamentably undergone many changes since the days of Barcelona's Gothic-era splendour.

Palau de la Generalitat
Palace

Map p60 (www.president.cat; Plaça de Sant Jaume; Ⓜ Liceu, Jaume I) Founded in the early 15th century, the Palau de la Generalitat is open on limited occasions only (the second and fourth weekends of the month, plus open-door days). The most impressive of the ceremonial halls is the **Saló de Sant Jordi**, named after St George, the region's patron saint. To see inside, book on the website.

Museu d'Idees i Invents de Barcelona
Museum

Map p60 (Museum of Ideas and Inventions; 📞93 332 79 30; www.mibamuseum.com; Carrer de la Ciutat 7; adult/child €8/6; 🕐10am-2pm & 4-7pm Tue-Fri, 10am-8pm Sat, to 2pm Sun; Ⓜ Jaume I) This small museum's collection makes for an amusing browse over an hour or so. You'll find both brilliant and bizarre inventions: square egg makers, absorbent pillows for flatulent folks, a chair for inserting suppositories, as well as more useful devices like the Lifestraw (filters contaminants from any drinking source) and gas glasses (adaptive eyecare for any prescription).

Plaça de Sant Josep Oriol
Square

Map p60 (Ⓜ Liceu) This small plaza flanking the majestic Església de Santa Maria del Pi is one of the prettiest in the Barri Gòtic. Its bars and cafes attract buskers and artists and make it a lively place to hang out. It is surrounded by quaint streets, many dotted with appealing cafes and shops.

Plaça Reial
Square

Map p60 (Ⓜ Liceu) One of the most photogenic squares in Barcelona, the Plaça Reial is a delightful retreat from the traffic and pedestrian mobs on the nearby Rambla. Numerous eateries, bars and nightspots lie beneath the arcades of 19th-century neoclassical buildings, with a buzz of activity at all hours.

Gran Teatre del Liceu
Architecture

Map p60 (📞93 485 99 14; www.liceubarcelona. com; La Rambla dels Caputxins 51-59; tour 20/80min €5.50/11.50; 🕐guided tour 10am, short tour 11.30am, noon, 12.30pm & 1pm; Ⓜ Liceu) If you can't catch a night at the opera, you can still have a look around one of Europe's greatest opera houses, known to locals as the Liceu. Smaller than Milan's La Scala but bigger than Venice's La Fenice, it can seat up to 2300 people in its grand horseshoe auditorium.

Mirador de Colom
Viewpoint

Map p116 (📞93 302 52 24; Plaça del Portal de la Pau; lift adult/child €4.50/3; 🕐8.30am-8pm; Ⓜ Drassanes) High above the swirl of traffic on the roundabout below, Columbus keeps permanent watch, pointing vaguely out to the Mediterranean. Built for the Universal Exhibition in 1888, the monument allows you to zip up 60m in the lift for bird's-eye views back up La Rambla and across the ports of Barcelona.

Església de Sants Just i Pastor
Church

Map p60 (📞93 301 74 33; www.basilicasantjust. cat; Plaça de Sant Just 5; 🕐11am-2pm & 5-8pm Mon-Sat, 10am-1pm Sun; Ⓜ Liceu or Jaume I) This somewhat neglected, single-nave church, with chapels on either side of the buttressing, was built in 1342 in Catalan Gothic style on what is reputedly the site of the oldest parish church in Barcelona. Inside, you can admire some fine stained-glass windows. In front of it, in a pretty little square that was used as a set (a smelly Parisian marketplace) in 2006 for *Perfume: The Story of a Murderer,* is what is claimed to be the city's oldest Gothic fountain.

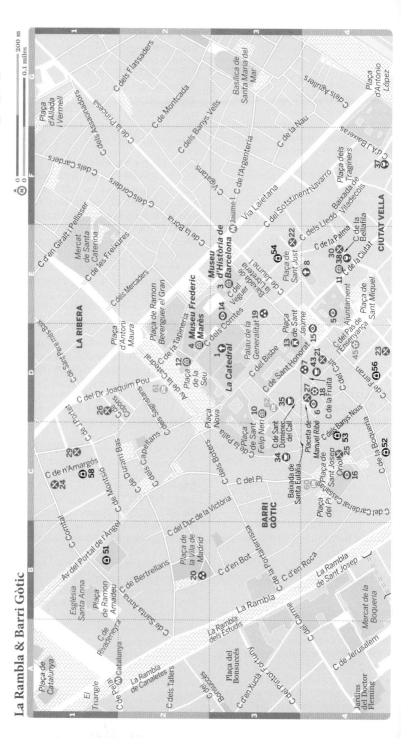

La Rambla & Barri Gòtic

LA RAMBLA & BARRI GÒTIC

200 m
0.1 miles

Plaça de Catalunya

El Triangle

Plaça de Ramon Amadeu

Església Santa Anna

C de Rivadeneyra

C de Santa Anna

La Rambla de Canaletes

La Rambla dels Estudis

C del Pintor Fortuny

Plaça del Bonsuccés

C d'en Xuclà

C del Carme

La Rambla de Sant Josep

Mercat de la Boqueria

Jardins del Doctor Fleming

C de Jerusalem

LA RIBERA

Plaça d'Allada i Vermell

C dels Flassaders

C de la Princesa

C dels Assaonadors

C de Montcada

Basílica de Santa Maria del Mar

C dels Banys Vells

C de la Nau

Plaça d'Antonio López

C d'A.J Baixeras

C dels Cardars

C dels Corders

C dels Mercaders

C de la Bòria

C de Sant Pere més Baix

Mercat de Santa Caterina

C de les Freixures

C d'en Giralt I Pellisser

Plaça de Ramon Berenguer el Gran

Plaça d'Antoni Maura

C de la Tapineria

Museu d'Història de Barcelona

C del Veguer

Plaça de Sant Just

Plaça dels Traginers

Baixada de Viladecols

Plaça de la Palma

C de la Ciutat

CIUTAT VELLA

Via Laietana

C del Sotstinent Navarro

C dels Lledó

C de la Palma

Baixada de la Llibreteria

Plaça de la Seu

La Catedral

Museu Frederic Marès

Palau de la Generalitat

Plaça de Sant Jaume

Plaça de Sant Honorat

Ajuntament

Plaça de Sant Miquel

Plaça del Pas de l'Ensenyança

C de Ferran

C del Call

C del Bisbe

C de Sant Honorat

C de la Fruita

C dels Banys Nous

Plaça de Manuel Ribé

Placeta del Call

C de Sant Domènec del Call

Plaça de Sant Felip Neri

C de Sant Sever

Plaça Nova

Pla de la Catedral

Av de la Catedral

C dels Capellans

C dels Boters

C del Pi

Baixada de Santa Eulàlia

Plaça de Sant Josep Oriol

Plaça del Pi

C del Cardenal Casañas

C de la Boqueria

BARRI GÒTIC

C del Duc de la Victòria

Plaça de la Vila de Madrid

C d'en Bot

C de la Portaferrissa

C d'en Roca

C de Bertrellans

Av del Portal de l'Àngel

C de n'Amargós

C Comtal

C del Pi I Molist

C de Duran I Bas

C de Montsió

C del Doctor Joaquim Pou

C d'En Comtes

C dels Sagristans

C de la Palla

C dels Comtes

La Pietat

Plaça del Rei

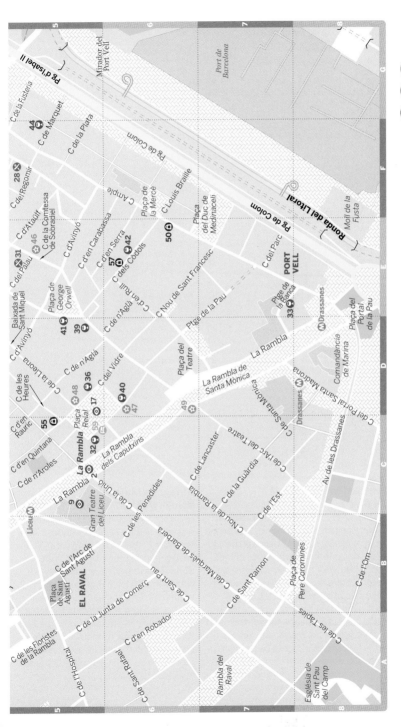

Pg d'Isabel II

Mirador del
Port Vell

Port de
Barcelona

C de la Fustería

C de Marquet

C de la Plata

Pg de Colom

44
C de Marquet

28

C del Regomir

Plaça de
la Mercè

C Ample

C Louis Braille

Plaça
del Duc de
Medinaceli

50

Pg de Colom

Ronda del Litoral

Molli de la
Fusta

C d'Ataülf

C de la Comtessa
de Sobradiel

C d'Avinyó

C d'en Carabassa

C d'Avinyó

46

C d'en Serra

42

C d'en Rull

C dels Codols

57

C del Parc

PORT
VELL

Baixada de
Sant Miquel

C del Palau

31

Plaça de
George
Orwell

C d'Avinyó

41

39

C de n'Aglà

C Nou de Sant Francesc

Ptge de la Pau

Ptge de
la Banca

33

Drassanes

Plaça del
Portal
de la Pau

C de les
Heures

C de la Lleona

C de n'Aglà

C del Vidre

Plaça del
Teatre

La Rambla

Comandància
de Marina

Plaça del
Portal
de la Pau

C d'en
Raurıc

48

36

17

40

47

La Rambla de
Santa Mònica

Drassanes

Comandància
de Marina

55

Plaça
Reial

32

59

La Rambla
dels Caputxins

49

C de Santa Mònica

C del Portal Santa Madrona

C d'en Quintana

C de n'Aroles

La Rambla

2

La Rambla

C de la Unió

C de l'Arc del Teatre

C de Lancaster

C de la Guàrdia

Av de les Drassanes

Liceu

9

Gran Teatre
del Liceu

C de les Penedides

C Nou de la Rambla

C de l'Est

C de l'Arc de
Sant Agustí

Plaça
de Sant
Agustí

EL RAVAL

C del Marquès de Barberà

C de Sant Pau

C de Sant Ramon

Plaça
de Pere
Coromines

C de n'Om

C de les Floristes
de la Rambla

C de la Junta de Comerç

C d'en Robador

C de les Tàpies

C de l'Hospital

C de Sant Rafael

Rambla del
Raval

Església de
Sant Pau
del Camp

La Rambla & Barri Gòtic

Centre d'Interpretació del Call
Historic Site

Map p60 (☎93 256 21 22; www.museuhistoria.bcn.cat; Placeta de Manuel Ribé; ⏰11am-2pm Tue-Fri, to 7pm Sat & Sun; MJaume I or Liceu) FREE Once a 14th-century house of the Jewish weaver Jucef Bonhiac, this small visitors centre is dedicated to the history of Barcelona's Jewish quarter, El Call. Glass sections in the ground floor allow you to inspect Bonhiac's former wells and storage space. The house, also known as the Casa de l'Alquimista (Alchemist's House), hosts a modest display of Jewish artefacts, including ceramics excavated in the area of El Call, along with explanations and maps of the one-time Jewish quarter.

Sinagoga Major
Synagogue

Map p60 (☎93 317 07 90; www.calldebarcelona.org; Carrer de Marlet 5; admission by suggested donation €2.50; ⏰10.30am-6.30pm Mon-Fri, to 2.30pm Sat & Sun; MLiceu) When an Argentine investor bought a run-down electrician's store with an eye to converting it into central Barcelona's umpteenth bar, he could hardly have known he had stumbled onto the remains of what could be the city's main medieval synagogue (some historians cast doubt on the claim). A guide will explain what is thought to be the significance of the site in various languages.

Temple Romà d'August
Ruin

Map p60 (Carrer del Paradis 10; ☺10am-2pm Mon,
to 7pm Tue-Sun; M Jaume I) FREE Opposite
the southeast end of La Catedral, narrow
Carrer del Paradis leads towards Plaça
de Sant Jaume. Inside no 10, an intriguing
building with Gothic and baroque touches,
are four columns and the architrave of Barcelona's main Roman temple, dedicated to
Caesar Augustus and built to worship his
imperial highness in the 1st century AD.

Via Sepulcral Romana
Archaeological Site

Map p60 (☎93 256 21 00; www.museuhistoria.
bcn.cat; Plaça de la Vila de Madrid; adult/child
€2/free; ☺11am-2pm Tue-Fri, to 7pm Sat & Sun;
M Catalunya) Along Carrer de la Canuda, a
block east of the top end of La Rambla, is
a sunken garden where a series of Roman
tombs lies exposed. A display in Spanish
and Catalan by the tombs explores burial
and funerary rites and customs. A few bits
of pottery (including a burial amphora with
the skeleton of a three-year-old Roman
child) accompany the display.

Domus de Sant Honorat
Archaeological Site

Map p60 (☎93 256 21 00; www.museuhistoria.
bcn.cat; Carrer de la Fruita 2; admission €2;
☺10am-2pm Sat & Sun; M Liceu) The remains
of a Roman *domus* (town house) have
been unearthed and opened to the public.
The house (and vestiges of three small
shops) lay close to the Roman forum and
the owners were clearly well off. Apart
from getting something of an idea of daily
Roman life through these remains, the
location also contains six medieval grain
silos installed at the time the Jewish quarter, El Call, was located in this area.

Museu del Calçat
Museum

Map p60 (Footwear Museum; ☎93 301 45 33;
Plaça de Sant Felip Neri 5; admission €2.50;
☺11am-2pm Tue-Sun; M Jaume I) This obscure
museum is home to everything from
Egyptian sandals to dainty ladies' shoes of
the 18th century. The museum and cobblers' guild, which has its roots in the city's
medieval past, were moved here shortly
after the civil war.

Eating

La Rambla is fine for people-watching,
but no great shakes for the palate. Instead
venture off into the streets that wind into
the Barri Gòtic and your belly (and wallet)
will be eternally grateful. Inside the medieval labyrinth, choices abound.

Caelum
Cafe €

Map p60 (☎93 302 69 93; www.caelumbarcelona.
com; Carrer de la Palla 8; ☺10.30am-8.30pm
Mon-Thu, 10.30am-11.30pm Fri & Sat, 11.30am-
9pm Sun; M Liceu) Centuries of heavenly
gastronomic tradition from across Spain
are concentrated in this exquisite medieval
space. The upstairs cafe is a dainty setting
for decadent cakes and pastries, while
going into the underground chamber with
its stone walls and flickering candles is like
stepping into the Middle Ages.

Rasoterra
Vegetarian €

Map p60 (☎93 318 69 26; Carrer del Palau 5; tapas
€5-8, lunch specials €7-10; ☺noon-5pm Tue, to
midnight Wed-Sun; ☑; M Jaume I) Rasoterra
cooks up first-rate vegetarian dishes in a
Zen-like setting with tall ceilings, low-play-
ing jazz and fresh flowers on the tables. The
creative, globally influenced menu changes
regularly and might feature Vietnamese-
style coconut pancakes with tofu and
vegetables, beluga lentils with basmati
rice, and pear and goat cheese quesadillas.
Good vegan and gluten-free options.

Cervecería Taller de Tapas
Tapas €

Map p60 (☎93 481 62 33; www.tallerdetapas.
com; Carrer Comtal 28; tapas €4-10; ☺8.30am-
1am Mon-Sat, from noon Sun; M Urquinaona)
Amid white stone walls and a beamed
ceiling, this buzzing, easygoing place
serves a broad selection of tapas as well
as changing daily specials like *cochin-
illo* (roast suckling pig). A smattering
of beers from across the globe – Leffe
Blond, Guinness, Brahma (Brazil) and Sol
(Mexico) – add to the appeal. It has a few
other locations around town, including a
well-placed spot with outdoor seating on
Plaça de Sant Josep Oriol (☎93 301 80 20;
Plaça de Sant Josep Oriol 9; ☺8.30am-1am Mon-
Sat, from noon Sun).

63

BARBARA BOENSCH/IMAGEBROKER/ROBERT HARDING ©

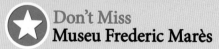

Don't Miss
Museu Frederic Marès

One of the wildest collections of historical curios lies inside this vast medieval complex, once part of the royal palace of the counts of Barcelona. A rather worn coat of arms on the wall indicates that it was also, for a while, the seat of the Spanish Inquisition in Barcelona. Frederic Marès i Deulovol (1893–1991) was a rich sculptor, traveller and obsessive collector, and displays of religious art and vast varieties of bric-a-brac litter the museum.

NEED TO KNOW

Map p60; 📞 93 256 35 00; www.museumares.bcn.es; Plaça de Sant Iu 5; admission €4.20, after 3pm Sun & 1st Sun of month free; 🕙10am-7pm Tue-Sat, 11am-8pm Sun; Ⓜ Jaume I

Cafè de l'Acadèmia   Catalan €€

Map p60 (📞 93 319 82 53; Carrer dels Lledó 1; mains €13-19; 🕙1.30-4pm & 8.45-11.30pm Mon-Fri; Ⓜ Jaume I) Expect a mix of traditional dishes with the occasional creative twist. At lunchtime, local *ajuntament* office workers pounce on the *menú del día* (daily set menu). In the evening it is rather more romantic, as low lighting emphasises the intimacy of the timber ceiling and wooden decor. On warm days, you can also dine on the pretty square at the front.

La Vinateria del Call   Spanish €€

Map p60 (📞 93 302 60 92; www.lavinateriadelcall. com; Carrer de Sant Domènec del Call 9; small plates €7-12; 🕙7.30pm-1am; Ⓜ Jaume I) In a magical setting in the former Jewish quarter, this tiny jewelbox of a restaurant serves up tasty Iberian dishes including Galician octopus, cider-cooked chorizo and the Catalan *escalivada* (roasted peppers, aubergine and onions) with anchovies. Portions are small and made for sharing, and there's an affordable selection of wines.

Allium
Catalan, Fusion €€

Map p60 (☎93 302 30 03; Carrer del Call 17; mains €8-16; ☺noon-4pm Mon-Tue, to 10.30pm Wed-Sat; Ⓜ Liceu) This inviting newcomer to Barri Gòtic serves beautifully prepared tapas dishes and changing specials (including seafood paella for one). The menu, which changes every two or three weeks, focuses on seasonal, organic cuisine. Allium's bright, modern interior sets it apart from other neighbourhood options; it's also open continuously, making it a good bet for those who don't want to wait until 9pm for a meal.

Onofre
Spanish €€

Map p60 (☎93 317 69 37; www.onofre.net; Carrer de les Magdalenes 19; mains €9-14; ☺10am-4pm & 7.30pm-midnight Mon-Sat; Ⓜ Jaume I) Famed for its wine selections, Onofre is a small, modern eatery (and wine shop and delicatessen) that has a strong local following for its delicious tapas plates, good affordable wines and great-value lunch specials (three-course prix-fixe for €10.75). Among the delectable tapas selections: Italian greens with foie shavings, duck confit, codfish carpaccio, oven-baked prawns, and warm goat cheese salad with ham and anchovies.

Cerería
Vegetarian €€

Map p60 (☎93 301 85 10; Baixada de Sant Miquel 3; mains €10-16; ☺7pm-midnight Tue-Sun; 📶📄; Ⓜ Jaume I) Black-and-white marble floors, a smattering of old wooden tables and ramshackle displays of instruments (most made on-site) lend a certain bohemian charm to this small vegetarian restaurant. The pizzas are delicious, and feature organic ingredients – as do the flavourful galettes, dessert crêpes and bountiful salads. Vegan options too.

Milk
Brunch €€

Map p60 (www.milkbarcelona.com; Carrer d'en Gignàs 21; mains €9-12; ☺9am-2am; 📶; Ⓜ Jaume I) Also known to many as an enticing cocktail spot, the Irish-run Milk's key role for Barcelona night owls is providing morning-after brunches (served till 4.30pm). Tuck into pancakes, eggs Benedict and other hangover dishes in a cosy lounge-like setting complete with ornate wallpaper, framed prints on the wall and pillow-lined seating.

Koy Shunka
Japanese €€€

Map p60 (☎93 412 79 39; www.koyshunka.com; Carrer de Copons 7; multicourse menus €77-110; ☺1.30-3pm Tue-Sun & 8.30-11pm Tue-Sat; Ⓜ Urquinaona) Down a narrow lane north of the cathedral, Koy Shunka opens a portal to exquisite dishes from Japan – mouthwatering sushi, sashimi, seared Wagyu beef and flavour-rich seaweed salads are served alongside inventive fusion dishes like steamed clams with sake or tempura of scallops and king prawns with Japanese mushrooms. Don't miss the house speciality of tender *toro* (tuna belly).

Pla
Fusion €€€

Map p60 (☎93 412 65 52; www.elpla.cat; Carrer de la Bellafila 5; mains €18-25; ☺7.30pm-midnight; 📄; Ⓜ Jaume I) One of Gòtic's long-standing favourites, Pla is a stylish, romantically lit medieval dining room where the cooks churn out such temptations as oxtail braised in red wine, seared tuna with oven-roasted peppers, and polenta with seasonal mushrooms. It has a tasting menu for €38 Sunday to Thursday.

Ⓠ Drinking & Nightlife

Ocaña
Bar

Map p60 (☎93 676 48 14; www.ocana.cat; Plaça Reial 13; ☺5pm-2.30am Mon-Fri, from 11am Sat & Sun; Ⓜ Liceu) Named after a flamboyant artist who once lived on Plaça Reial, Ocaña is a beautifully designed space with fluted columns, candlelit chandeliers and plush furnishings. Sit on the terrace and watch the passing people parade, or head downstairs to the Moorish-inspired Apotheke bar or the chic lounge a few steps away, where DJs spin for a mix of beauties and bohemians on weekend nights.

Sor Rita
Bar

Map p60 (Carrer de la Mercè 27; ☺7pm-2.30am; Ⓜ Jaume I) A lover of all things kitsch, Sor Rita is pure eye candy, from its leopard print wallpaper to its shoe-festooned ceiling, and deliciously irreverent decorations inspired by Almodóvar's films. It's a fun and festive scene, with special-event nights throughout the week, including tarot readings on Mondays, €5 all-you-can-eat snack buffets on Tuesdays, karaoke Wednesdays and gin specials on Thursdays.

Oviso   Bar

Map p60 (Carrer d'Arai 5; ⏰10am-2.30am; 📶; MLiceu) Oviso is a popular budget-friendly restaurant with outdoor tables on the plaza, but shows its true bohemian colours by night, with a mixed crowd, a rock-and-roll vibe and a rustic decorated two-room interior plastered with curious murals – geese taking flight, leaping dolphins and blue peacocks framing the brightly painted concrete walls.

La Cerveteca   Bar

Map p60 (Carrer de Gignàs 25; ⏰6-11pm Sun-Thu, to midnight Fri & Sat; MJaume I) An unmissable stop for beer lovers, La Cerveteca serves an impressive variety of global craft brews. In addition to scores of bottled brews, there's a frequent rotation of what's on draught. Cheeses, *jamon ibérico* and other charcuterie selections are on hand, including *cecina* (cured horse meat). The standing cask tables (with a few seats at the back) are a fine setting for an early evening pick me up.

Salterio   Cafe

Map p60 (Carrer de Sant Domènec del Call 4; ⏰2pm-midnight; MJaume I) A wonderfully photogenic spot tucked down a tiny lane in the Call, Salterio serves Turkish coffee, authentic mint teas and snacks amid stone walls, incense and ambient Middle Eastern music. If hunger strikes, try the *sardo* (grilled flat-bread covered with pesto, cheese or other toppings).

Čaj Chai   Cafe

Map p60 (📞93 301 95 92; www.cajchai.com; Carrer de Sant Domènec del Call 12; ⏰3-10pm Mon, 10.30am-10pm Tue-Sun; MJaume I) Inspired by Prague's bohemian tearooms, this bright and buzzing cafe in the heart of the old Jewish quarter is a tea connoisseur's para-dise. Čaj Chai stocks over 100 teas from China, India, Korea, Japan, Nepal, Morocco and beyond. It's a much-loved local haunt.

Marula Cafè   Bar

Map p60 (www.marulacafe.com; Carrer dels Escudellers 49; ⏰11pm-5am Wed-Sun; MLiceu) A fantastic funk find in the heart of the Barri Gòtic, Marula will transport you to the 1970s and the best in funk and soul. James Brown fans will think they've died and gone to heaven. It's not, however, a monothematic place and DJs slip in other tunes, from breakbeat to house.

Polaroid   Bar

Map p60 (Carrer dels Còdols 29; ⏰7pm-2.30am; MDrassanes) For a dash of 1980s nostalgia, Polaroid is a blast from the past with its wall-mounted VHS tapes, old film posters, comic-book-covered tables, action-figure displays and other kitschy decor. Not surprisingly, it draws a fun, unpretentious crowd who comes for cheap *cañas* (draught beer), mojitos and free popcorn.

Barcelona Pipa Club   Bar

Map p60 (📞93 302 47 32; www.bpipaclub.com; Plaça Reial 3; ⏰10pm-4am; MLiceu) This club is like an apartment, with interconnecting rooms and knick-knacks – notably the pipes after which the place is named. Buzz at the door and head two floors up. There is occasional live music.

L'Ascensor   Bar

Map p60 (Carrer de la Bellafila 3; ⏰6pm-midnight Mon-Thu, to 3am Fri & Sat; MJaume I) Named after the lift (elevator) doors that serve as the front door, this elegant drinking den gathers a faithful crowd who come for old-fashioned cocktails and lively conversation against a soundtrack of up-tempo jazz and funk.

El Paraigua   Live Music

Map p60 (📞93 302 11 31; www.elparaigua.com; Carrer del Pas de l'Ensenyança 2; ⏰10.30am-1am Sun, Tue & Wed, to 2am Thu-Sat; MLiceu) A tiny chocolate box of dark tinted Modernisme, the 'Umbrella' has been serving up drinks since the 1960s. The turn-of-the-20th-

QUIM ROSER/AGE FOTOSTOCK/ROBERT HARDING ©

 Don't Miss
Museu d'Història de Barcelona

One of Barcelona's most fascinating museums takes you back through the centuries to the very foundations of Roman Barcino. You'll stroll over ruins of the old streets, sewers, laundries and wine- and fish-making factories that flourished here following the town's founding by Emperor Augustus around 10 BC. Equally impressive is the building itself, which was once part of the Palau Reial Major (Grand Royal Palace) on Plaça del Rei, among the key locations of medieval princely power in Barcelona.

NEED TO KNOW

Map p60; ☏93 256 21 00; www.museuhistoria.bcn.cat; Plaça del Rei; adult/child €7/free, free 1st Sun of month & 3-8pm Sun; ☺10am-7pm Tue-Sat, 10am-8pm Sun; Ⓜ Jaume I

---

century decor was transferred here from a shop knocked down elsewhere in the district and cobbled back together to create this cosy locale.

Bosc de les Fades   Lounge
(Passatage de la Banca 5; ☺11am-1.30am; Ⓜ Drassanes) The 'Forest of the Faeries' is touristy but offers a whimsical retreat from the busy Ramblas nearby. Lounge chairs and lamplit tables are scattered beneath an indoor forest complete with trickling fountain and grotto. Prices are steep (€8 for a cocktail).

Entertainment

Harlem Jazz Club   Jazz
Map p60 (☏93 310 07 55; www.harlemjazzclub. es; Carrer de la Comtessa de Sobradiel 8; admission around €7-8; ☺8pm-5am Tue-Sat; Ⓜ Drassanes) This narrow, old-city dive is one of the best spots in town for jazz, as well as funk, Latin, blues and gypsy jazz. It attracts a mixed crowd who maintains a respectful silence during the acts. Most concerts start around 10pm. Get in early if you want a seat in front of the stage.

Jamboree — Live Music

Map p60 (📞93 319 17 89; www.masimas.com/jamboree; Plaça Reial 17; admission €10-20; ⏰8pm-6am; Ⓜ Liceu) For over half a century, Jamboree has been bringing joy to the jivers of Barcelona, with high-calibre acts featuring jazz trios, blues, Afrobeats, Latin sounds and big-band sounds. Two concerts are held most nights (at 8pm and 10pm), after which Jamboree morphs into a DJ-spinning club at midnight. WTF jam sessions are held Mondays (entrance a mere €5). Buy tickets online to save a few euros.

Karma — Club

Map p60 (📞93 302 56 80; www.karmadisco.com; Plaça Reial 10; ⏰midnight-5.30am Tue-Sun; Ⓜ Liceu) During the week Karma plays good, mainstream indie music, while on weekends the DJs spin anything from rock to disco. A golden oldie in Barcelona, tunnel-shaped Karma is small and becomes quite tightly packed (claustrophobic for some) with a good-natured crowd of locals and out-of-towners.

Sidecar Factory Club — Live Music

Map p60 (📞93 302 15 86; www.sidecarfactoryclub.com; Plaça Reial 7; admission €8-18; ⏰10pm-5am Mon-Sat; Ⓜ Liceu) With its entrance on Plaça Reial, you can come here for a meal before midnight or a few drinks at ground level (which closes by 3am at the latest), or descend into the red-tinged, brick-vaulted bowels for live music most nights. Just about anything goes here, from UK indie through to country punk, but rock and pop lead the way. Most shows start around 10pm. DJs take over at 12.30am to keep things going.

Gran Teatre del Liceu — Theatre

Map p60 (📞93 485 99 00; www.liceubarcelona.com; La Rambla dels Caputxins 51-59; ⏰box office 1.30-8pm Mon-Fri & 1hr before show Sat & Sun; Ⓜ Liceu) Barcelona's grand old opera house, restored after fire in 1994, is one of the most technologically advanced theatres in the world. To take up a seat in the grand auditorium, returned to all its 19th-century glory but with the very latest in acoustic accoutrements, is to be transported to another age. Tickets can cost anything from €9 for a cheap seat behind a pillar to €205 for a well-positioned night at the opera.

Teatre Principal — Live Music

Map p60 (📞93 412 31 29; www.teatreprincipalbcn.com; La Rambla 27; concerts from €20; Ⓜ Liceu) Following a €6 million renovation, this historic theatre has been transformed into a lavish concert space and nightclub. It hosts a range of sounds from flamenco to indie rock.

Gran Teatre del Liceu
ELAN FLEISHER/ROBERT HARDING ©

🔒 Shopping

A handful of interesting shops dot La Rambla, but the real fun starts inside the labyrinth. Young fashion on Carrer d'Avinyó, a mixed bag on Avinguda del Portal de l'Àngel, some cute old shops on Carrer de la Dagueria and lots of exploring in tight old lanes awaits.

Emprentes de Catalunya
Handicrafts

Map p60 (🖉 93 467 46 60; Carrer dels Banys Nous 11; 🕙10am-8pm Mon-Sat, to 2pm Sun; Ⓜ Liceu) A celebration of Catalan products, this nicely designed store is a great place to browse for unique gifts. You'll find jewellery with designs inspired by Roman iconography (as well as works that reference Gaudí and Barcelona's Gothic era), plus pottery, wooden toys, silk scarves, notebooks, housewares and more.

B Lab
Clothing, Accessories

Map p60 (🖉 93 184 38 38; www.b-lab.eu; Carrer Ample 9; 🕙10am-2pm & 4-9pm Mon-Sat; Ⓜ Drassanes) This creative little boutique for men and women sells beautifully crafted dresses, sneakers, graphic- and embroidered T-shirts, chunky jewellery and wooden sunglasses, mostly created by Barcelona designers.

Taller de Marionetas Travi
Marionettes

Map p60 (🖉 93 412 66 92; www.marionetastravi. com; Carrer de n'Amargós 4; 🕙noon-9pm Mon-Sat; Ⓜ Urquinaona) Opened in the 1970s, this atmospheric shop sells beautifully handcrafted marionettes. Don Quixote, Sancho and other iconic Spanish figures are on hand, as well as unusual works from other parts of the world – including rare Sicilian puppets and pieces from Myanmar (Burma) and Indonesia.

La Talenta
Vintage

Map p60 (🖉 93 412 38 79; latalentabarcelona. com; Carrer dels Còdols 23; 🕙noon-8pm Tue-Sat; Ⓜ Drassanes) This atmospheric shop is a great spot for browsing. La Talenta has an intriguing mix of vintage objects (opera glasses, postcards, furniture, old bicycles suspended from the ceiling), as well as crafty, design-minded items (wooden boxes with images of Barcelona, jewellery and accessories, paper-doll kits, coffee-table books), and original artwork.

Herboristeria del Rei
Beauty

Map p60 (🖉 93 318 05 12; www.herboristeriadel-rei.blogspot.com; Carrer del Vidre 1; 🕙4-8pm Tue-Fri, 10am-8pm Sat; Ⓜ Liceu) Once patronised by Queen Isabel II, this timeless corner store flogs all sorts of weird and wonderful herbs, spices and medicinal plants. It's been doing so since 1823 and the decor has barely changed since the 1860s. However, some of the products have, and you'll find anything from fragrant soaps to massage oil nowadays. Film director Tom Tykwer shot scenes of *Perfume: The Story of a Murderer* here.

El Ingenio
Novelties, Toys

Map p60 (🖉 93 317 71 38; www.el-ingenio.com; Carrer d'en Rauric 6; 🕙10am-1.30pm & 4.15-8pm Mon-Fri, 10am-2pm & 5-8.30pm Sat; Ⓜ Liceu) In this whimsical fantasy store you will find elegant Venetian masks, marionettes, theatrical accessories, flamenco costumes, gorilla heads, yo-yos, kazoos, unicycles and other novelty items. It's a great place to pick up a few gifts for kids back home.

La Manual Alpargatera
Shoes

Map p60 (🖉 93 301 01 72; lamanualalpargatera.es; Carrer d'Avinyó 7; 🕙9.30am-1.30pm & 4.30-8pm; Ⓜ Liceu) Everyone from Salvador Dalí to Jean Paul Gaultier has ordered a pair of *espadrilles* (rope-soled canvas shoes or sandals) from this famous store, which is the birthplace of the iconic footware. The shop was founded just after the Spanish Civil War, though the roots of the simple shoe design date back thousands of years.

Fires, Festes i Tradicions
Food

Map p60 (🖉 93 269 12 61; Carrer de la Dagueria 13; 🕙4-8.30pm Mon, 10am-8.30pm Tue-Sat; Ⓜ Jaume I) Whether assembling a picnic or hoping to bring home a few edible momentos, don't miss this little shop, which stocks a wide range of specialities from Catalunya, including jams, sweets, sausages and cheeses.

El Raval

Long one of the most rough-and-tumble parts of Barcelona, El Raval is now hip in a grungy, inner-city way. *Barcelonins* have even invented a verb for rambling around El Raval: *ravalejar*.

The northern half of El Raval is the best place to start your ramble – this part of the *barri* has an almost respectable air about it. Spend a day wandering along the art-shop filled Carrer del Pintor Fortuny, lunching in the colourful Mercat de la Boqueria and dedicating a few hours to the fascinating MACBA. Join the youthful set of hedonists on La Rambla del Raval and check out the strip's assortment of bars. Don't miss the striking cylindrical designer hotel Barceló Raval and its fashionable restaurant.

Night time is El Raval's forte. This is where you will find some of the more eccentric, trendy and downright ancient bars and clubs.

La Confitería (p82)

El Raval Highlights

MACBA (p81)

Usually referred to by its acronym MACBA, the Museu d'Art Contemporani de Barcelona, set on Plaça de Ángels (a hangout for local skateboarders), is stuffed with over seven decades' worth of modern art. This is the place to view the cutting edge of the contemporary scene in rooms flooded with natural light, courtesy of huge south-facing windows. Catalan and Spanish paintings form the backbone of the collection. Below: MACBA; architect: Richard Meier & Partners

Mercat de la Boqueria (p82)

Plump and seductive fruits and vegetables, gleaming seafood counters, the earthy scent of artisanal cheeses. Mercat de la Boqueria is all this and much more. It's the city's oldest and most atmospheric market, a noisy melange of history, heritage and street theatre. Not surprisingly, it's also one of the biggest tourist magnets – particularly the enticing row of tapas counters in the back.

MARCO CRISTOFORI/CORBIS ©

Palau Güell (p76)

Mega-rich industrialist Eusebi Güell and Modernista architect Gaudí are as synonymous with Barcelona as they are with each other. This gilded mansion, with its toadstool chimneys and gabled frontage, captures Gaudí in a youthful, less flamboyant incarnation. Art fiends flock here to gain an insight into a genius in the making.

Right: Chimneys, Palau Güell

Bars (p82)

Long known for its seedy nightlife and louche drinking holes, El Raval's abundant bars have been sanitised in recent years, replicating what happened in La Ribera's El Born district in the 1990s. Nonetheless, the neighbourhood still retains 'edge', along with enough grungy, open-all-night places to keep any Hemingway-emulating barfly happy for weeks.

Neighbourhood Eateries (p77)

Sitting in one of the most exciting parts of town, El Raval's ever-evolving restaurant scene is characterised by a diverse ethnic make-up and a hungry army of students. To meet the local need, the district's traditional eating houses have been complemented in recent years by vegetarian self-service joints, juice bars and the odd classy candlelit nook.

El Raval Walk

Edgy street art, hedonistic nightspots and colourful characters are part of the urban backdrop of ever-evolving El Raval. This journey takes in some of its diverse highlights with stops at bohemian drinking dens, architectural masterpieces and one magnificent food market (bring an appetite).

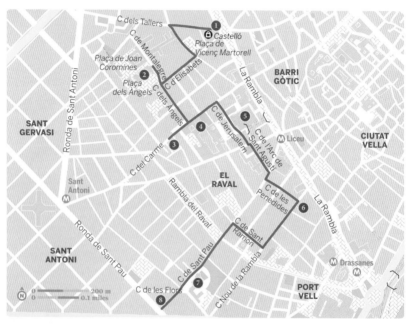

WALK FACTS

- **Start** La Rambla de Canaletes
- **Finish** La Confitería
- **Distance** 2.8km
- **Duration** Two hours

❶ Carrer des Tallers

Just off La Rambla, this narrow **pedestrian lane** has rhythm in its soul, with a smattering of CD and record stores as well as guitar shops. For a broad collection of sounds from Spain and beyond, stop in **Discos Castelló** (p85).

❷ MACBA

Stroll past **Plaça de Vicenç Martorell**, a pleasant slice of local life, and make your way over to the **MACBA** (p81), which was a major catalyst to the cultural rebirth of El Raval. The ultra-modern all-white design by American architect Richard Meier was controversial for its dramatic contrast to the surrounding historic buildings.

❸ Bar Muy Buenas

For a refreshment, stop in **Bar Muy Buenas** (p83) on Carrer del Carme. Opened as a milk bar in the late 19th century, it retains much of its original Modernista decor. It's a welcoming spot for a tipple and snacks.

4 Antic Hospital de la Santa Creu

Up the road, have a wander through the peaceful courtyard of the **Antic Hospital de la Santa Creu** (p76), the city's main hospital in the 15th century. The impressive Gothic buildings now house cultural institutions, including a large library.

5 Hotel España

After a few nibbles at La Boqueria, stroll over to **Hotel España** for classic Catalan fare. The famous dining rooms are part of the 1903 design by Domènech i Montaner and there is a magnificent alabaster fireplace designed by Eusebi Arnau.

6 Palau Güell

After a few nibbles at La Boqueria, stroll down Carrer de les Penedides to one of El Raval's star attractions. The beautifully restored **Palau Güell** (p76) showcases the early work of Barcelona's favourite architect. The classic Gaudí elements are at play, including colourful mosaic-covered chimney pots.

7 Església de Sant Pau del Camp

Next, stroll over to Barcelona's oldest church. Along the way, you'll pass the pedestrian-filled **La Rambla del Raval**, which has a fraction of the crowds of its cousin to the east. **Església de Sant Pau del Camp** has some wonderful Visigothic sculptural decoration on its doorway and a serene air. The cloister is the best example of Romanesque architecture in the city.

8 La Confitería

End your stroll at **La Confitería** (p82), one of El Raval's charming watering holes. Once a barber shop and then confectioner's, it was converted to a bar in 1998. Most of the elements are the real deal.

 The Best...

PLACES TO EAT

Bar Pinotxo One of the best tapas bars in La Boqueria. (p80)

Suculent Rich and imaginative cooking from Michelin-starred chef Carles Abellan. (p80)

Granja M Viader Rich cups of hot chocolate are served up in this delightful Catalan-style milk bar. (p83)

Mam i Teca Slow Food-loving joint that cooks up delectable Catalan specials. (p77)

Elisabets A neighbourhood charmer that always packs a lunchtime crowd. (p77)

PLACES TO DRINK

Bar Marsella Lots of tipplers have sipped at this historic spot, including Hemingway. (p83)

La Confitería Mural-filled bar with 19th-century decor and excellent house-made vermouth. (p82)

33|45 Trendy cocktail bar that draws a fashionista crowd. (p83)

LIVE MUSIC

Jazz Sí Club This tiny spot has eclectic programming, including authentic Flamenco. (p84)

23 Robadors Small jazz-loving joint. (p84)

Discover El Raval

Getting There & Away

- **Metro** El Raval is encircled by three Metro lines. Línies 1, 2 and 3 stop at strategic points around the district, so nothing is far from a Metro stop. The Línia 3 stop at Liceu is a convenient exit point.

 Sights

Palau Güell
Palace

Map p78 (☎93 472 57 75; www.palauguell.cat; Carrer Nou de la Rambla 3-5; adult/concession €12/8; ⊙10am-8pm Tue-Sun; Ⓜ Drassanes) Finally reopened in its entirety in May 2012 after several years of refurbishment, this is a magnificent example of the early days of Gaudí's fevered architectural imagination – the extraordinary neo-Gothic mansion, one of the few major buildings of that era raised in Ciutat Vella, gives an insight into its maker's prodigious genius.

Antic Hospital de la Santa Creu
Historic Building

Map p78 (Former Hospital of the Holy Cross; ☎93 270 16 21; www.bnc.cat; Carrer de l'Hospital 56; ⊙9am-8pm Mon-Fri, to 2pm Sat; Ⓜ Liceu) FREE Behind La Boqueria stands the Antic Hospital de la Santa Creu, which was once the city's main hospital. Begun in 1401, it functioned until the 1930s, and was considered one of the best in Europe in its medieval heyday. It is also the place where Antoni Gaudí died in 1926. Today it houses the **Biblioteca de Catalunya**, and the **Institut d'Estudis Catalans** (Institute for Catalan Studies). The hospital's Gothic chapel, **La Capella** (☎93 442 71 71; www.bcn.cat/lacapella; ⊙noon-2pm & 4-8pm Tue-Sat, 11am-2pm Sun & holidays; Ⓜ Liceu) FREE, shows temporary exhibitions.

Centre de Cultura Contemporània de Barcelona
Building

Map p78 (CCCB; ☎93 306 41 00; www.cccb.org; Carrer de Montalegre 5; adult/senior & student/ child under 16yr 2 exhibitions €8/6/free, 1 exhibition €6/4/free, free on Sun 3-8pm; ⊙11am-8pm Tue-

Palau Güell
MURAT TANER/GETTY IMAGES ©

A complex of auditoriums, exhibition spaces and conference halls opened here in 1994 in what had been an 18th-century hospice, the Casa de la Caritat. The courtyard, with a vast glass wall on one side, is spectacular. With 4500 sq metres of exhibition space in four separate areas, the centre hosts a constantly changing program of exhibitions, film cycles and other events.

Església de Sant Pau del Camp
Church

Map p78 (Carrer de Sant Pau 101; adult/concession €3/2; ⏱10am-1.30pm & 4-7.30pm Mon-Sat; **M** Paral·lel) The best example of Romanesque architecture in the city is the dainty little cloister of this church. Set in a somewhat dusty garden, the 12th-century church also boasts some Visigothic sculptural detail on the main entrance.

Eating

For contrast alone, El Raval is possibly the most interesting part of the old town. Timeless classics of Barcelona dining are scattered across what was long the old city's poorest *barrio* (district), and since the late 1990s, battalions of hip new eateries and artsy restaurants can be found in the area around MACBA.

Elisabets
Catalan €

Map p78 (☎93 317 58 26; Carrer d'Elisabets 2-4; mains €8-10; ⏱7.30am-11pm Mon-Thu & Sat, until 2am Fri, closed Aug; **M** Catalunya) This unassuming restaurant is popular for no-nonsense local fare. The walls are dotted with old radio sets and the *menú del día* (set menu; €10.85) varies daily. If you prefer *a la carta*, try the *ragú de jabalí* (wild boar stew) and finish with *mel i mató* (a Catalan dessert made from cheese and honey). Those with a post-midnight hunger on Friday nights can probably get a meal here as late as 1am.

Pla dels Àngels
Mediterranean €

Map p78 (☎93 329 40 47; Carrer de Ferlandina 23; set lunch €6.75-10.30, set dinner €15, mains €8-10; ⏱1.30-11.30pm daily; **M** Universitat)

Just opposite the MACBA, this is a suitably colourful and lively little bistro with brightly painted walls and tightly squeezed tables in the back room. More space is to be had in the bar area, at the front, though it's not as pretty. The dishes span the Mediterranean, and can be quite quirky, with salads like mango, tofu, mint and oregano, and pear, chestnut and pine nut soup.

Sésamo
Vegetarian €

Map p78 (☎93 441 64 11; Carrer de Sant Antoni Abat 52; tapas €6; ⏱8pm-midnight Tue-Sun; 🍴; **M** Sant Antoni) Widely held to be the best vegie restaurant in the city (admittedly not as great an accolade as it might be elsewhere), Sésamo is a cosy, fun place. The menu is mostly tapas, and most people go for the seven-course tapas menu (wine included; €25), but there are a few more substantial dishes. Nice touches include the home-baked bread and cakes.

El Colectivo
Cafe €

Map p78 (☎93 318 63 80; Carrer del Pintor Fortuny 22; bocadillos from €4; ⏱9am-9pm Mon-Wed, 9am-midnight Thu, 9am-2am Fri & Sat; 🛜; **M** Catalunya) A relaxed little cafe on a quiet Raval street, El Colectivo makes excellent cake (carrot, pineapple, you name it), creative *bocadillos* (filled rolls) and good coffee. The shop-window seating is perfect for street watching, the decor is simple and minimal with a single row of wooden tables, and there is always good jazz playing in the background. Tapas is served on Thursdays and Fridays.

Mam i Teca
Catalan €€

Map p78 (☎93 441 33 35; Carrer de la Lluna 4; mains €9-12; ⏱1-4pm & 8pm-midnight Mon, Wed-Fri & Sun, 8pm-midnight; **M** Sant Antoni) A tiny place with half a dozen tables, Mam i Teca is as much a lifestyle choice as a restaurant. Locals drop in and hang about at the bar, and diners are treated to Catalan dishes made with locally sourced products and adhering to Slow Food principles. Try, for example, cod fried in olive oil with garlic and red pepper, or pork ribs with chickpeas.

El Raval

EL RAVAL

200 m
0.1 miles

N

CIUTAT
VELLA

BARRI
GÒTIC

Plaça
Nova

Plaça de
Sant Felip
Neri

Plaça de la
Boqueria

Plaça de
St Josep
Oriol

Plaça de
Sant
Agustí

Plaça de
Ramon
Amadeu

Plaça de
la Vila de
Madrid

Plaça de
Vicenç
Martorell

Plaça del
C Bonsucces

Plaça del
Pi

Plaça dels
Àngels

Plaça de
Joan
Coromines

Plaça de
Castella

Plaça de la
Universitat

Plaça de
Terenci Moix

Plaça del
Pes de
la Palla

Mercat de la
Boqueria

MACBA

Catalunya M

Universitat M

Liceu M

La Rambla
de Canaletes

La Rambla
dels Estudis

La Rambla
dels Estudis

La Rambla de
Sant Josep

La Rambla

Av del Portal de l'Àngel

C de Montsió

C de Duran i Bas

C dels Boters

C de la Palla

C de n'Aroles

C de Ferran

C de la Boqueria

C del Petritxol

C del Pi

C d'en Bot

C d'en Roca

C de la Portaferrissa

C de la Canuda

C de Bertrellans

C de Santa Anna

C de Pelai

C de Jovellanos

C dels Tallers

C dels Tallers

C de Gravina

C de Ramelleres

C de les Ramelleres

C del Bonsuccés

C d'en Xuclà

C del Pintor Fortuny

C del Carme

C del Notariat

C dels Bisbes

C de Montalegre

C dels Àngels

C del Doctor Dou

C de Jerusalem

C de les Floristes de la Rambla

C de les
Egipcíaques

Jardins del
Doctor
Fleming

C de Joaquín Costa

C del Peu de la Creu

C de la Lluna

C de Ferlandina

C de Sant Vicenç

C del Lleó

C del Tigre

C de Valldonzella

41
35
36
34
28
4
1
18
22
14
13
26
32
12
38
37
40
11
10
23
8
2
20
6
3

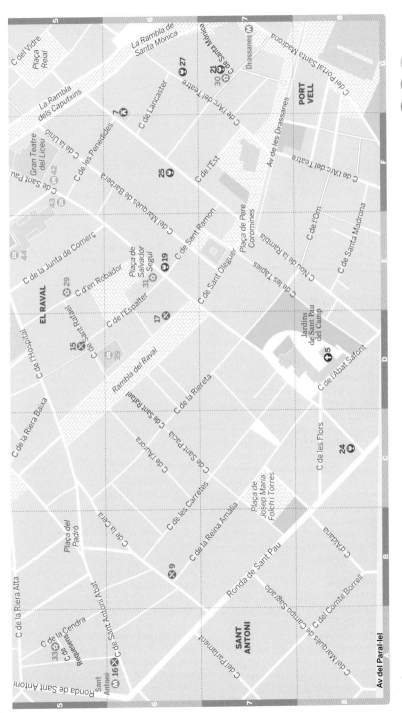

EL RAVAL

79

El Raval

Caravelle
International €€

Map p78 (☑ 93 317 98 92; Carrer del Pintor Fortuny 31; mains €10-13; ⏰ 8.30am-6.30pm Mon-Wed, 8.30am-1am Thu, 10.30am-1am Sat, 10.30am-6.30pm Sun; Ⓜ Liceu) This bright little joint, beloved of the hipster element of El Raval and anyone with a discerning palate, offers tacos as you've never tasted them (cod, lime alioli and radish; pulled pork with roast corn and avocado), a superior steak sandwich on homemade brioche with pickled celeriac and all manner of soul food. Drinks are every bit as inventive – try the homemade ginger beer or grapefruit soda.

Bar Pinotxo
Tapas €€

Map p78 (www.pinotxobar.com; Mercat de la Boqueria; mains €8-15; ⏰ 6am-4pm Mon-Sat; Ⓜ Liceu) Bar Pinotxo is arguably La Boqueria's, and even Barcelona's, best tapas bar. It sits among the half-dozen or so informal eateries within the market, and the popular owner, Juanito, might serve up chickpeas with a sweet sauce of pine nuts and raisins, a fantastically soft mix of potato and spinach sprinkled with coarse salt, baby soft baby squid with cannellini beans, or a quivering cube of caramel-sweet pork belly.

Suculent
Catalan €€

Map p78 (☑ 93 443 65 79; www.suculent.com; Rambla del Raval 39; mains €11-20; ⏰ 1-4pm & 8.30-11.30pm Wed-Sun, closed Sun night; Ⓜ Liceu) Michelin-starred chef Carles Abellan (of Comerç 24 fame) adds to his stable with this old-style bistro, which showcases the best of Catalan cuisine. From the cod brandade to the oxtail stew with truffled sweet potato, only the best ingredients are used. The prices can mount up a bit, but this is a great place to sample the regional highlights.

Restaurant el Cafetí
Catalan €€

Map p78 (☑ 93 329 24 19; www.elcafeti. com; Carrer de Sant Rafael 18; mains €12-18, menú del dia €10; ⏰ 1.30-3.30pm & 8.30-11.30pm Tue-Sun, closed Aug; Ⓜ Liceu) This diminutive eatery is filled with an-

MACBA; ARCHITECT: RICHARD MEIER & PARTNERS.
TRAVELSTOCK44/JUERGEN HELD/GETTY IMAGES ©

Don't Miss
MACBA

Designed by Richard Meier and opened in 1995, MACBA has become the city's foremost contemporary art centre, with captivating exhibitions for the serious art lover. The permanent collection is on the ground floor and dedicates itself to Spanish and Catalan art from the second half of the 20th century, with works by Antoni Tàpies, Joan Brossa and Miquel Barceló, among others, though international artists, such as Paul Klee, Bruce Nauman and John Cage, are also represented. The gallery is dedicated to temporary visiting exhibitions that are almost always challenging and intriguing, and the extensive bookshop is fantastic for books about art, quirky gifts and small design objects.

NEED TO KNOW

Map p78; Museu d'Art Contemporani de Barcelona; ☑93 412 08 10; www.macba.cat; Plaça dels Àngels 1; adult/concession €10/8; ☺11am-7.30pm Mon & Wed-Fri, 10am-9pm Sat, 10am-3pm Sun & holidays; Ⓜ Universitat

tique furniture and offers traditional local cooking, with one or two unorthodox variations. Paella and other rice dishes dominate. The entrance is down the little Passatge de Bernardí Martorell.

Can Lluís   Catalan €€
Map p78 (www.restaurantcanlluis.cat; Carrer de la Cera 49; mains €9-19, menú del día €9.80;

☺Mon-Sat Sep-Jul; Ⓜ Sant Antoni) Three generations have kept this spick and span old-time classic in business since 1929. Beneath the olive-green beams in the back dining room you can see the spot where an anarchist's bomb went off in 1946, killing the then owner. Expect fresh fish and seafood. The *llenguado* (sole) is oven cooked with whisky and raisins.

81

CHRIS MELLOR/GETTY IMAGES ©

⭐ Don't Miss
Mercat de la Boqueria

Mercat de la Boqueria is possibly La Rambla's most interesting building, not so much for its Modernista-influenced design (it was actually built over a long period, from 1840 to 1914, on the site of the former St Joseph monastery), but for the action of the food market within.

NEED TO KNOW

Map p78 ; 📞 93 318 25 84; www.boqueria.info; La Rambla 91; 🕘 8am-8.30pm Mon-Sat; Ⓜ Liceu

---

🍷 Drinking & Nightlife

La Confitería   Bar
Map p78 (Carrer de Sant Pau 128; 🕘 7.30pm-3am Mon-Thu, 1pm-3am Fri-Sun; Ⓜ Paral·lel) This is a trip into the 19th century. Until the 1980s it was a confectioner's shop, and although the original cabinets are now lined with booze, the look of the place has barely changed in its conversion into a laid-back bar. A quiet enough spot for a house *vermut* (€3; add your own soda) in the early evening, it fills with theatregoers and local partiers later at night.

Casa Almirall   Bar
Map p78 (www.casaalmirall.com; Carrer de Joaquín Costa 33; 🕘 6pm-2.30am Mon-Thu, 6.30pm-3am Fri, noon-3am Sat, noon-1.30am Sun; Ⓜ Universitat) In business since the 1860s, this unchanged corner bar is dark and intriguing, with Modernista decor and a mixed clientele. There are some great original pieces in here, like the marble counter, and the cast-iron statue of the muse of the Universal Exposition, held in Barcelona in 1888.

Negroni   Cocktail Bar
Map p78 (www.negronicocktailbar.com; Carrer de Joaquín Costa 46; 🕘 7pm-2.30am Mon-Thu, 7pm-

3am Fri & Sat; **M** Liceu) Good things come in small packages and this dark, teeny cocktail bar confirms the rule. The mostly black decor lures in a largely student set to try out the cocktails, among them, of course, the celebrated Negroni, a Florentine invention with one part Campari, one part gin and one part sweet vermouth.

33|45 Bar

Map p78 (Carrer de Joaquín Costa 4; ⏱10am-2.30am daily, from 4pm Mon; **M** Universitat) A super-trendy bar on a street that's not short of them, this place has rather excellent mojitos – even pink, strawberry ones – and a fashionable crowd. The main area has DJ music and lots of excited noise-making, while the back room is scattered with sofas and armchairs for a post-dancing slump. On occasional Sundays this is a venue for lunchtime live gigs.

Granja M Viader Cafe

Map p78 (📞93 318 34 86; www.granjaviader.cat; Carrer d'en Xuclà 6; ⏱9am-1.30pm & 5-9pm Mon-Sat; **M** Liceu) For more than a century, people have flocked down this alley to get to the cups of homemade hot chocolate and whipped cream (ask for a *suís*) ladled out in this classic Catalan-style milk bar-cum-deli. The Viader clan invented Cacaolat, a forerunner of kids' powdered-chocolate beverages. The interior is delightfully vintage and the atmosphere always upbeat.

Bar Marsella Bar

Map p78 (Carrer de Sant Pau 65; ⏱10pm-2.30am Mon-Wed, 10pm-3am Thu-Sat; **M** Liceu) This bar has been in business since 1820, and has served the likes of Hemingway, who was known to slumped here over an *absenta* (absinthe). The bar still specialises in absinthe, a drink to be treated with respect. Your glass comes with a lump of sugar, a fork and a little bottle of mineral water. Hold the sugar on the fork, over your glass, and drip the water onto the sugar so that it dissolves into the absinthe, which turns yellow. The result should give you a warm glow.

Bar Muy Buenas Bar

Map p78 (Carrer del Carme 63; ⏱9am-2.30am Mon-Thu, 9am-3am Fri, 10.30am-3am Sat & 6pm-2am Sun; **M** Liceu) What sets the Muy Buenas apart is the spectacular Modernista woodwork in its facade and bar area. Aside from this, it's a good spot for a quiet mojito, though it can get pretty lively on Friday and Saturday nights. You may catch a little live music or even a poetry reading, and you can nibble on a limited menu of Middle Eastern titbits.

Bar Pastís Bar

Map p78 (www.barpastis.com; Carrer de Santa Mònica 4; ⏱7.30pm-2am daily; **M** Drassanes) A French cabaret theme (with lots of Piaf in the background) dominates this tiny, cluttered classic. It's been going, on and

Bar Marsella
MATT MUNRO/LONELY PLANET ©

off, since the end of WWII. You'll need to be in here before 9pm to have a hope of sitting or getting near the bar. On some nights it features live acts, usually performing French *chansons* (songs).

London Bar
Bar

Map p78 (Carrer Nou de la Rambla 34-36; ⏱6pm-3am Mon-Thu & Sun, 6pm-3.30am Fri, Sat; MLiceu) Open since 1909, this Modernista bar started as a hang-out for circus hands and was later frequented by the likes of Picasso, Miró and Hemingway. Today it fills to the brim with punters at the long front bar and rickety old tables. On occasion, you can attend concerts at the small stage right up the back.

Marmalade
Bar

Map p78 (www.marmaladebarcelona.com; Carrer de la Riera Alta 4-6; ⏱6.30pm-2.30am Mon-Wed, 10am-2.30am Thu-Sun; MSant Antoni) The golden hues of this backlit bar and restaurant beckon seductively through the glass facade. There are various distinct spaces, decorated in different but equally sumptuous styles, and a pool table next to the bar. Cocktails are big business here, and a selection of them are €5 all night.

Moog
Club

Map p78 (www.masimas.com/moog; Carrer de l'Arc del Teatre 3; admission €10; ⏱midnight-5am Mon-Thu & Sun, midnight-6am Fri & Sat; MDrassanes) This fun and minuscule club is a standing favourite with the downtown crowd. In the main dance area, DJs dish out house, techno and electro, while upstairs you can groove to a nice blend of indie and occasional classic-pop throwbacks.

⭐ Entertainment

Filmoteca de Catalunya
Cinema

Map p78 (📞93 567 10 70; www.filmoteca. cat; Plaça de Salvador Seguí 1-9; adult/concession €4/2 ; ⏱4-10pm Tue-Sun; MLiceu) After almost a decade of planning and preparations, the Filmoteca de Catalunya (Catalonia's national cinema) moved into this modern 6000-sq-metre building

in 2012. It's a glass, metal and concrete beast that hulks in the midst of the most louche part of the Raval, but the building's interior shouts revival, with light and space, wall-to-wall windows, skylights and glass panels that let the sun in.

Jazz Sí Club
Live Music

Map p78 (📞93 329 00 20; www.tallerdemusics. com; Carrer de Requesens 2; admission €4-9, incl drink; ⏱8.30-11pm Tue-Sat, 6.30-10pm Sun; MSant Antoni) A cramped little bar run by the Taller de Músics (Musicians' Workshop) serves as the stage for a varied program of jazz jams through to some good flamenco (Friday nights). Thursday night is Cuban night, Tuesday and Sunday nights feature rock, and the rest are devoted to jazz and/or blues sessions. Concerts start around 9pm but the jam sessions can get going earlier.

23 Robadors
Live Music

Map p78 (Carrer d'en Robador 23; admission varies; ⏱8pm-3am daily; MLiceu) On what remains a sleazy Raval street, where a hardy band of streetwalkers, junkies and other misfits hang out in spite of all the work being carried out to gentrify the area, a narrow little bar has made a name for itself with its shows and live music. Jazz is the name of the game, but you'll also find live poetry, flamenco and more.

Cangrejo
Gay

Map p78 (📞93 301 29 78; Carrer de Montserrat 9; ⏱11pm-3am Fri & Sat; MDrassanes) This altar to kitsch, a dingy dance hall that has transgressed since the 1920s, is run by the luminous underground cabaret figure of Carmen Mairena and exudes a gorgeously tacky feel, especially with the midnight drag shows on Friday and Saturday. Due to its popularity with tourists, getting in is all but impossible unless you turn up early.

Gipsy Lou
Live Music

Map p78 (www.gipsylou.com; Carrer de Ferlandina 55; ⏱7pm-2.30am Sun-Thu, 7pm-3am Sat; MSant Antoni) A louche little bar that packs 'em in for live music from rumba to pop to flamenco, along with occasional storytelling events, and whatever else Felipe feels like putting on. There are decent bar snacks to keep you going on a long night of pisco sours, the house special.

🔒 Shopping

The area has a handful of art galleries around MACBA, along with a burgeoning secondhand and vintage clothes scene on Carrer de la Riera Baixa. Carrer dels Tallers is one of the city's main music strips.

Fantastik   Arts & Crafts
Map p78 (www.fantastik.es; Carrer de Joaquín Costa 62; ⊙11am-2pm & 4-8.30pm Mon-Fri, noon-9pm Sat, closed Sun; Ⓜ Universitat) Over 400 products, including a Mexican skull rattle, robot moon explorer from China and recycled plastic zebras from South Africa, are to be found in this colourful shop, which sources its items from Mexico, India, Bulgaria, Russia, Senegal and 20 other countries. It's a perfect place to buy all the things you don't need but can't live without.

La Portorriqueña   Coffee
Map p78 (Carrer d'en Xuclà 25; ⊙9am-2pm & 5-8pm Mon-Fri, 9am-2pm Sat; Ⓜ Catalunya) Coffee beans from around the world, freshly ground before your eyes, has been the winning formula in this store since 1902. It also offers all sorts of chocolate goodies. The street is good for little old-fashioned food boutiques.

Holala! Plaza   Fashion
Map p78 (Plaça de Castella 2; ⊙11am-9pm Mon-Sat; Ⓜ Universitat) Backing on to Carrer de Valldonzella, where it boasts an exhibition space (Gallery) for temporary art displays,

this Ibiza import is inspired by that island's long established (and somewhat commercialised) hippie tradition. Vintage clothes are the name of the game, along with an eclectic program of exhibitions and activities.

Discos Castelló   Music
Map p78 (Carrer dels Tallers 7; ⊙10am-8.30pm Mon-Sat; Ⓜ Catalunya) Castelló used to dominate this street of instrument and CD shops, but the recession took its toll and now only this store remains, selling new and second-hand CDs of all types of music from heavy metal to classical, along with a selection of related books and paraphernalia.

Teranyina   Arts & Crafts
Map p78 (www.teresarosa.com; Carrer del Notariat 10; ⊙11am-3pm & 5-8pm Mon-Fri; Ⓜ Catalunya) Artist Teresa Rosa Aguayo runs this textile workshop in the heart of the artsy bit of El Raval. You can join courses at the loom, admire some of the rugs and other works that Teresa has created, and, of course, buy them.

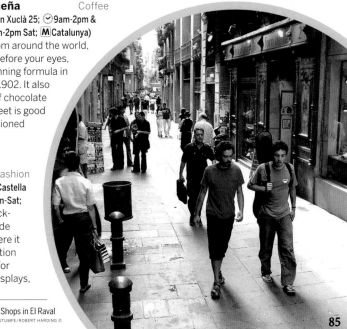

Shops in El Raval
JUERGEN STUMPE/ROBERT HARDING ©

La Ribera

La Ribera is a fascinating blend of history and cutting edge. It has a warren of medieval buildings inhabited by celebrated museums, award-winning restaurants and eye-catching boutiques. The south part of the district, known as El Born, should be your first port of call. Here you'll find the magnificent Gothic Basílica de Santa Maria del Mar and the atmospheric Carrer de Montcada, a street lined with Gothic and baroque mansions as well as the city's major museums.

Passeig del Born was Barcelona's main square from the 13th to the 18th centuries and still has an air of excitement around it – dozens of bars, cafes and some good restaurants line it, and the streets that cross this short drag are packed with some impressive (quite high-end) shopping. It's a popular night-time area for locals, especially in the summer when terraces get full and bars throw open their doors.

El Xampanyet (p104)

La Ribera Highlights

El Born Reborn (p99)

Barcelona rarely stands still, especially in El Born, the tight grid of streets south of Carrer de la Princesa that has been transformed into its most à la mode neighbourhood. Passeig del Born and the Plaça de Santa María del Mar are the hottest strips: trendy boutiques merge with hip bars, specialist shops and experimental cuisine. The renaissance began in the 1990s but shows no signs of abating. Below: Plaça de Santa María del Mar

1

2 ## Palau de la Música Catalana (p102)

Give a Modernista architect (Lluís Domènech i Montaner) carte blanche in a music theatre and this is what you get: a splendiferous quasi-palace. Dripping in intricate details, the 1908 palace is music recreated in stone and stained glass with fine acoustics to match. For the most intimate picture, take a guided tour. For a full musical explosion, attend a performance.

ADRIENNE BRESNAHAN/GETTY IMAGES ©

Basílica de Santa Maria del Mar (p99) 3

DAVID CLAPP/GETTY IMAGES ©

The Barri Gòtic might be Barcelona's quintessential medieval quarter, but you have to roam a few blocks east to view its greatest Gothic monument. This 14th-century church exhibits the purest manifestation of the Gothic genre. The exterior is rather monastic, but inside, soaring columns, a light-filled apse and magnificent stained-glass windows create a sense of solemn beauty.

JEAN-PIERRE LESCOURRET/GETTY IMAGES ©

4 Parc de la Ciutadella (p94)

For a long time, La Ciutadella was the city's only green space and it still serves as a vital setting for a bit fresh air for residents living in the narrow lanes of the Ciutat Vella (Old City). Aside from offering the standard diversions of walking, jogging and lounging on the grass for an afternoon siesta, the park has a zoo, a Gaudíesque fountain, curious sculptures and the Catalan parliament. Above: Parlament de Catalunya

5 Museu Picasso (p92)

Set in five adjacent Gothic-baroque mansions, this art museum showcases Picasso's early career. Works that predate the painter's Cubist reinvention in Paris offer insight into his youthful development. They also emphasise the role that Barcelona has played in influencing him. For late-career fans, a trio of rooms is dedicated to Picasso's reevaluation of Velázquez's *Las Meninas*.

La Ribera Walk

The star of the Ciutat Vella (Old City), La Ribera is packed with great monuments that span the centuries. Former jousting grounds, medieval merchant houses, one magnificent Gothic church and a celebrated music hall from the 20th century are all part of La Ribera's enchanting mix.

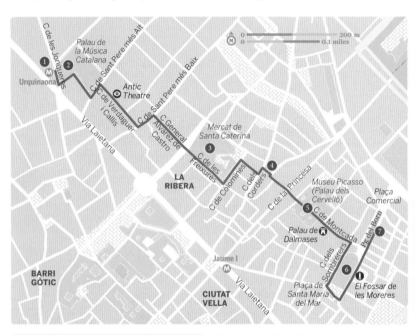

❶ La Caixa

An outstanding example of Modernista architecture, **La Caixa** savings bank pays homage to Barcelona's Gothic past, with its faux bell tower, arched windows, stained glass and sculpture. Note the statue of a woman holding a (savings) box in the corner. The logo of La Caixa – a blue star with a yellow circle above a red circle – was designed by Joan Miró and symbolizes a person dropping a coin into a piggy bank.

❷ Palau de la Música Catalana

Around the corner you'll find the extravagant **Palau de la Música Catalana** (p102), designed by Domènech i Montaner in the early 1900s. Sculptures of mythic figures (like flag-holding St George, a patron saint of Catalonia) and famous composers as well as ordinary Catalan citizens adorn the facade. To see the theatre, come back for a guided tour or an evening concert.

❸ Mercat de Santa Caterina

Make your way through the narrow lanes of La Ribera, passing by the **Antic Theatre**

(Carrer de Verdaguer i Callís 12) with its pleasant courtyard cafe. The next stop is the **Mercat de Santa Caterina** (p95), a modern version of a 19th-century market. In addition to a bounty of meats, fish, cheeses, olives and eateries, the market holds the remains of a 15th-century monastery.

④ Capella d'en Marcús

At the corner of Carrer dels Corders and the northern end of the street, just beyond the 19th-century Carrer de la Princesa, stands a Romanesque **chapel**, originally built in the 12th century. The Capella d'en Marcús once served as a wayfarers' stop on the road northeast out of medieval Barcelona.

⑤ Carrer de Montacada

During the Middle Ages **Carrer de Monta-cada** was the city's most stylish address for the merchant classes. The bulk of the great mansions remaining today date to the 14th and 15th centuries, and several have been converted into major museums, like the **Museu Picasso** (p92). By night, the baroque courtyard of the medieval Palau de Dalmases at number 20 hosts live music.

⑥ Basílica de Santa Maria del Mar

Barcelona's most stirring **Gothic structure** (p99) looms majestically above the compact cobblestone lanes of El Born. Inside, a real sense of light and space pervades the entire sanctuary of the church. Opposite the church's southern flank at El Fossar de les Moreres, an eternal flame commemorates the Catalan resistance fighters, buried here after the siege of Barcelona ended in defeat in September 1714 during the War of the Spanish Succession.

⑦ Passeig del Born

One of Barcelona's prettiest **pedestrian lanes** has a graceful setting amid outdoor cafes and bars. Still a favourite with prom-enading residents, the Passeig del Born was Barcelona's main square from the 13th to 18th centuries. Jousting tournaments, executions and other public entertainments took place here in the Middle Ages.

The Best...

PLACES TO EAT

Bormuth Serves both classic and new wave tapas, plus tasty vermouths. (p100)

Le Cucine Mandarosso Hearty Italian dishes, cooked to perfection. (p102)

Passadís Del Pep A much-loved local seafood haunt. (p103)

El Atril A brilliant menu of global fusion. (p101)

PLACES TO DRINK

La Vinya del Senyor Great wine list and outdoor seating. (p103)

Juanra Falces White-jacketed waiters serve up artful elixirs. (p103)

El Xampanyet One of Barcelona's most famous (and jovial) *cava* bars. (p104)

Miramelindo Stylish spot on buzzing Passeig del Born. (p103)

ARTFUL SPACES

Basílica de Santa Maria del Mar Sublime Gothic cathedral. (p99)

Palau de la Musica Catalana A fairy-tale-like music hall. (p102)

Parc de la Ciutadella Pleasant green space with a dramatic cascade. (p94)

Seafood tapas
MICHAEL HEFFERNAN/LONELY PLANET ©

Don't Miss
Museu Picasso

The setting alone, in five contiguous medieval stone mansions, makes the Museu Picasso unique (and worth the probable queues). The pretty courtyards, galleries and staircases pre-served in the first three of these buildings are as delightful as the collection inside. The exhibitions showcase Picasso's early career. Works that pre-date the painter's Cubist reinvention in Paris offer insight into his youthful development. They also emphasise the role that Barcelona has played in influencing one of the giants of the art world.

Map p96

☎ 93 256 30 00

www.museupicasso.bcn.es

Carrer de Montcada 15-23

adult/senior & child under 16yr/ student €11/ free/6, temporary exhibitions €6/ free/2.90, 3-8pm Sun & 1st Sun of month free

🕓 9am-7pm Tue-Sun, until 9.30pm Thu

Ⓜ Jaume I

The Collection

While the collection concentrates on Picasso's formative years, there is enough material from subsequent periods to give you a thorough impression of his versatility and genius. Above all, you come away feeling that Picasso was the true original, always one step ahead of himself (let alone anyone else) in his search for new forms of expression.

Early Work

A visit starts with sketches and oils from Picasso's earliest years in Málaga and La Coruña – around 1893–95. Some of his self-portraits and the portraits of his father, which date from 1896, are evidence enough of his precocious talent. *Retrato de la Tía Pepa* (*Portrait of Aunt Pepa*), done in Málaga in 1896, shows the incredible maturity of his brushstrokes and his ability to portray character – at the tender age of 15. Picasso painted the enormous *Ciència i Caritat* (*Science and Charity*) the same year, showcasing his masterful academic techniques of portraiture. His ingeniousness extends to his models too. His father stands in for the doctor, and the sick woman and child are modelled by a beggar whom he hired off the street along with her offspring.

Blue Period

Other highlights include paintings from Picasso's Blue Period. *Woman with Bonnet* is an important work from this time, depicting a captive from the Saint-Lazare women's prison and veneral disease hospital which Picasso visited when in Paris. This visit started Picasso's fascination with people in the down-and-out layers of society. His nocturnal blue-tinted views of *Terrats de Barcelona* (*Roofs of Barcelona*) and *El Foll* (*The Madman*) are cold and cheerless, yet somehow alive. During this period he frequently painted the city rooftops from different perspectives. He also did many drawings of beggars, the blind and the impoverished elderly throughout 1903 and 1904 – *El Foll* is one of the most impressive from those series.

Don't Miss List

BY MALÉN GUAL, CURATOR AT MUSEU PICASSO

1 SCIENCE AND CHARITY

In 1897, Picasso started work on a canvas that would strengthen his position in the Spanish art world: *Science and Charity*. Following the guidelines of social realism and in an absolutely academic style, the work is the postscript to that first period of his youth. It was painted when he was only 15 years old.

2 DWARF-DANCER (LA NANA)

When Picasso painted this in 1901, his work was influenced by Toulouse-Lautrec. However, unlike Lautrec's work, there is very little drawing in his oils. The application of the brushstroke is harsh, the colours are warm and vehement, and the paint is often applied in medium and light brushstrokes. He searched for subjects for his paintings in dancehalls and cabarets, like Le Moulin Rouge.

3 EL PASEO DEL COLOM

In 1917, Picasso came to Barcelona with the Russian Ballets in pursuit of one of the Russian ballerinas, Olga Kokhlova. In *El Paseo del Colom*, Passeig de Colon is seen from the Ranzini guest house where Olga was staying. The painting combines Cubism with Divisionism.

4 HARLEQUIN

Here Picasso opts for a return to Classicism, not only in the execution but also in the softness and subtlety of the tonalities, which is reminiscent of the harlequins of 1905. Picasso presented the work at the art exhibition of 1919.

5 LAS MENINAS SUITE

Between August and December 1957, Picasso carried out an exhaustive analysis of Velázquez's *Las Meninas*. This suite of 58 works is a comprehensive study of rhythm, colour and movement. It is also a constant play of imagination in metamorphosing the personalities of a number of the components of the work. However, his faithfulness and respect towards the atmosphere of Velázquez's work are evident through all the compositions.

93

Discover La Ribera

Getting There & Away

- **Metro** Línia 4 coasts down the southwest flank of La Ribera, stopping at Urquinaona, Jaume I and Barceloneta. Línia 1 also stops nearby, at Urquinaona and Arc de Triomf (the nearest stop for the Parc de la Ciutadella).

Sights

Museu Picasso   Museum
See p92

Parc de la Ciutadella   Park
Map p96 (Passeig de Picasso; **M** Arc de Triomf)
FREE Come for a stroll, a picnic, a visit to the zoo or to inspect Catalonia's regional parliament, but don't miss a visit to this, the most central green lung in the city. Parc de la Ciutadella is perfect for winding down.

After the War of the Spanish Succession, Felipe V razed a swath of La Ribera to build a huge fortress (La Ciutadella), designed to keep watch over Barcelona. It became a loathed symbol of everything Catalans hated about Madrid and the Bourbon kings, and was later used as a political prison. Only in 1869 did the central government allow its demolition, after which the site was turned into a park and used for the Universal Exhibition of 1888.

The monumental **cascada** (waterfall) near the Passeig de Pujades park entrance, created between 1875 and 1881 by Josep Fontserè with the help of an enthusiastic young Gaudí, is a dramatic combination of statuary, rugged rocks, greenery and thundering water – all of it perfectly artificial. Nearby, you can hire a rowing boat to paddle about in the small lake.

To the southeast, in what might be seen as an exercise in black humour, the fort's former arsenal now houses the **Parlament de Catalunya** (www.parlament. cat; ☺ guided tours 10am-1pm Sat, Sun & holidays). You can join free guided tours, in Catalan and Spanish only, on Saturdays and Sundays. The building is open for

Mercat de Santa Caterina
MATT MUNRO/LONELY PLANET ©

independent visiting on 11 September from 10am to 7pm. On show to the public are the sweeping Escala d'Honor (Stairway of Honour) and the several solemn halls that lead to the Saló de Sessions, the semicircular auditorium where parliament sits. In the lily pond at the centre of the garden in front of the building is a statue of a seemingly heartbroken woman, *Desconsol* (Distress; 1907), by Josep Llimona.

The Passeig de Picasso side of the park is lined with several buildings constructed for, or just before, the Universal Exhibition. The medieval-looking caprice at the top end is the most engaging. Known as the **Castell dels Tres Dragons** (Castle of the Three Dragons), it long housed the Museu de Zoologia, which has since moved to the Fòrum area and is now known as the Museu Blau. Domènech i Montaner put the 'castle's' trimmings on a pioneering steel frame. The coats of arms are all invented and the whole building exudes a teasing, playful air. It was used as a cafe-restaurant during the Universal Exhibition of 1888.

To the south is L'Hivernacle, an elaborate greenhouse. Next come the former Museu de Geologia and L'Umbracle, a palm house. On Passeig de Picasso itself is Antoni Tàpies' typically impenetrable **Homenatge a Picasso**. Water runs down the panes of a glass box full of bits of old furniture and steel girders.

Northwest of the park, Passeig de Lluís Companys is capped by the Modernista **Arc de Triomf** (Passeig de Lluís Companys; MArc de Triomf), designed by Josep Vilaseca as the principal Exhibition entrance, with unusual, Mudéjar-style brickwork. Josep Llimona did the main reliefs. Just what the triumph was eludes us, especially since the Exhibition itself was a commercial failure. It is perhaps best thought of as a bricks-and-mortar embodiment of the city's general fin-de-siècle feel-good factor.

Mercat de Santa Caterina — Market

Map p96 (✆ 93 319 17 40; www.mercatsanta caterina.com; Avinguda de Francesc Cambó 16; ⏱ 7.30am-2pm Mon, to 3.30pm Tue, Wed & Sat, to 8.30pm Thu & Fri, closed afternoons Jul & Aug; M Jaume I) Come shopping for your tomatoes at this extraordinary-looking produce market, designed by Enric Miralles and Benedetta Tagliabue to replace its 19th-century predecessor. Finished in 2005, it is distinguished by its kaleidoscopic and undulating roof, held up above the bustling produce stands, restaurants, cafes and bars by twisting slender branches of what look like grey steel trees.

Zoo de Barcelona — Zoo

Map p96 (✆ 902 457545; www.zoobarcelona.cat; Parc de la Ciutadella; adult/child €19.90/€11.95; ⏱ 10am-5.30pm Nov-Mar, to 7pm Apr, May, Sep, Oct, to 8pm Jun-Aug; ⛹; M Barceloneta) The zoo is a great day out for kids, with 7500 critters that range from geckos to gorillas, lions and elephants – there are more than 400 species, plus picnic areas dotted all around and a wonderful adventure playground. There are pony rides, a petting zoo and a mini-train meandering through the grounds. A new marine zoo being built on the coast of El Fòrum northeast of the city centre will ease the currently slightly crowded space, although the recession has meant plans are stalled for the time being.

Museu de la Xocolata — Museum

Map p96 (✆ 93 268 78 78; www.museuxocolata. cat; Carrer del Comerç 36; adult/senior & student/ child under 7yr/€5/4.25/free; ⏱ 10am-7pm Mon-Sat, to 3pm Sun & holidays; ⛹; M Jaume I) Chocoholics have a hard time containing themselves in this museum dedicated to the fundamental foodstuff, particularly when faced with tempting displays of cocoa-based treats in the cafe at the exit. The displays trace the origins of chocolate, its arrival in Europe, and the many myths and images associated with it. Among the informative stuff and machinery used in the production of chocolate are large chocolate models of emblematic buildings such as La Sagrada Família, along with various characters, local and international.

La Ribera

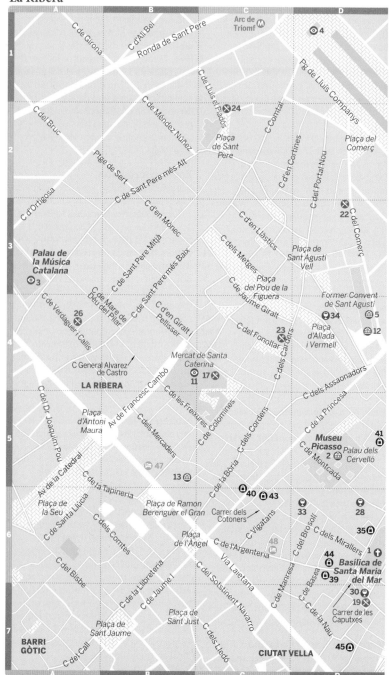

Arc de Triomf

4

Pg de Lluís Companys

C de Girona

C d'Ali Bei

Ronda de Sant Pere

C de Lluís el Piadós

24

C de Méndez Núñez

Plaça de Sant Pere

C del Bruc

Plaça del Comerç

C d'en Cortines

C del Portal-Nou

Ptge de Sert

C de Sant Pere més Alt

C del Comerç

22

C d'Ortigosa

C d'en Monec

C d'en Llàstics

Plaça de Sant Agustí Vell

Palau de la Música Catalana

3

C de Sant Pere Mitjà

C dels Metges

Plaça del Pou de la Figuera

Plaça de Jaume Giralt

Former Convent de Sant Agustí

34

5

C de Verdaguer i Callís

26

C de Mare de Déu del Pilar

C de Sant Pere més Baix

C d'en Giralt i Pellisser

C del Fonollar

23

C dels Carders

Plaça d'Allada i Vermell

12

C General Alvarez de Castro

LA RIBERA

Mercat de Santa Caterina

17

11

C dels Assaonadors

C de Francesc Cambó

C de les Freixures

C dels Colomines

C de la Princesa

Plaça d'Antoni Maura

C dels Mercaders

C dels Corders

Museu Picasso

2

41

Palau dels Cervelló

C del Dr Joaquim Pou

C de la Bòria

C de Montcada

47

13

40

43

33

28

Av de la Catedral

C de la Tapineria

Plaça de Ramon Berenguer el Gran

Carrer dels Cotoners

C Vigatans

35

1

Plaça de la Seu

Plaça de Santa Llúcia

C dels Comtes

Plaça de l'Àngel

C de l'Argenteria

48

C del Brosoli

C dels Mirallers

44

Basílica de Santa Maria del Mar

39

C del Bisbe

C de la Llibreteria

Via Laietana

C del Sotstinent Navarro

C de Manresa

C de Basea

30

19

Carrer de les Caputxes

C de Jaume I

Plaça de Sant Jaume

Plaça de Sant Just

C dels Lledó

C de la Nau

BARRI GÒTIC

C del Call

CIUTAT VELLA

45

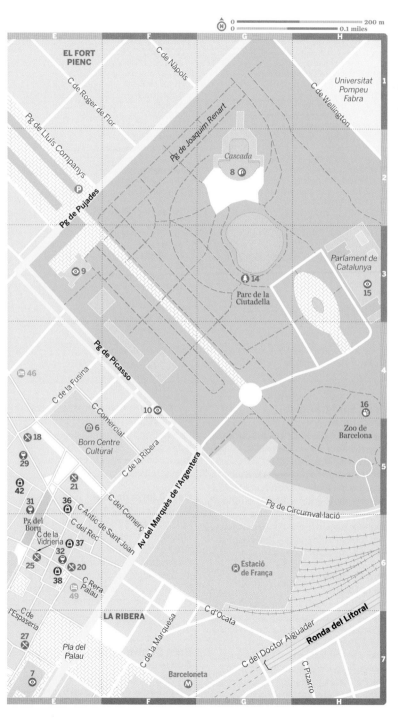

0
200 m
0
0.1 miles

EL FORT PIENC

C de Nàpols

Universitat Pompeu Fabra

C de Roger de Flor

C de Wellington

Pg de Lluís Companys

Pg de Joaquim Renart

Cascada
8 🔘

Pg de Pujades

P

🔘 9

Parlament de Catalunya

🔘 15

🧍 14

Parc de la Ciutadella

Pg de Picasso

C de la Fusina

📷 46

C Comercial

10 🔘

16 ✛

Zoo de Barcelona

🏛 6

Born Centre Cultural

C de la Ribera

C de la Ribera

Av del Marquès de l'Argentera

❌ 18

🍴 29

🍴 21

🔒 42

31

36 🔒

C Antic de Sant Joan

C del Comerç

Pg de Circumval·lació

Pg del Born

C del Rec

C de la Vidrieria 🔒 37

32 🔒

❌ 25

🔒 20

38 🔒

C Rera Palau

📷 49

Estació de França

C de l'Espaseria

LA RIBERA

C de la Marquesa

C d'Ocata

Ronda del Litoral

❌ 27

Pla del Palau

Barceloneta Ⓜ

C del Doctor Aiguader

C Pizarro

7 🔘

La Ribera

Arxiu Fotogràfic de Barcelona
Gallery

Map p96 (📞 93 256 34 20; www.bcn.cat/arxiu/fotografic; Plaça de Pons i Clerch 2, 2A; ⊕10am-7pm Mon-Sat; Ⓜ Jaume I) **FREE** On the 2nd floor of the former Convent de Sant Agustí is the modest exhibition space of this city photo archive. Photos on show are generally related to the city, as the photo collection is principally devoted to that theme, from the late 19th century until the late 20th century.

Museu del Rei de la Màgia
Museum

Map p96 (📞 93 318 71 92; www.elreydelamagia.com; Carrer de les Jonqueres 15; admission €3; ⊕11am-2pm & 4-8pm Thu-Sun, closed Sun morning Jul & Aug; 🚼; Ⓜ Jaume I) This museum is a timeless curio. It is the scene of magic shows, home to collections of material that hark back to the 19th-century origins of the associated magic shop (p105) at

Carrer de la Princesa 11 (which holds everything from old posters and books for learning tricks to magic wands and trick cards) and the place for budding magicians of all ages to enrol in courses. Seeing is believing.

Casa Llotja de Mar
Architecture

Map p96 (La Llotja; 📞 93 547 88 49; www.casal-lotja.com; Passeig d'Isabel II 1; Ⓜ Barceloneta) The centrepiece of the city's medieval stock exchange (more affectionately known as La Llotja) is the fine Gothic Saló de Contractacions (Transaction Hall), built in the 14th century. Pablo Picasso and Joan Miró attended the art school that was housed in the Saló dels Cònsols from 1849.

Born Centre Cultural
Historic Building

Map p96 (📞 93 256 68 51; www.elborncentre-cultural.bcn.cat; Plaça Comercial 12; centre free,

EURASIA/GETTY IMAGES ©

 ## Don't Miss
Basílica de Santa Maria del Mar

At the southwest end of Passeig del Born stands the apse of Barcelona's finest Catalan Gothic church, Santa Maria del Mar (Our Lady of the Sea). Built in the 14th century with record-breaking alacrity for the time (it took just 54 years), the church is remarkable for its architectural harmony and simplicity.

NEED TO KNOW

Map p96; ☏ 93 310 23 90; Plaça de Santa Maria del Mar; ⏱9am-1.30pm & 4.30-8.30pm Mon-Sat, 10.30am-1.30pm & 4.30-8.30pm Sun; Ⓜ Jaume I

exhibition spaces adult/child €6/free; ⏱10am-8pm Tue-Sun; Ⓜ Barceloneta) Launched to great fanfare in 2013, as part of the events held for the tercentenary of the Catalan defeat in the War of the Spanish Succession, this shiny new cultural space is housed in the former Mercat del Born, a handsome 19th-century structure of slatted iron and brick.

Excavation in 2001 unearthed the remains of whole streets flattened to make way for the much-hated citadel (*ciutadella*) – these are now on show on the exposed subterranean level.

 # Eating

If you'd mentioned El Born (El Borne in Spanish) in the early 1990s, you wouldn't have raised much interest. Now the area is peppered with bars, dance dives, groovy designer stores and restaurants. El Born is where Barcelona is truly cooking – avant-garde chefs and fusion masters have zeroed in on this southern corner of La Ribera to conduct their culinary experiments. If you don't want to play such wild games, there's plenty of the traditional stuff to choose from, too.

Bormuth
Tapas €

Map p96 (93 310 21 86; Carrer del Rec 31; tapas from €3.50; 5pm-midnight Mon & Tue, noon-1am Wed, Thu & Sun, noon-2.30am Fri & Sat; M Jaume I) Opened on the pedestrian Carrer del Rec in 2013, Bormuth has tapped into the vogue for old-school tapas with modern-times service and decor, and serves all the old favourites – *patatas bravas, ensaladilla* (Russian salad), tortilla – along with some less predictable and superbly prepared numbers (try the chargrilled red pepper with black pudding). The split-level dining room is never less than animated, but there's a more peaceful space with a single long table if you can assemble a group.

La Llavor dels Orígens
Catalan €

Map p96 (93 310 75 31; www.lallavordelsorigens.com; Carrer de la Vidrieria 6-8; mains €8-11; 12.30pm-midnight; M Jaume I) In this treasure chest of Catalan regional products, the shop shelves groan under the weight of bottles and packets of goodies. It also has a long menu of smallish dishes, such as *sopa de carbassa i castanyes* (pumpkin and chestnut soup) or *mandonguilles amb alberginies* (rissoles with aubergine), that you can mix and match over wine by the glass.

Bar Joan
Catalan €

Map p96 (93 310 61 50; Mercat de Santa Caterina; menú del día €11, tapas from €3; 7.30am-2pm Mon, to 3.30pm Tue, Wed & Sat, to 8.30pm Thu & Fri, closed afternoons Jul & Aug; M Jaume I) Along with the popular Cuines de Santa Caterina, there are a couple of bar-eateries in the Mercat de Santa Caterina. Bar Joan is known especially to locals for its *arròs negre* (cuttlefish-ink rice) on Tuesday at lunchtime and paella on Thursdays. It's a simple spot, with only tapas or the *menú del día* (daily set menu), but it's friendly and good value.

Left: A tapas restaurant; **Below:** *Jamón* tapas

En Aparté — French €

Map p96 (☏ 93 269 13 35; www.enaparte.es; Carrer Lluis el Piados 2; mains €7-10; ☺10am-1am Tue-Thu, 10am-2am Fri & Sat, noon-1am Sun; 🛜; Ⓜ Arc de Triomf or Urquinaona) A great low-key place for good-quality French food, just off the quiet Plaça de Sant Pere. The restaurant is small but spacious, with sewing-machine tables and vintage details, and floor-to-ceiling windows that bring in some early-afternoon sunlight.

Bubó — Pastelería €

Map p96 (☏ 93 268 72 24; www.bubo.es; Carrer de les Caputxes 6 & 10; tapas from €5; ☺10am-9pm Mon-Thu & Sun, 10am-midnight Fri & Sat; Ⓜ Barceloneta) Carles Mampel is a wizard of desserts. It is hard to walk by his bar and pastry shop without trying one of his fantasy-laden creations. Try saying no to a mousse of *gianduia* (a dark hazelnut cream) with mango cream, spiced caramelised hazelnuts, and a hazelnut biscuit.

El Atril — International €€

Map p96 (☏ 93 310 12 20; www.atrilbarcelona. com; Carrer dels Carders 23; mains €11-15; ☺6pm-midnight Mon, noon-midnight Tue-Thu, noon-1am Fri & Sat, 11.30am-11.30pm Sun; Ⓜ Jaume I) Aussie owner Brenden is inspired by culinary influences from all over the globe, so while you'll see plenty of tapas (the *patatas bravas* are recommended for their homemade sauce), you'll also find kangaroo fillet, salmon and date rolls with mascarpone, chargrilled turkey with fried yucca, and plenty more. If the weather is good or there's no room in the cosy dining room, there are tables outside in a lively square.

Casa Delfín — Spanish €€

Map p96 (☏ 93 319 50 88; www.tallerdetapas. com; Passeig del Born 36; mains €10-15; ☺8am-midnight daily, until 1am Fri & Sat; Ⓜ Barceloneta) One of Barcelona's culinary delights, Casa Delfín is everything you dream of

101

DE AGOSTINI/S. VANNINI/GETTY IMAGES ©

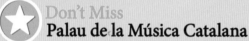

Don't Miss
Palau de la Música Catalana

This concert hall is a high point of Barcelona's Modernista architecture, a symphony in tile, brick, sculpted stone and stained glass. Built by Domènech i Montaner between 1905 and 1908 for the Orfeó Català musical society, it was conceived as a temple for the Catalan Renaixença (Renaissance).

NEED TO KNOW
📞 93 295 72 00; www.palaumusica.org; Carrer de Sant Francesc de Paula 2; adult/child €17/free; ⏱guided tours 10am-3.30pm daily; Ⓜ Urquinaona

when you think of Catalan (and Mediterranean) cooking. Start with the tangy and sweet *calçots* (a cross between a leek and an onion; February and March only) or salt-strewn *padron* peppers, moving on to grilled sardines speckled with parsley, then tackle the meaty monkfish roasted in white wine and garlic.

Cal Pep Tapas €€
Map p96 (📞 93 310 79 61; www.calpep.com; Plaça de les Olles 8; mains €12-20; ⏱7.30-11.30pm Mon, 1-3.45pm & 7.30-11.30pm Tue-Fri, 1-3.45pm Sat, closed last 3 weeks Aug; Ⓜ Barceloneta) It's getting a foot in the door here that's the problem – there can be queues

out into the square with people trying to get in. And if you want one of the five tables out the back, you'll need to call ahead. Most people are happy elbowing their way to the bar for some of the tastiest gourmet seafood tapas in town.

Le Cucine Mandarosso Italian €€
Map p96 (📞 93 269 07 80; www.lecucine-mandarosso.com; Carrer Verdaguer i Callis 4; mains €12-14, menú del día €11; ⏱1.30-4pm & 9pm-midnight Tue-Sat; Ⓜ Urquinaona) This is comfort food done to perfection – the menu changes daily, with only a handful of mains to choose from, most of which are pasta, and one or two fish or meat.

The antipasti can be vegetables, or fresh cheese, such as the wonderfully creamy *burrata* (fresh cheese made from mozzarella and cream), buffalo-milk mozzarella, or smoked *scamorza* and *provola* cheese.

Comerç 24 International €€€

Map p96 (93 319 21 02; www.carlesabellan.com; Carrer del Comerç 24; mains €24-32; 1.30-3.30pm & 8.30-11pm Tue-Sat; Barceloneta) Michelin-starred chef Carles Abellán playfully reinterprets the traditional (suckling pig 'Hanoi style'), as well as more international classics, such as the bite-sized mini-pizza sashimi with tuna; *melón con jamón,* a *millefeuille* of layered caramelised Iberian ham and thinly sliced melon; or oxtail with cauliflower purée. If your budget will stretch to it, try a little of almost everything with the Menú del Gran Festival (€116).

Passadís Del Pep Seafood €€€

Map p96 (93 310 10 21; www.passadis.com; Pla del Palau 2; mains €18-23; 1.15-3.45pm Mon-Sat; Barceloneta) There's no sign, but locals know where to head for a seafood feast. They say that the restaurant's raw materials are delivered daily from fishing ports along the Catalan coast. There is no menu – what's on offer depends on what the sea has surrendered on the day – but you can count on something along the lines of fresh seafood and/or fish, a bit of *jamón* (cured ham), tomato bread and grilled vegetables. Just head down the long, ill-lit corridor and entrust yourself to its care.

Drinking & Nightlife

Countless bars dot the elongated Passeig del Born and the web of streets winding off it and around the Basílica de Santa Maria del Mar – the area has an ebullient, party feel.

Mudanzas Bar

Map p96 (93 319 11 37; Carrer de la Vidrieria 15; 9.30am-2.30am Mon-Fri, 5pm-3am Sat

& Sun; ; Jaume I) This was one of the first bars to get things into gear in El Born and it still attracts a faithful crowd. It's a straightforward place for a beer, a chat and perhaps a sandwich. Oh, and it has a nice line in rums and malt whiskey.

La Vinya del Senyor Wine Bar

Map p96 (93 310 33 79; www.lavinyadelsenyor.com; Plaça de Santa Maria del Mar 5; noon-1am Mon-Thu, noon-2am Fri & Sat, noon-midnight Sun; Jaume I) Relax on the *terrassa,* which lies in the shadow of Basílica de Santa Maria del Mar, or crowd inside at the tiny bar. The wine list is as long as *War and Peace* and there's a table upstairs for those who opt to sample by the bottle rather than the glass.

Juanra Falces Cocktail Bar

Map p96 (93 310 10 27; Carrer del Rec 24; 8pm-3am, from 10pm Mon & Sun; Jaume I) Transport yourself to a Humphrey Bogart movie in this narrow little bar, formerly (and still, at least among the locals) known as Gimlet. White-jacketed bar staff with all the appropriate aplomb will whip you up a gimlet or any other classic cocktail (around €10) your heart desires.

Rubí Bar

Map p96 (647 773707; Carrer dels Banys Vells 6; 7.30pm-2.30am; Jaume I) With its boudoir lighting and cheap mojitos, Rubí is where El Born's cognoscenti head for a nightcap – or several. It's a narrow, cosy space – push through to the back where you might just get one of the coveted tables – with superior bar food, from Vietnamese rolls to more traditional selections of cheese and ham.

Miramelindo Bar

Map p96 (93 310 37 27; Passeig del Born 15; 8pm-2.30am; Jaume I) A spacious tavern in a Gothic building, this remains a classic on Passeig del Born for mixed drinks, while soft jazz and soul sounds float overhead. Try for a comfy seat at a table towards the back before it fills to bursting. A couple of similarly barn-sized places line this side of the *passeig.*

El Xampanyet
Wine Bar

Map p96 (☎93 319 70 03; Carrer de Montcada 22; ⏰noon-3.30pm & 7-11pm Tue-Sat, noon-4pm Sun; Ⓜ Jaume I) Nothing has changed for decades in this, one of the city's best-known cava bars. Plant yourself at the bar or seek out a table against the decoratively tiled walls for a glass or three of the cheap house cava and an assortment of tapas, such as the tangy *boquerons en vinagre* (fresh anchovies in vinegar).

Upiaywasi
Bar

Map p96 (☎93 268 01 54; www.upiaywasi.com; Carrer d'Allada Vermell 11; ⏰12.30pm-2am Mon-Thu, 11am-3am Fri & Sat, 11am-1am Sun; Ⓜ Barceloneta) Slide into this dimly lit bar, which crosses a chilled ambiance with Latin American music. A mix of sofas and intimate table settings, chandeliers and muted decorative tones lend the place a pleasingly conspiratorial feel. During the day most people will be found on the terrace.

⭐ Entertainment

Palau de la Música Catalana
Classical Music

Map p96 (☎93 295 72 00; www.palaumusica.org; Carrer de Sant Francesc de Paula 2; ⏰box office 9.30am-9pm Mon-Sat; Ⓜ Urquinaona) A feast for the eyes, this Modernista confection is also the city's most traditional venue for classical and choral music, although it has a wide-ranging program, including flamenco, pop and – particularly – jazz. Just being here for a performance is an experience. Sip a pre-concert tipple in the foyer, its tiled pillars all a-glitter. Head up the grand stairway to the main auditorium, a whirlpool of Modernista whimsy.

🔒 Shopping

The former commercial heart of medieval Barcelona is today still home to a cornucopia of old-style specialist food and drink shops, a veritable feast of aroma and atmosphere. They have been joined, since the late 1990s, by a raft of hip little fashion stores.

Loisaida
Clothing, Antiques

Map p96 (☎93 295 54 92; www.loisaid-abcn.com; Carrer dels Flassaders 42; ⏰11am-9pm Mon-Sat, 11am-2pm & 4-8pm Sun; Ⓜ Jaume I) A sight in its own right, housed in what was once the coach house and stables for the Royal Mint, Loisaida (from the Spanglish for 'Lower East Side') is a deceptively large emporium of colourful, retro and somewhat preppy clothing for men and women, costume jewellery, music from the 1940s and '50s and some covetable antiques.

El Xampanyet

There is more womenswear and some very cute children's lines a few doors away at **No 32** (Map p96; ☎93 295 54 92; Carrer dels Flassaders 32; ◷11am-9pm Mon-Sat, 11am-2pm & 4-8pm Sun; Ⓜ Jaume I).

Casa Gispert — Food

Map p96 (☎93 319 75 35; www.casagispert. com; Carrer dels Sombrerers 23; ◷9.30am-2pm & 4-8.30pm Tue-Fri, 10am-2pm & 5-8.30pm Sat; Ⓜ Jaume I) The wonderful, atmospheric and wood-fronted Casa Gispert has been toasting nuts and selling all manner of dried fruit since 1851. Pots and jars piled high on the shelves contain an unending variety of crunchy titbits: some roasted, some honeyed, all of them moreish. Your order is shouted over to the till, along with the price, in a display of old-world accounting.

Vila Viniteca — Drink

Map p96 (☎902 32 77 77; www.vilaviniteca.es; Carrer dels Agullers 7; ◷8.30am-8.30pm Mon-Sat; Ⓜ Jaume I) One of the best wine stores in Barcelona (and Lord knows, there are a few), this place has been searching out the best in local and imported wines since 1932. On a couple of November evenings it organises what has by now become an almost riotous wine-tasting event in Carrer dels Agullers and surrounding lanes, at which cellars from around Spain present their young new wines. At No 9 it has another store devoted to gourmet food products.

Coquette — Fashion

Map p96 (☎93 295 42 85; www.coquettebcn. com; Carrer del Rec 65; ◷11am-3pm & 5-9pm Mon-Fri, 11.30am-9pm Sat; Ⓜ Barceloneta) With its spare, cut-back and designer look, this fashion store is attractive in its own right. Women can browse through casual, feminine wear by such designers as Humanoid, Vanessa Bruno, UKE and Hoss Intropia, and others, with a further collection nearby at Carrer de Bonaire 5 (Map p96; ☎93 310 35 35; Carrer de Bonaire 5; ◷11am-3pm & 5-9pm Mon-Fri, 11.30am-8.30pm Sat; Ⓜ Barceloneta).

El Magnífico — Coffee

Map p96 (☎93 319 39 75; www.cafeselmagnifico. com; Carrer de l'Argenteria 64; ◷10am-8pm Mon-Sat; Ⓜ Jaume I) All sorts of coffee has been roasted here since the early 20th century. The variety of coffee (and tea) available is remarkable – and the aromas hit you as you walk in. Across the road, the same people run the exquisite and much newer tea shop **Sans i Sans** (☎93 310 25 18; Carrer de l'Argenteria 59; Ⓜ Jaume I).

El Rei de la Màgia — Speciality

Map p96 (☎93 319 39 20; www.elreydelamagia. com; Carrer de la Princesa 11; ◷11am-2pm & 5-8pm Mon-Fri, 11am-2pm Sat; Ⓜ Jaume I) For more than 100 years, the people behind this box of tricks have been keeping locals both astounded and amused. Should you decide to stay in Barcelona and make a living as a magician, this is the place to buy levitation brooms, glasses of disappearing milk and decks of magic cards.

Nu Sabates — Shoes, Accessories

Map p96 (☎93 268 03 83; www.nusabates. com; Carrer dels Cotoners 14; ◷11am-9pm Mon-Sat; Ⓜ Jaume I) A couple of modern-day Catalan cobblers have put together some original handmade leather shoes (and a handful of bags and other leather items) in their stylish locale.

Custo Barcelona — Fashion

Map p96 (☎93 268 78 93; www.custo-barce-lona.com; Plaça de les Olles 7; ◷10am-9pm Mon-Sat, noon-8pm Sun; Ⓜ Jaume I) The psychedelic decor and casual atmosphere lend this avant-garde Barcelona fashion store a youthful edge. Custo presents daring new women's and men's collections each year on the New York catwalks. The dazzling colours and cut of anything from dinner jackets to hot pants are for the uninhibited. It has five other stores around town.

Barceloneta & the Waterfront

Barcelona's long, sundrenched waterfront provides a pleasant escape when you need a break from Gothic lanes and Modernista architecture. Heading northeast from the Ciutat Vella, you'll soon find yourself amid tempting seafood restaurants and waterfront bars, with a palm-lined promenade taking cyclists, joggers and strollers out to the beaches, which run some 4km up to Parc del Fòrum.

Abutting the waterfront is Barceloneta, an old fishing quarter laid out in the mid-18th century with narrow grid-like streets and an earthy feel. Countless seafood eateries and a handful of bohemian drinking dens lurk in this labyrinth.

On summer days, the area fills with sunseekers making their way to and from the people-packed sands nearby. There are beaches all the way north to El Fòrum. Along the sand, rustic summertime shacks called *chringuitos* (beach bars) dole out music and cocktails day and night.

Rambla de Mar (p110); designer: Viaplana & Piñon **107**

Barceloneta & the Waterfront Highlights

Beaches (p114)

Other cities may have their diamond-dust beaches, but how often are they juxtaposed with 2000 rollercoaster years of history? Seven broad scimitars of sand lie within soccer-ball-lobbing distance of the Ciutat Vella (Old City) and a slew of other heavyweight sights. In addition to frolicking in the sea, highlights include cycling the promenade, dining off Port Olímpic marina and having a sunset cocktail overlooking Barceloneta beach.

Seafood (p115)

In Barcelona, cooking is a form of alchemy, with the city exhibiting some of Spain's most daring and avant-garde cuisine. But down in the salty 18th-century grid of La Barceloneta, fresh seafood is served with less pretension. Roam the streets between tightly packed, family-run restaurants and look for local specialities such as *arròs negre* (squid-ink rice) and scallops in *cava* (Catalan sparkling wine).

L'Aquàrium (p112)

There are approximately 450 species of aquatic animals in this water-side aquarium, but it's the sharks that leave the biggest impression. An 80m-long underwater tunnel keeps the beasts at bay behind worryingly thin Plexiglas. After you've scared the wits out of the kids, calm them down in the museum's Mediterranean-themed interactive section. Afterwards, you can take a scenic stroll along Barcelona's revitalised Port Vell.

3

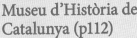

4

Museu d'Història de Catalunya (p112)

Catalan pride runs deep in Barcelona, a fiercely independent city with a history that often has more in common with Sardinia than Seville. To understand the complexities, head first to this multifarious museum, where you can learn about the unique story of Catalunya, from Stone Age peoples to the post-Franco years, with interactive displays on Roman rule, the Middle Ages, the Spanish Civil War and other pivotal epochs.

5

Museu Marítim (p114)

For a break from the art and architecture of the Ciutat Vella, dip into this fascinating museum set inside a massive Gothic shipyard. Barcelona is Europe's largest Mediterranean port, with a maritime legacy surpassed only by Venice's and the Museu Marítim is more than the usual stash of naval ephemera. Despite ongoing renovations the museum retains its prize exhibit: a replica of a 16th-century Spanish flagship.

Barceloneta & the Waterfront Walk

Once an industrial wasteland, Barcelona's waterfront was transformed for the 1992 Olympics, with artificial beaches, sculptures, marinas and a seaside promenade. This breezy ramble takes you through the former fishing village of La Barceloneta and past serene beaches out to Port Olímpic.

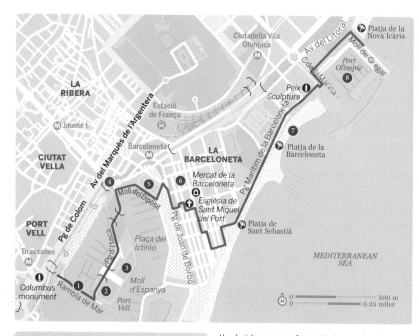

WALK FACTS

- **Start** Port Vell
- **Finish** Port Olímpic
- **Distance** 4.2km
- **Duration** Two hours

1 Rambla de Mar

With your back to the Columbus monument, take a stroll out along the **Rambla de Mar**, a narrow pedestrian walkway out over the harbour. A natural continuation of La Rambla, this swing bridge provides a tranquil spot to take in the breezy views over Port Vell and Barcelona's much cleaned-up waterfront extension. Every hour or so,

the bridge opens for entering and exiting sailboats.

2 Maremàgnum

Anchoring the western side of the Rambla de Mar is **Maremàgnum** (p123), a bubbling leisure centre with chirpy waterside restaurants, bars, shops and cinemas.

3 L'Aquàrium

Next door you'll find one of Europe's largest aquariums, **L'Aquàrium** (p112), which is home to more than 11,000 different sea critters. The most spectacular is a varied collection of sharks, seen through a glass tunnel. Intrepid divers can even go for a swim with these massive predators.

4 Barcelona Head

As you make your way over to Barceloneta, you'll pass the colourful **Barcelona Head sculpture** by famous American pop artist Roy Lichtenstein. Unveiled in 1992, the sculpture pays homage to Gaudí and other Modernistas in its *trencadis* (use of broken tiles to form mosaics).

5 Museu d'Història de Catalunya

Housed in former warehouses, **Museu d'Història de Catalunya** (p112) provides a potted history of Catalonia. It also boasts a top-floor restaurant-bar with terrace. Downstairs, a series of upscale seafood eateries offer open-air dining facing the marina.

6 Barceloneta

Walk down Passeig de Joan de Borbó, a street that crackles with activity and draws a cross-section of society. Make your way into the compact lanes of **Barceloneta**, which still retains a bit of its salty character from when those crowded dwellings were mostly home to dockworkers and mariners. Stroll past the Baroque Església de Sant Miquel del Port and pass the lively Mercat de la Barceloneta.

7 Platja de la Barceloneta

The narrow streets of Barceloneta can feel claustrophobic after awhile, but luckily the expansive seafront is just steps away. Barcelona's inner-city beach **Platja de la Barceloneta** is packed with people and activity. A series of bars on the sand churn out meals, cocktails and music for the hordes of sun worshippers. Up in the northeast corner, a string of hip bar-restaurants get especially busy on languid summer nights.

8 Port Olímpic

A long promenade shadows the waterfront up to the marina of **Port Olímpic**, which was created for the 1992 Olympics and is jammed with seafood restaurants. An eye-catcher on the approach from Barceloneta is Frank Gehry's giant copper *Peix* (Fish) sculpture. Just to the north is the agreeable Platja de Nova Icària.

 The Best...

PLACES TO EAT

Can Majó Open-air seafood feasts near the beachfront. (p118)

Jai-Ca Great anytime spot for seafood plates and cold drinks. (p116)

La Cova Fumada Hole-in-the-wall joint serving incredible food. (p115)

Can Recasens Romantic spot with market-fresh fare in Poblenou. (p119)

Barraca Sparkling waterfront restaurant with unique seafood combinations. (p118)

PLACES TO DRINK

Can Paixano *Cava* bar that's perfect for an afternoon pick-me-up. (p121)

Absenta Kitsch-filled bar serving absinthe and housemade vermouth. (p121)

Opium Mar Ever popular seaside club and beachfront bar. (p121)

Ké? Bohemian-esque drinking spot in the heart of Barceloneta. (p122)

SEASIDE ACTIVITIES

Orsom Take a sunset sail aboard a catamaran. (p123)

El Fòrum Bike to this post-millennial development along the waterfront. (p115)

Boardriders Barceloneta Go Stand-up paddleboarding, then cool off in the Mediterranean. (p123)

Rambla del Mar; designer: Viaplana & Piñon
MANFRED GOTTSCHALK/GETTY IMAGES ©

Discover Barceloneta & the Waterfront

⟷ Getting There & Away

○ **Foot** From the old city, La Rambla and Via Laietana are the main pedestrian access points across busy Ronda del Litoral.

○ **Metro** Go to Drassanes (Línia 3) to reach Port Vell; Barceloneta (Línia 4) has its own stop for the neighbourhood. Línia 4 continues out to Ciutadella Vila Olímpica (best stop for Port Olímpic) and El Maresme Fòrum near Parc del Fòrum.

◉ Sights

Port Vell & La Barceloneta

Museu d'Història de Catalunya   Museum

Map p116 (Museum of Catalonian History; ☎93 225 47 00; www.mhcat.net; Plaça de Pau Vila 3; adult/child €4.50/3.50, 1st Sun of month free; ⊙10am-7pm Tue & Thu-Sat, to 8pm Wed, to 2.30pm Sun; Ⓜ Barceloneta) Inside the **Palau de Mar**, this worthwhile museum takes you from the Stone Age through to the early 1980s. It is a busy hotchpotch of dioramas, artefacts, videos, models, documents and interactive bits: all up, an entertaining exploration of 2000 years of Catalan history.

See how the Romans lived, listen to Arab poetry from the time of the Muslim occupation of the city, peer into the dwelling of a Dark Ages family in the Pyrenees, try to mount a knight's horse or lift a suit of armour.

When you have had enough of all this, descend into a civil-war air-raid shelter, watch a video in Catalan on post-Franco Catalonia, or head upstairs to the first-rate rooftop restaurant and cafe, **1881** (☎93 221 00 50; www.sagardi.com; mains €14-28; ⊙10am-midnight Tue-Sun; 🛜).

The temporary exhibitions are often as interesting as the permanent display. Outside the museum, you'll find a string of elegant open-air restaurants serving up classic seafood dishes.

L'Aquàrium   Aquarium

Map p116 (☎93 221 74 74; www.aquariumbcn.com; Moll d'Espanya; admission adult/child €20/15, dive €300; ⊙9.30am-11pm Jul & Aug, to 9pm Sep-Jun; Ⓜ Drassanes) It is hard not to shud-

Transbordador Aeri
SIQUI SANCHEZ/GETTY IMAGES ©

der at the sight of a shark gliding above you, displaying its toothy, wide-mouthed grin. But this, the 80m shark tunnel, is the highlight of one of Europe's largest aquariums. The aquarium has the world's best Mediterranean collection and plenty of colourful fish from as far off as the Red Sea, the Caribbean and the Great Barrier Reef. All up, some 11,000 fish (including a dozen sharks) of 450 species reside here.

Back in the shark tunnel, which you reach after passing a series of themed fish tanks with everything from bream to sea horses, various species of shark (white tip, sand tiger, bonnethead, black tip, nurse and sandbar) flit around you, along with a host of other critters, including flapping rays and bloated sunfish. An interactive zone, Planeta Aqua, is host to a family of Antarctic penguins and a tank of rays that you watch close up.

Divers with a valid dive certificate may dive in the main tank with the sharks.

Pailebot de Santa Eulàlia   Ship
Map p116 (Moll de la Fusta; adult/child €1/ free; ⏱10am-8.30pm Tue-Fri & Sun, 2-8.30pm

Sat; Ⓜ Drassanes) This 1918 three-mast schooner, restored by the Museu Marítim, is moored along the palm-lined promenade Moll de la Fusta. You can see it perfectly well without going aboard, and there's not an awful lot to behold below decks. Admission is free with a paid Museu Marítim ticket. At 10am on Saturdays it sets sail for a three-hour cruise along the coast (adult/child €12/6). Reserve a spot by emailing reserves.mmaritim@ diba.cat.

Transbordador Aeri   Cable Car
Map p116 (www.telefericodebarcelona.com; Passeig Escullera; one way/return €11/16.50; ⏱11am-7pm; ☐17, 39 or 64, Ⓜ Barceloneta) This cable car strung across the harbour to Montjuïc provides an eagle-eye view of the city. The cabins float between the Torre de Sant Sebastià (in La Barceloneta) and Miramar (Montjuïc), with a midway stop at the Torre de Jaume I in front of the World Trade Center. At the top of the Torre de Sant Sebastià is a restaurant, **Torre d'Alta Mar** (☑93 221 00 07; www.torredealtamar.com; Passeig de Joan Borbó 88; mains around €35; ⏱1-3.30pm

BARBARA BOENSCH/IMAGEBROKER/ROBERT HARDING ©

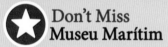

Don't Miss
Museu Marítim

These mighty Gothic shipyards shelter the Museu Marítim, a remarkable relic from Barcelona's days as the seat of a seafaring empire. Highlights include a full-sized replica (made in the 1970s) of Don Juan of Austria's 16th-century flagship, fishing vessels, antique navigation charts and dioramas of the Barcelona waterfront.

The pleasant museum cafe offers courtyard seating and a decent *menú del día* (set-price menu) at lunchtime. Also in the courtyard, you can have a look at a swollen replica of the *Ictíneo,* one of the world's first submarines. It was invented and built in 1858 by Catalan polymath Narcis Monturiol.

NEED TO KNOW

Map p116; ☏93 342 99 20; www.mmb.cat; Avinguda de les Drassanes; adult/child €5/2, free 3-8pm Sun; ◷10am-8pm; Ⓜ Drassanes

Tue-Sat & 8-11.30pm daily; 🚍17, 39, 57 or 64, ⓂBarceloneta).

Platjas   Beaches
Map p120 (🚍36 or 41, ⓂCiutadella Vila Olímpic, Bogatell, Llacuna or Selva de Mar) A series of pleasant beaches stretches northeast from the Port Olímpic marina. They are largely artificial, but this doesn't stop an estimated seven million bathers from piling in every year!

Port Olímpic, El Poblenou & El Fòrum

Museu del Disseny
de Barcelona   Museum
Map p120 (☏93 256 68 00; www.museudeld-isseny.cat; Plaça de les Glòries Catalanes 37; ⓂGlòries) Barcelona's design museum lies inside a new monolithic building with geometric facades and a rather brutal-ist appearance – it has been unkindly

nicknamed *la grapadora* (the stapler) by locals.

The museum, expected to open by early 2015, will house a dazzling collection of ceramics, decorative arts and textiles, taken from its old location in the Palau Reial de Pedralbes.

Torre Agbar
Architecture

Map p120 (www.torreagbar.com; Avinguda Diagonal 225; M Glòries) Barcelona's very own cucumber-shaped tower, Jean Nouvel's luminous Torre Agbar is among the most daring additions to the skyline since the first towers of La Sagrada Família went up. Completed in 2005, it shimmers at night in shades of midnight blue and lipstick red.

At the time of research, the Hyatt group was in negotiations to purchase the building and transform it into a luxury hotel.

El Fòrum
Neighbourhood

Map p120 (93 356 10 50; M El Maresme Fòrum) Once an urban wasteland, this area has seen dramatic changes in recent years, with sparkling new buildings, open plazas and waterfront recreation areas. The most striking element is the eerily blue, triangular *2001: A Space Odyssey*–style **Edifici Fòrum** building by Swiss architects Herzog & de Meuron.

Museu de la Música
Museum

Map p120 (93 256 36 50; www.museumusica.bcn.cat; Carrer de Lepant 150; adult/student €5/4, 3-8pm Sun free; 10am-6pm Tue-Sat, to 8pm Sun; M Monumental) Some 500 instruments (less than a third of those held) are on show in this museum, housed on the 2nd floor of the administration building in L'Auditori, the city's main classical-music concert hall.

Museu Blau
Museum

Map p120 (Blue Museum; 93 256 60 02; www.museublau.bcn.cat; Parc del Fòrum; adult/child €6/free; 10am-7pm Tue-Sat, to 8pm Sun; M El Maresme Fòrum) Set inside the futuristic Edifici Fòrum, the Museu Blau takes visitors on a journey all across the natural world. Multimedia and interactive exhibits explore topics like the history of evolution, earth's formation and the great scientists who have helped shaped human knowledge. There are also specimens from the animal, plant and mineral kingdoms – plus dinosaur skeletons – all rather dramatically set amid the sprawling 9000 sq metres of exhibition space.

Eating

Port Vell & La Barceloneta

For good food and atmosphere, head around to La Barceloneta, the lanes of which fairly bristle with everything from good-natured, noisy tapas bars to upmarket seafood restaurants. Almost everything shuts on Sunday and Monday evenings.

La Cova Fumada
Tapas €

Map p116 (93 221 40 61; Carrer del Baluard 56; tapas €3.50-7.50; 9am-3.20pm Mon-Wed, 9am-3.20pm & 6-8.20pm Thu & Fri, 9am-1.20pm Sat; M Barceloneta) There's no sign and the setting is decidedly downmarket, but this tiny, buzzing family-run tapas spot always packs in a crowd. The secret? Mouthwatering *pulpo* (octopus), *calamar, sardinias* and 15 or so other small plates cooked to perfection in the small open kitchen near the door. The *bombas* (potato croquettes served with *alioli*) and grilled *carxofes* (artichokes) are good, and everything is amazingly fresh.

Vaso de Oro
Tapas €

Map p116 (Carrer de Balboa 6; tapas €4-12; 10am-midnight; M Barceloneta) Always packed, this narrow bar gathers a festive, beer-swilling crowd who come for fantastic tapas. Fast-talking, white-jacketed waiters will serve up a few quick quips with your plates of grilled *gambes* (prawns), *foie a la plancha* (grilled liver pâté) or *solomillo* (sirloin) chunks. Want something a little different to drink? Ask for a *flauta cincuenta* – half lager and half dark beer.

Port Vell & La Barceloneta

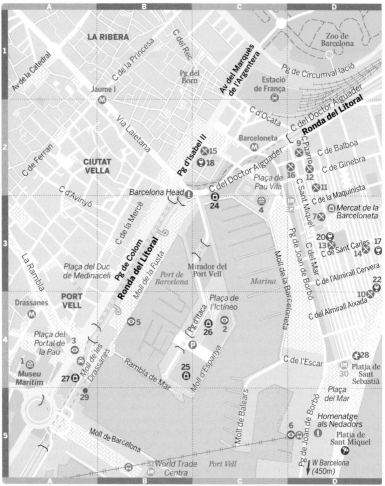

Jai-Ca
Seafood €

Map p116 (☎93 268 32 65; Carrer de Ginebra 13; tapas €4-7; ☺9am-11.30pm Mon-Sat; Ⓜ Barceloneta) Jai-Ca is a much-loved eatery that serves up juicy grilled prawns, flavour-rich anchovies, tender octopus, decadent razor clams and other seafood favourites to ever-growing crowds as the evening progresses. The *turbio* (Galician white wine), sangria and cold draughts are ideal refreshment after a day on the beach.

Bitácora
Tapas €

Map p116 (Carrer de Balboa 1; tapas €4-9; ☺10am-11pm Mon-Fri, to 5pm Sat; Ⓜ Barceloneta) This youthful little gem is a neighbourhood favourite for its simple but congenial ambience and well-priced tapas plates, which come in ample portions. There's also a small hidden terrace at the back. Top picks: *ceviche de pescado* (fish ceviche), *chipirones* (baby squid) and *gambas a la plancha* (grilled shrimp).

Port Vell & La Barceloneta

Maians   Tapas €

Map p116 (☎93 221 10 20; Carrer de Sant Carles 28; tapas €4-7; ◷1-4pm & 8-11pm Tue-Sat; Ⓜ Barceloneta) This tiny jovial bar and eatery in Maians serves excellent tapas to a hip, largely neighbourhood crowd. Highlights include the not-to-be-missed *cazón en adobo* (marinated fried dogfish) and *mejillones a la marinera* (mussels in a rich tomato broth) followed by hearty *arroz negra* (paella with cuttlefish).

Baluard Barceloneta   Bakery €

Map p116 (Carrer del Baluard 36; pastries €1-2.70; ◷8am-9pm; Ⓜ Barceloneta) One of the best bakeries in the city, Baluard serves up warm flaky croissants, perfect baguettes, moist muffins, and a range of tempting pastries and tarts (try one with figs or wild berries).

117

Can Maño
Spanish €

Map p116 (Carrer del Baluard 12; mains €7-12; ⏱9am-4pm Tue-Sat & 8-11pm Mon-Fri; MBarceloneta) It may look like a dive, but you'll need to be prepared to wait before being squeezed in at a packed table for a raucous night of *raciones* (full-plate-size tapas serving; posted on a board at the back) over a bottle of *turbio* – a cloudy white plonk. The seafood is abundant with first-rate squid, shrimp and fish served at rock-bottom prices.

Barraca
Seafood €€€

Map p116 (☑93 224 12 53; www.barraca-barcelona.com; Passeig Maritim de la Barceloneta 1; mains €19-29; ⏱1pm-midnight; MBarceloneta) Recently opened, this lively, buzzing space has a great location fronting the Mediterranean – a key reference point in the excellent seafood dishes served up here. Come here with a big appetite and gorge yourself; start off with a cauldron of chili-infused clams, cockles and mussels before moving on to the lavish paellas and other rice dishes which steal the show.

Can Majó
Seafood €€€

Map p116 (☑93 221 54 55; www.canmajo.es; Carrer del Almirall Aixada 23; mains €16-26; ⏱1-4pm Tue-Sun & 8-11.30pm Tue-Sat; 🚌45, 57, 59, 64 or 157, MBarceloneta) Located virtually on the beach (with tables outside in summer), Can Majó has a long and steady reputation for fine seafood, particularly its rice dishes and bountiful *suquets* (fish stews). The bouillabaisse of fish and seafood is succulent. Sit outside (there are heat lamps in winter) and admire the beach goers as you dine.

Restaurant 7 Portes
Seafood €€€

Map p116 (☑93 319 30 33; www.7portes.com; Passeig d'Isabel II 14; mains €16-32; ⏱1pm-1am; MBarceloneta) Founded in 1836 as a

Left: The waterfront at night; **Below:** A dish of cockles
(LEFT) MATT MUNRO/LONELY PLANET ©; (BELOW) ENCANTADISIMO/GETTY IMAGES ©

cafe and converted into a restaurant in 1929, Restaurant 7 Portes is a classic. It exudes an old-world atmosphere with its wood panelling, tiles, mirrors and plaques naming some of the famous people – such as Orson Welles – who have passed through.

Paella is the speciality here, or go for the surfeit of seafood in the *gran plat de marisc* (which literally translates as 'big plate of seafood').

Port Olímpic, El Poblenou & El Fòrum

Can Recasens   Catalan €€
Map p120 (93 300 81 23; Rambla del Poblenou 102; mains €6-14; 9pm-1am Mon-Sat & 1-4pm Sat; M Poblenou) One of Poblenou's most romantic settings, Can Recasens hides a warren of warmly lit rooms full of oil paintings, flickering candles, fairy lights and baskets of fruit. The food

is outstanding, with a mix of salads, fondues, smoked meats, cheeses, and open-faced sandwiches piled high with delicacies like wild mushrooms and brie, *escalivada* (grilled vegetables) and gruyere, and spicy chorizo.

Els Pescadors   Seafood €€€
Map p120 (93 225 20 18; www.elspescadors. com; Plaça de Prim 1; mains €18-34; 1-3.45pm & 8-11.30pm; M Poblenou) Set on a picturesque square lined with low houses and bella ombre trees long ago imported from South America, this quaint family restaurant continues to serve some of the city's great grilled fish and seafood-and-rice dishes. There are three dining areas inside: two quite modern, while the main one preserves its old tavern flavour. On warm nights, though, try for a table outside.

119

Port Olímpic, El Poblenou & El Fòrum

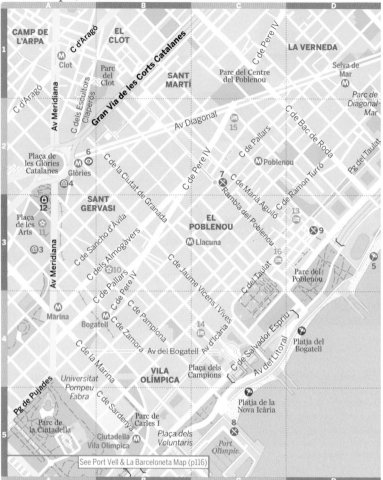

El Cangrejo Loco   Seafood €€€

Map p120 (☎ 93 221 05 33; www.elcangre-joloco.com; Moll de Gregal 29-30; mains €15-28, menú del día €26; ☉ 1-4pm & 8pm-midnight; ⓂCiutadella Vila Olímpica) Of the hive of eating activity along the docks of Port Olímpic, the 'Mad Crab' is among the best. Fish standards, such as sea bass and monkfish, are served in various guises and melt in the mouth. For utter decadence, there's a seafood platter, which has lobster, prawns, razor clams, crayfish and other delights.

🍷 Drinking & Nightlife

The northeastern end of the beach on the Barceloneta waterfront near Port Olímpic is a pleasant corner of evening chic that takes on a balmy, almost Caribbean air in the warmer months. A selection of restaurant-lounges and trendy bar-clubs vies for your attention. Several other attractive options are scattered about away from this core of night-time entertainment.

Port Olímpic, El Poblenou & El Fòrum

Can Paixano   Wine Bar

Map p116 (☎93 310 08 39; Carrer de la Reina Cristina 7; tapas €3-6; ☺9am-10.30pm Mon-Sat; Ⓜ Barceloneta) This lofty old champagne bar has long been run on a winning formula. The standard poison is bubbly rosé in elegant little glasses, combined with bite-sized *bocadillos* (filled rolls). This place is jammed to the rafters, and elbowing your way to the bar to ask harried staff for menu items can be a titanic struggle.

Absenta   Bar

Map p116 (Carrer de Sant Carles 36; ☺7pm-2am Wed-Thu, from 1pm Sat & Sun; Ⓜ Barceloneta) Decorated with old paintings, vintage lamps and curious sculpture (including a dangling butterfly woman and face-painted TVs), this whimsical and creative drinking den takes its liquor seriously. Stop in for the house-made vermouth or for more bite try one of the many absinthes on hand. Absenta gathers a hipsterish but easygoing crowd.

Bar Leo   Bar

Map p116 (Carrer de Sant Carles 34; ☺noon-9.30pm; Ⓜ Barceloneta) Bar Leo is a hole-in-the-wall drinking spot plastered with images of late Andalucian singer and heart-throb Bambino, and a jukebox mostly dedicated to flamenco. For a youthful, almost entirely *barcelonin* crowd, Bar Leo is it! It's liveliest on weekends.

Opium Mar   Club

Map p116 (☎902 26 74 86; www.opiummar.com; Passeig Marítim de la Barceloneta 34; admission €10-20; ☺8pm-6am; Ⓜ Ciutadella Vila Olímpica)

This seaside dance place has a spacious dance floor that attracts a mostly North American crowd. It only begins to fill from about 3am and is best in summer, when you can spill onto a terrace overlooking the beach. The beachside outdoor section works as a chilled restaurant-cafe.

CDLC   Lounge

Map p116 (www.cdlcbarcelona.com; Passeig Marítim de la Barceloneta 32; ⊙noon-4am; MⒸiutadella Vila Olímpica) Seize the night by the scruff at the Carpe Diem Lounge Club, where you can lounge in Asian-inspired surrounds. Ideal for a slow warm-up before heading to the nearby clubs. You can come for the food (quite good, but pricey) or wait until about midnight, when they roll up the tables and the DJs and dancers take full control.

Ké?   Bar

Map p116 (Carrer del Baluard 54; ⊙noon-2am; MBarceloneta) An eclectic and happy crowd hangs about this small bohemian bar run by a friendly Dutchman. Pull up a padded 'keg chair' or grab a seat on one of the worn lounges at the back and join in the animated conversation wafting out over the street. It has outdoor seating in summer and is just a few steps from Barceloneta's market.

Santa Marta   Bar

Map p116 (Carrer de Guitert 60; ⊙9.30am-midnight; 🚌45, 57, 59 or 157, MBarceloneta) This chilled bar just back from the beach attracts a garrulous mix of locals and expats, who come for light meals, beers and prime people-watching at one of the outdoor tables near the boardwalk. It has some tempting food too: a mix of local and Italian items, with a range of satisfying sandwiches.

Shôko   DJ

Map p116 (www.shoko.biz; Passeig Marítim de la Barceloneta 36; ⊙noon-3am Tue-Sun; MⒸiutadella Vila Olímpica) This stylish restaurant, club and beachfront bar brings in a touch of the Far East via potted bamboo, Japanese electro and Asian-Med fusion cuisine. As the food is cleared away, Shôko transforms into a deep-grooving nightspot with DJs spinning for the beautiful crowd. The open-sided beachfront lounge is a popular spot for a sundowner.

Razzmatazz   Live Music

Map p120 (📞93 320 82 00; www.sala-razzmatazz.com; Carrer de Pamplona 88; admission €12-32; ⊙midnight-3.30am Thu, to 5.30am Fri & Sat; MMarina, Bogatell) Bands from far and wide occasionally create scenes of near hysteria in this, one of the city's classic live-music and clubbing venues. Bands can appear throughout the week (check the website), with different start times. On weekends the live music then gives way to club sounds.

 Entertainment

L'Auditori   Classical Music

Map p120 (📞93 247 93 00; www.auditori.org; Carrer de Lepant 150; admission €10-51; ⊙box office 5-9pm Tue-Fri, 10am-1pm & 5-9pm Sat; MMonumental) Barcelona's modern home for serious music lovers, L'Auditori puts on plenty of orchestral, chamber, religious and other music. The ultramodern building (designed by Rafael Moneo) is home to the Orquestra Simfònica de Barcelona i Nacional de Catalunya.

Teatre Nacional
de Catalunya   Performing Arts

Map p120 (📞93 306 57 00; www.tnc.cat; Plaça de les Arts 1; admission €12-30; ⊙box office 3-8pm Wed-Fri, 3-9.30pm Sat, 3-6pm Sun & 1hr before show; MGlòries or Monumental) Ricard Bofill's ultraneoclassical theatre, with its bright, airy foyer, hosts a wide range of performances, including dramas, comedies, musicals and dance performances. Some shows are free.

Waterfront Markets

On weekends, Port Vell springs to life with a handful of markets selling a mix of antiques, contemporary art and crafts at key points along the waterfront.

At the base of La Rambla, the small **Port Antic** (Map p116; Plaça del Portal de la Pau; ⏰10am-8pm Sat & Sun; Ⓜ Drassanes) market is a requisite stop for strollers and antique hunters.

Near the Palau de Mar, you'll find **Feria de Artesanía del Palau de Mar** (Map p116; Moll del Dipòsit; ⏰11am-8pm Sat & Sun; Ⓜ Barceloneta), with artisans selling a range of crafty items, including jewellery, graphic T-shirts, handwoven hats, fragrant candles and soaps, scarves and decorative items.

Take a stroll along the pedestrian-only Rambla de Mar to reach the weekend art fair **Mercado de Pintores** (Map p116; Passeig d'Ítaca; ⏰10am-8pm Sat & Sun; Ⓜ Drassanes), with a broad selection of paintings both collectable and rather forgettable.

🔒 Shopping

Els Encants Vells   Market
Map p120 (Fira de Bellcaire; ☎93 246 30 30; www.encantsbcn.com; Plaça de les Glòries Catalanes; ⏰8am-8pm Mon, Wed, Fri & Sat; Ⓜ Glòries) In a gleaming open-sided complex near Plaça de les Glòries Catalanes, the 'Old Charms' flea market is the biggest of its kind in Barcelona. Over 500 vendors ply their wares beneath massive mirror-like panels. It's all here, from antique furniture through to secondhand clothes. A lot of it is junk, but occasionally you'll stumble across a *ganga* (bargain).

Maremàgnum   Mall
Map p116 (www.maremagnum.es; Moll d'Espanya 5; ⏰10am-10pm; Ⓜ Drassanes) Created out of largely abandoned docks, this buzzing shopping centre, with its bars, restaurants and cinemas, is pleasant enough for a stroll virtually in the middle of the old harbour. The usual labels are on hand, including the youthful Spanish chain Mango, mega-retailer H&M and eye-catching fashions from Barcelona-based Desigual. Football fans will be drawn to the paraphernalia at FC Botiga.

🤸 Sports & Activities

Boardriders
Barceloneta   Water Sports
Map p116 (☎93 221 44 91; Carrer de la Drassana 10; ⏰10am-8pm Mon-Sat, from 11am Sun; Ⓜ Barceloneta) Facing the seafront, Boardriders rents out surfboards (per hour/half-day €12/25), stand-up paddleboards (per hour/half-day €15/30) and wetsuits. It also sells clothes and gear.

Orsom   Cruise
Map p116 (☎93 441 05 37; www.barcelona-orsom.com; Moll de les Drassanes; adult/child €16.50/11; ⏰Apr-Oct; Ⓜ Drassanes) Aboard a large sailing catamaran, Orsom makes the 90-minute journey to Port Olímpic and back. There are three departures per day (four on weekends in July and August), and the last is a jazz cruise, scheduled around sunset. The same company also runs five daily, 50-minute speedboat tours (adult/child €12.50/11).

La Sagrada Família & L'Eixample

By far the most extensive of Barcelona's districts, this sprawling grid is full of subidentities. Almost all the city's Modernista buildings were raised in L'Eixample. The pick of them line Passeig de Gràcia, but hundreds adorn the area. Work on Gaudí's La Sagrada Família church continues.

As Barcelona's population exploded, the medieval walls were knocked down by 1856. In 1869, work began on L'Eixample (the Extension) to fill the open country that then lay between Barcelona and Gràcia. Building continued until well into the 20th century. Well-to-do families snapped up prime plots and raised fanciful buildings in the eclectic style of the Modernistas.

Shoppers converge on Passeig de Gràcia and La Rambla de Catalunya. At night, mainly from Thursday to Saturday, Carrer d'Aribau and nearby streets are home to a buzzing nightlife scene. The 'Gaixample', around Carrer del Consell de Cent and Carrer de Muntaner, is the centre of gay nightlife.

Casa Batlló (p147)

La Sagrada Família & L'Eixample Highlights

La Sagrada Família (p130)

Spain's biggest tourist attraction, La Sagrada Família, is a unique, extraordinary piece of architecture. Conceived as atonement for Barcelona's sins of modernity, this giant church became Gaudí's holy mission and, in medieval fashion, is still under construction 100 years after its inception. At once ancient and thoroughly modern, La Sagrada Família is packed with religious iconography and symbolism, and leaves no one unmoved.

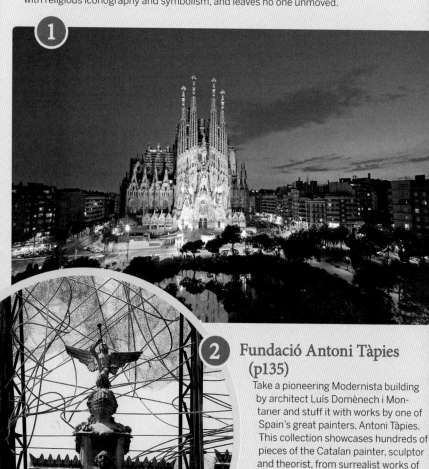

Fundació Antoni Tàpies (p135)

Take a pioneering Modernista building by architect Luís Domènech i Montaner and stuff it with works by one of Spain's great painters, Antoni Tàpies. This collection showcases hundreds of pieces of the Catalan painter, sculptor and theorist, from surrealist works of the 1940s to imaginative sculpture-like pieces of 1970s Abstract Expression.

KRZYSZTOF DYDYNSKI / GETTY IMAGES ©

La Pedrera (p142)

One of Passeig de Gràcia's most captivating Modernista structures, La Pedrera is in the top tier of Gaudí's achievements. Officially called Casa Milà after its owners, it was nicknamed La Pedrera (The Stone Quarry) by bemused locals who watched Gaudí build it from 1905 to 1910. Conceived as an apartment block, it bears all the trademarks of Gaudí: swirling staircases, hallucinogenic curves and not a straight line in sight.

CULTURA TRAVEL/QUIM ROSER/GETTY IMAGES©

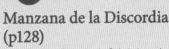

Shopping on Passeig de Gràcia (p151)

Once a lane that linked Barcelona to the village of Gràcia, the elegant, tree-lined Passeig de Gràcia has metamorphosed into the city's most opulent boulevard. Heaving with posh hotels and punctuated with architectural nods to Catalonia's Modernista movement, it is feted most for its shopping. Luxury labels share space with the odd indie fashion guerrilla.

Above: Vinçon (p152)

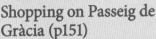

Manzana de la Discordia (p128)

One block on Passeig de Gràcia is embellished with buildings by the three enfants terribles of early-20th-century Modernisme. Each building has a unique style. Puig i Cadafalch's Casa Amatller (p134) is gabled and faintly Dutch, Domènech i Montaner's Casa Lleó Morera (p135) has a regal quality and Gaudí's Casa Batlló (p147) is downright other-worldly.

Above: Casa Amatller; architect: Josep Puig i Cadafalch

La Sagrada Família & L'Eixample Walk

L'Eixample is packed with Modernista treasures. Start with the three unique buildings of the Manzana de la Discordia and end at La Sagrada Família.

WALK FACTS

- **Start** Passeig de Gràcia
- **Finish** La Sagrada Família
- **Distance** 3km
- **Duration** 1.5 hours

1 Casa Lleó Morera

Near Carrer del Consell de Cent, have a look at the heavily ornamented facade of **Casa Lleó Morera** (p135), designed by Domènech i Montaner. Note the fine-featured sculptures of maidens holding the latest in early 20th-century technology: the telephone, the phonograph, the telegraph and the camera.

2 Casa Amatller

A few doors up, you'll see Puig i Cadafalch's **Casa Amatller** (p134), which has a stepped Flemish Renaissance roof and a medievalesque facade adorned with whimsical statuary. Near the entrance portal, St George is impaling the dragon and there are more curious creatures on the second floor, including a monkey hammering on a forge.

3 Casa Batlló

Casa Batlló (p147) shimmers in Gaudíesque extravagance. Its symbolic meaning is open to interpretation but is undoubtedly connected with Catalan identity: a Carnaval celebration (the masklike balconies, the facade glittering like confetti), a fish (with scales and bonelike columns) and an abstract St George (the swordlike chimney) slaying the dragon (the scaly roof).

④ Fundació Antoni Tàpies

Just around the corner is another of Domènech i Montaner's fine works, which today houses the **Fundació Antoni Tàpies** (p135). The symmetrical brick exterior shows Muslim influences, while the wiry sculpture on the roof is a Tàpies creation and represents a chair jutting out of a cloud.

⑤ La Pedrera

Up the road is Casa Milà, better known as **La Pedrera** (p142) for its grey stone facade. The undulating walls and rippling wrought-iron balconies show organic influences. Up top stand the famous stone chimneys that resemble helmeted warriors, but you'll have to pay to see them.

⑥ Casa Thomas

Casa Thomas was one of Domènech i Montaner's earlier efforts. The ceramic details are a trademark and the massive ground-level wrought-iron decoration is magnificent. Wander inside to the Cubiña design store to admire his interior work.

⑦ Casa Llopis i Bofill

Casa Llopis i Bofill is an interesting block of flats designed by Antoni Gallissà. The graffiti-covered facade is particularly striking. The use of parabolic arches on the ground floor is a clear Modernista touch, as are the wrought-iron balconies.

⑧ La Sagrada Família

Strolling around **La Sagrada Família** (p130), you'll notice the wildly different styles of the Nativity Facade, completed during Gaudí's lifetime, and the Passion Facade, designed by Josep Maria Subirachs in the 1980s. Other key things to look for: the Risen Christ teetering halfway up the Passion Facade, eight completed belltowers with a different apostle seated at each and the image of Gaudí himself in the Passion Facade.

 The Best...

PLACES TO EAT

Tapaç 24 Innovative chef Carles Abellàn creates some of Barcelona's best tapas. (p140)

Cerveseria Catalana Great-value neighbourhood haunt that draws crowds any time of day. (p143)

Cinc Sentits Tasting menus that showcase the best of Catalan cooking. (p148)

Cata 1.81 Lovely setting for gourmet tapas and wines by the glass. (p146)

PLACES TO DRINK

Monvínic Enchanting setting amid one of Spain's best wine bars. (p150)

La Fira Funhouse ambience and a staggering drinks selection. (p150)

Les Gens Que J'Aime Stylish but unpretentious gem in L'Eixample. (p151)

Dry Martini Classy bar serving Barcelona's best gin and tonics. (p149)

PLACES TO SHOP

Vinçon Beautifully designed furniture and housewares in a Modernista building. (p152)

El Corte Inglés Sprawling department store that often has unbeatable sales. (p153)

El Bulevard dels Antiquaris Dozens of antique shops. (p152)

Spanish-style antipasto

Don't Miss
La Sagrada Família

If you have time for only one sightseeing outing, this should be it. La Sagrada Família inspires awe by its sheer verticality and magnificently elaborate design – inside and out. It may be unfinished, but it attracts over 3 million visitors a year and is the most visited monument in Spain. There's much to explore here – symbol-rich facades, an other-worldly interior and the on-site Museu Gaudí, which houses materials on the master's life and work.

Map p136

☎ 93 207 30 31

www.sagrada
familia.org

Carrer de Mallorca 401

adult/child under
10yr/senior &
student €13/
free/11

🕙 9am-8pm Apr-
Sep, to 6pm Oct-Mar

Ⓜ Sagrada Família

The Design

Gaudí devised a temple 95m long and 60m wide, able to seat 13,000 people. It was to have a central tower 170m high above the transept (representing Christ) and another 17 of 100m or more. The 12 towers along the three facades represent the Apostles, while the remaining five represent the Virgin Mary and the four Evangelists. With his characteristic dislike for straight lines (he said there were none in nature), Gaudí gave his towers swelling outlines inspired by the weird peaks of the holy mountain Montserrat outside Barcelona, and encrusted them with a tangle of sculpture that seems an outgrowth of the stone.

Building planners estimate that the church will be completed in 2026, roughly 140 years after construction began. Already, some of the oldest parts of the church, especially the apse, have required restoration work.

The Interior

Inside, the roof is held up by a forest of extraordinary angled pillars. As the pillars soar towards the ceiling, they sprout a web of supporting branches, creating the effect of a forest canopy. The tree image is in no way accidental – Gaudí envisaged such an effect. Everything was thought through, including the shape and placement of windows to create the mottled effect of sunlight pouring through the branches of a thick forest.

Visiting La Sagrada Família

Although essentially a building site, the completed sections and the museum may be explored at leisure. Fifty-minute guided tours (€4.50) are offered. Alternatively, pick up an audio tour (€4.50). Enter from Carrer de Sardenya and Carrer de la Marina. Once inside, €4.50 will get you into lifts that rise up the towers of the Nativity and Passion facades. These two facades, each with four sky-scraping towers, are the sides of the church. The main Glory Facade, on which work is underway, closes off the southeast end on Carrer de Mallorca.

1 PASSION FACADE
Among the *Fachada de la Pasión*'s stand-out features are the angled columns, the dramatic scenes from Jesus' last hours, an extraordinary rendering of the Last Supper and a bronze door that reads like a sculptured book. But the most surprising view is from inside the door on the extreme right (especially in the afternoon with the sun in the west).

2 MAIN NAVE
The majestic *Nave Principal* showcases Gaudí's use of tree motifs for columns to support the domes. But it's the skylights that give the nave its luminous quality, with light flooding into the apse and main altar from the skylight 75m above the floor.

3 SIDE NAVE AND NATIVITY TRANSEPT
Although beautiful in its own right, this is the perfect place to view the sculpted treelike columns and get an overall perspective of the main nave. Turn around and you're confronted with the inside of the Nativity Facade, an alternative view that most visitors miss. The stained-glass windows are superb.

4 NATIVITY FACADE
The *Fachada del Nacimiento* is Gaudí's grand hymn to Creation. Begin by viewing it front-on, then draw close (but to one side) to make out the details of its sculpted figures. The complement to the finely wrought detail is the majesty of the four parabolic towers, which are topped by Venetian stained glass.

5 MODEL OF COLÒNIA GÜELL
The most interesting model in the Museu Gaudí is the church at Colònia Güell. It's upside down because that's how Gaudí worked to best study the building's form and structural balance.

La Sagrada Família

A TIMELINE

1882 Francesc del Villar is commissioned to construct a neo-Gothic church.

1883 Antoni Gaudí takes over as chief architect, and plans a far more ambitious church to hold 13,000 faithful.

1926 Death of Gaudí; work continues under Domènec Sugrañes. Much of the **apse ❶** and **Nativity Facade ❷** is complete.

1930 **Bell towers ❸** of the Nativity Facade completed.

1936 Construction is interrupted by Spanish Civil War; anarchists destroy Gaudí's plans.

1939-40 Architect Francesc de Paula Quintana i Vidal restores the crypt and meticulously reassembles many of Gaudí's lost models, some of which can be seen in the **museum ❹**.

1976 Completion of **Passion Facade ❺**.

1986-2006 Sculptor Josep Subirachs adds sculptural details to the Passion Facade including the panels telling the story of Christ's last days, amid much criticism for employing a style far removed from what was thought typical of Gaudí.

2000 **Central nave vault ❻** completed.

2010 Church completely roofed over; Pope Benedict XVI consecrates the church; work begins on a high-speed rail tunnel that will pass beneath the church's **Glory Facade ❼**.

2026–28 Projected completion date.

TOP TIPS

» **Light** The best light through the stained-glass windows of the Passion Facade bursts through into the heart of the church in the late afternoon.

» **Time** Visit at opening time on week-days to avoid the worst of the crowds.

» **Views** Head up the Nativity Facade bell towers for the views, as long queues generally await at the Passion Facade towers.

Spiral staircase

Nativity Facade
Gaudí used plaster casts of local people and even of the occasional corpse from the local morgue as models for the portraits in the Nativity scene.

Central nave vault

Apse
Built just after the crypt in mostly neo-Gothic style, it is capped by pinnacles that show a hint of the genius that Gaudí would later deploy in the rest of the church.

Bell towers
The towers (eight completed) of the three facades represent the 12 Apostles. Lifts whisk visitors up one tower of the Nativity and Passion Facades (the latter gets longer queues) for fine views.

Completed church
Along with the Glory Facade and its four towers, six other towers remain to be completed. They will represent the four Evangelists, the Virgin Mary and, soaring above them all over the transept, a 170m colossus symbolising Christ.

Glory Facade
This will be the most fanciful facade of all, with a narthex boasting 16 hyperboloid lanterns topped by cones that will look something like an organ made of melting ice cream.

Museu Gaudí
Jammed with old photos, drawings and restored plaster models that bring Gaudí's ambitions to life, the museum also houses an extraordinarily complex plumb-line device he used to calculate his constructions.

Escoles de Gaudí

Crypt
The first completed part of the church, the crypt is in largely neo-Gothic style and lies under the transept. Gaudí's burial place here can be seen from the Museu Gaudí.

Passion Facade
See the story of Christ's last days from Last Supper to burial in an S-shaped sequence from bottom to top of the facade. Check out the cryptogram in which the numbers always add up to 33, Christ's age at his death.

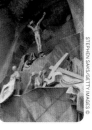

Discover La Sagrada Família & L'Eixample

⟷ Getting There & Away

○ **Metro** Four Metro lines criss-cross L'Eixample, three stopping at Passeig de Gràcia for the Manzana de la Discordia. Línia 3 stops at Diagonal for La Pedrera, while Línies 2 and 5 stop at Sagrada Família.

○ **Train** FGC lines from Plaça de Catalunya take you one stop to Provença, in the heart of L'Eixample.

◎ Sights

L'Esquerra de L'Eixample

Casa Amatller Architecture

Map p136 (☎93 487 72 17; www.amatller.org; Passeig de Gràcia 41; tour €10; ☉tour Sat; Ⓜ Passeig de Gràcia) **FREE** One of Puig i Cadafalch's most striking bits of Modernista fantasy, Casa Amatller combines Gothic window frames with a stepped gable borrowed from Dutch urban architecture. But the busts and reliefs of dragons, knights and other characters dripping off the main facade are pure caprice.

The pillared foyer and staircase lit by stained glass are like the inside of some romantic castle.

The building was renovated in 1900 for the chocolate baron and philanthropist Antoni Amatller (1851–1910) and it will one day open partly to the public. Renovation – still continuing at the time of research – will see the 1st (main) floor converted into a museum with period pieces, while the 2nd floor will house the Institut Amatller d'Art Hispanic (Amatller Institute of Hispanic Art).

For now, you can wander into the foyer, admire the staircase and lift, and head through the shop to see the latest temporary exhibition out the back. Depending on the state of renovation, it is also possible to join a 1½-hour guided tour of the 1st floor, with its early-20th-century furniture and decor intact, and Amatller's photo studio. These are generally held on Saturdays; check the website for details.

Amatller was a keen traveller and photographer (his absorbing shots of turn-of-the-20th-century Morocco are

Casa Amatller
DE AGOSTINI/C. MAURY/GETTY IMAGES ©

occasionally on show). The tour also includes a tasting of Amatller chocolates in the original kitchen.

Casa Lleó Morera Architecture

Map p136 (📞93 676 27 33; www.casalleomorera. com; Passeig de Gràcia 35; adult/concession/ child under 12yr €15/€13.50/free; 🕓guided tour in English 10am Mon-Sat; 🅼Passeig de Gràcia) Domènech i Montaner's 1905 contribution to the Manzana de la Discordia, with Modernista carving outside and a bright, tiled lobby in which floral motifs predominate, is perhaps the least odd-looking of the three main buildings on the block. In 2014 part of the building was opened to the public (by guided tour only), so you can appreciate the 1st floor, giddy with swirling sculptures, rich mosaics and whimsical decor.

Fundació Antoni Tàpies Gallery

Map p136 (📞93 487 03 15; www.fundaciotapies. org; Carrer d'Aragó 255; adult/concession €7/5.60; 🕓10am-7pm Tue-Sun; 🅼Passeig de Gràcia) The Fundació Antoni Tàpies is both a pioneering Modernista building (completed in 1885) and the major collection

of leading 20th-century Catalan artist Antoni Tàpies. A man known for his esoteric work, Tàpies died in February 2012, aged 88; he leaves behind a powerful range of paintings and a foundation intended to promote contemporary artists.

The building, designed by Domènech i Montaner for the publishing house Editorial Montaner i Simón (run by a cousin of the architect), combines a brick-covered iron frame with Islamic-inspired decoration. Tàpies crowned it with the meanderings of his own mind, a work called *Núvol Cadira* (Cloud and Chair) that spirals above the building like a storm.

Museu del Modernisme Català Museum

Map p136 (📞93 272 28 96; www.mmcat.cat; Carrer de Balmes 48; adult/concession €10/€8.50; 🕓10am-8pm Mon-Sat, to 2pm Sun; 🅼Passeig de Gràcia) Housed in a Modernista building, the ground floor seems like a big Modernista furniture showroom. Several items by Antoni Gaudí, including chairs from Casa Batlló and a mirror from Casa Calvet, are supplemented by a host of items by his

135

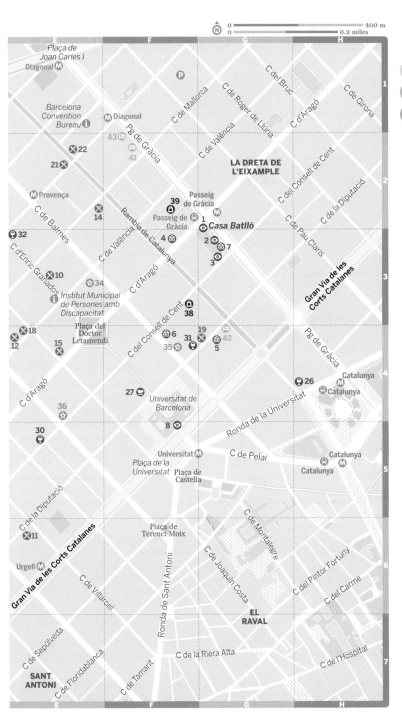

L'Esquerra de L'Eixample

lesser-known contemporaries, including some typically whimsical, mock medieval pieces by Puig i Cadafalch.

Fundación Francisco Godia   Gallery

Map p136 (☎93 272 31 80; www.fundacionfgodia.org; Carrer de la Diputació 250; adult/student/child under 6yr €6/3/free; ⏰10am-8pm Mon & Wed-Sat, 10am-3pm Sun; Ⓜ Passeig de Gràcia) Francisco Godia (1921–90), head of one of Barcelona's great establishment families, liked fast cars (he came sixth in the 1956 Grand Prix season driving Maseratis) and fine art. An intriguing mix of medieval art, ceramics and modern paintings make up this varied private collection. Housed in Casa Garriga Nogués, this is a stunning, carefully restored Modernista residence originally built for a rich banking family by Enric Sagnier in 1902–05.

Museu del Perfum   Museum

Map p136 (☎93 216 01 21; www.museudelperfum.com; Passeig de Gràcia 39; adult/child €5/3;

⏰10.30am-2pm & 4.30-8pm Mon-Fri, 11am-2pm Sat; Ⓜ Passeig de Gràcia) Housed in the back of the **Regia** (www.regia.es; ⏰9.30am-8.30pm Mon-Fri, 10.30am-8.30pm Sat) perfume store, this museum contains everything from ancient Egyptian and Roman (the latter mostly from the 1st to 3rd centuries AD) scent receptacles to classic eau de cologne bottles – all in all, some 5000 bottles of infinite shapes, sizes and histories.

Universitat de Barcelona   Architecture

Map p136 (☎93 402 11 00; www.ub.edu; Gran Via de les Corts Catalanes 585; ⏰9am-9pm Mon-Fri; Ⓜ Universitat) Although a university was first set up on what is now La Rambla in the 16th century, the present, glorious mix of (neo) Romanesque, Gothic, Islamic and Mudéjar architecture is a caprice of the 19th century (built 1863–82). Wander into the main hall, up the grand staircase and around the various leafy cloisters, or take a stroll in the rear gardens.

La Dreta de L'Eixample

La Sagrada Família   Church
See p130

Recinte Modernista de Sant Pau   Architecture
(📞93 553 78 01; www.santpaubarcelona.org; Carrer de Cartagena 167; adult/concession/child €8/5.60/free; ⊙10am-6.30pm Mon-Sat, to 2.30pm Sun; Ⓜ Hospital de Sant Pau) Domènech i Montaner outdid himself as architect and philanthropist with the Modernista Hospital de la Santa Creu i de Sant Pau, redubbed in 2014 the 'Recinte Modernista'. It was long considered one of the city's most important hospitals, and only recently repurposed, its various spaces becoming cultural centres, offices and something of a monument.

The complex, including 16 pavilions – together with the Palau de la Música Catalana, a joint World Heritage site – is lavishly decorated and each pavilion is unique.

Fundació Suñol   Gallery
Map p144 (📞93 496 10 32; www.fundaciosunol.org; Passeig de Gràcia 98; adult/concession/child €4/2/free; ⊙11am-2pm & 4-8pm Mon-Fri, 4-8pm Sat; Ⓜ Diagonal) Rotating exhibitions of portions of this private collection of mostly 20th-century art (some 1200 works in total) offer anything from Man Ray's photography to sculptures by Alberto Giacometti. The gallery is spread over two floors, and you are most likely to see works by Spanish artists – anyone from Picasso to Jaume Plensa – along with a sprinkling of others from abroad.

A visit here makes a refreshing pause between the crush of crowded Modernista monuments on this boulevard. Indeed, you get an interesting side view of one of them, La Pedrera, from out the back.

Palau del Baró Quadras   Architecture
Map p144 (📞93 467 80 00; Avinguda Diagonal 373; ⊙8am-8pm Mon-Fri; Ⓜ Diagonal) FREE Puig i Cadafalch designed Palau del Baró Quadras (built 1902–06) in an exuberant Gothic-inspired style. The main facade is its most intriguing, with a soaring, glassed-in gallery. Take a closer look at the gargoyles and reliefs – the pair of toothy fish and the sword-wielding knight clearly have the same artistic signature as the architect behind Casa Amatller. Decor inside is eclectic, but dominated by Middle Eastern and East Asian themes. Much of the building is closed to the public, however you can visit the ground floor.

Església de la Puríssima Concepció I Assumpció de Nostra Senyora   Church
Map p144 (📞93 457 65 52; Carrer de Roger de Llúria 70; ⊙7.30am-1pm & 5-9pm; Ⓜ Passeig de Gràcia) One hardly expects to run into

LA SAGRADA FAMÍLIA & L'EIXAMPLE SIGHTS

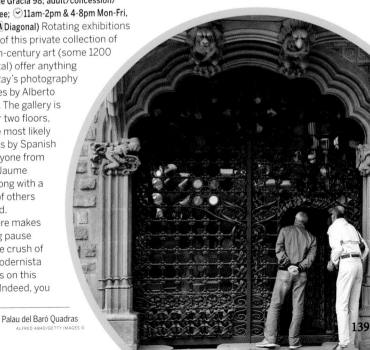

Palau del Baró Quadras
ALFRED ABAD/GETTY IMAGES ©

Below: Seafood tapas; **Right:** A restaurant in L'Eixample
(BELOW) MICHAEL HEFFERNAN/LONELY PLANET ©; (RIGHT) ELAN FLEISHER/LOOK/ROBERT HARDING ©

a medieval church on the grid-pattern streets of the late-19th-century city extension, yet that is just what this is. Transferred stone by stone from the old centre in 1871–88, this 14th-century church has a pretty 16th-century cloister with a peaceful garden. Behind is a Romanesque-Gothic bell tower (11th to 16th century), moved from another old town church that didn't survive, Església de Sant Miquel. This is one of a handful of such old churches shifted willy-nilly from their original locations to L'Eixample.

🍴 Eating

Most of this huge area's many varied and enticing restaurants are concentrated in the Quadrat d'Or between Carrer de Pau Claris and Carrer de Muntaner, Avinguda Diagonal and Gran Via de les Corts Catalanes.

La Dreta de L'Eixample

Tapas 24   Tapas €€
Map p144 (📞93 488 09 77; www.carlesabellan.com; Carrer de la Diputació 269; tapas €4-9; ⏰9am-midnight Mon-Sat; Ⓜ Passeig de Gràcia) Carles Abellan, master of Comerç 24 in La Ribera, runs this basement tapas haven known for its gourmet versions of old faves. Specials include the *bikini* (toasted ham and cheese sandwich – here the ham is cured and the truffle makes all the difference) and a thick black *arròs negre de sípia* (squid-ink black rice).

Can Kenji   Japanese €€
Map p144 (📞93 476 18 23; www.cankenji.com; Carrer del Rosselló 325; mains €8-14; ⏰1-3.30pm & 8.30-11pm Mon-Sat; Ⓜ Verdaguer) If you want to go Japanese in Barcelona, this is the place. The chef of this understated little *izakaya* (the Japanese version of a tavern) gets his ingredients fresh from the city's markets, with traditional Japanese recipes receiving a

Mediterranean touch, so you'll get things like sardine tempura with an aubergine, miso and anchovy puree, or *tataki* (lightly grilled meat) of *bonito* (tuna) with *salmorejo* (a Córdoban cold tomato and bread soup). This is fusion at its very best.

Granja Petitbo   Mediterranean €€

Map p144 (93 265 65 03; www.granjapetitbo. com; Passeig de Sant Joan 82; sandwiches €5-6, menú del día €12.90; 8.30am-10pm Mon-Wed, 8.30am-midnight Thu, 8.30am-1am Fri, 10am-1am Sat, 10am-5pm Sun; ; Girona) High ceilings, battered leather armchairs and dramatic flower arrangements set the tone in this sunny little corner cafe, beloved of local hipsters and young families, who up until now have been ill-served in this part of town. As well as an all-day parade of homemade cakes, freshly squeezed juices and superior coffee, there's a brunch menu on weekends, and a *menú del día* (daily set menu) during the week.

Casa Amalia   Catalan €€

Map p144 (93 458 94 58; Passatge del Mercat 4-6; mains €8-17; 1-3.30pm & 9-10.30pm Tue-Sat, 1-3.30pm Sun; Girona) This very local restaurant is popular for its hearty Catalan cooking that uses fresh produce, mainly sourced from the busy market next door. On Thursdays during winter Casa Amalia offers the mountain classic, *escudella* (soup). Otherwise, you might try light variations on local cuisine, such as the *bacallà al allioli de poma* (cod in an apple-based aioli sauce). The three-course *menú del día* is exceptional lunchtime value at €12.

Casa Alfonso   Spanish €€

Map p144 (93 301 97 83; www.casaalfonso. com; Carrer de Roger de Llúria 6; tapas from €4, mains €18-28; 8am-1am Mon-Sat; Urquinaona) In business since 1934, Casa Alfonso is perfect for a morning coffee or a tapas stop at the long marble bar. Timber panelled and festooned with old photos, posters and swinging hams, it attracts a faithful local clientele at all hours

141

ARTUR DEBAT/GETTY IMAGES ©

Don't Miss
La Pedrera

This undulating beast is another madcap Gaudí masterpiece, built in 1905–10 as a combined apartment and office block. Formally called Casa Milà, after the businessman who commissioned it, it is better known as La Pedrera (the Quarry) because of its uneven grey stone facade, which ripples around the corner of Carrer de Provença.

The Fundació Caixa Catalunya has opened the top-floor apartment, attic and roof, together called the Espai Gaudí (Gaudí Space), to visitors. The roof is the most extraordinary element, with its giant chimney pots looking like multicoloured medieval knights.

One floor below the roof, where you can appreciate Gaudí's taste for parabolic arches, is a modest museum dedicated to his work.

The next floor down is the apartment (El Pis de la Pedrera). It is fascinating to wander around this elegantly furnished home, done up in the style a well-to-do family might have enjoyed in the early 20th century. The sensuous curves and unexpected touches in everything from light fittings to bedsteads, from door handles to balconies, might seem admirable to us today, but not everyone thought so at the time. The story goes that one tenant, a certain Mrs Comes i Abril, had complained that there was no obvious place to put her piano in these wavy rooms. Gaudí's response was simple: 'Madame, I suggest you take up the flute.'

On summer evenings, La Pedrera usually stages a series of concerts on the roof.

NEED TO KNOW

Map p144; Casa Milà; ☎93 484 59 00; www.lapedrera.com; Carrer de Provença 261-265; adult/student/child €16.50/14.85/8.25; ☺9am-8pm Mar-Oct, to 6.30pm Nov-Feb; Ⓜ Diagonal

for its *flautas* (thin custom-made ba-guettes with your choice of filling), hams, cheeses, hot dishes and homemade des-serts, but there are also more substantial dishes, mostly involving huge hunks of grilled meat. Consider rounding off with an *alfonsito* (miniature Irish coffee).

De Tapa Madre   Catalan €€

Map p144 (☎ 93 459 31 34; www.detapamadre. cat; Carrer de Mallorca 301; tapas from €4; ☺ 8am-midnight Mon-Fri, 10am-midnight Sat, noon-midnight Sun; ⓜ Verdaguer) A chatty atmosphere greets you from the bar the moment you swing open the door. A few tiny tables line the window, but head upstairs for more space in the gallery, which hovers above the array of tapas on the bar below, or go deeper inside past the bench with the ham legs. The *arròs caldós amb llagostins* (a hearty rice dish with king prawns) is delicious.

Alkímia   Catalan €€€

(☎ 93 207 61 15; www.alkimia.cat; Carrer de l'Indústria 79; mains €18-29; ☺ 1.30-3.30pm & 8-11pm Mon-Fri; ⓜ Sagrada Família) Jordi Vilà, a culinary alchemist, serves up refined Catalan dishes with a twist in this elegant, white-walled locale well off the tourist trail. Dishes such as his *arròs de nyora i safrà amb escamarlans de la costa* (saffron and sweet-chilli rice with crayfish) earned Vilà his first Michelin star. He presents a series of set menus from €68 to €130.

Casa Calvet   Catalan €€€

Map p144 (☎ 93 412 40 12; www.casacalvet.es; Carrer de Casp 48; mains €26-31; ☺ 1-3.30pm & 8.30-11pm Mon-Sat; ⓜ Urquinaona) An early Gaudí masterpiece loaded with his trademark curvy features now houses a swish restaurant (just to the right of the building's main entrance). Dress up and ask for an intimate *taula cabina* (wooden booth). You could opt for sole and lobster on mashed leeks, with balsamic vinegar and Pedro Ximénez reduction, and artichoke chips. It has various tasting menus for up to €70, and a lunch menu for €34.

L'Esquerra de L'Eixample

Cerveseria Catalana   Tapas €

Map p136 (☎ 93 216 03 68; Carrer de Mallorca 236; tapas €4-11; ☺ 9.30am-1.30am; ⓜ Passeig de Gràcia) The 'Catalan Brewery' is good for breakfast, lunch and dinner. Come for your morning coffee and croissant, or wait until lunch to enjoy choosing from the abundance of tapas and *montaditos* (canapés). You can sit at the bar, on the pavement terrace or in the restaurant at the back. The variety of hot tapas, salads and other snacks draws a well-dressed crowd of locals and outsiders.

Copasetic   Cafe €

Map p136 (☎ 93 532 76 66; www.copaseticbar-celona.com; Carrer de la Diputació 55; mains €8-12; ☺ 7pm-midnight Mon, noon-midnight Tue & Wed, noon-1am Thu, noon-3am Fri, 10.30am-3am Sat, 10.30am-6pm Sun; ⓜ Rocafort) A fun and friendly new cafe, decked out with retro furniture. The menu holds plenty for everyone, whether your thing is eggs Benedict, wild-berry tartlets or a juicy fat burger. There are lots of vegetarian, gluten-free and organic options, and superb (and reasonably priced) brunches on weekends. Wednesday night is ladies' night, with cheap cocktails.

Fastvínic   Cafe €

Map p136 (☎ 93 487 32 41; www.fastvinic.com; Carrer de la Diputació 251; sandwiches €4.25-12; ☺ noon-midnight Mon-Sat; ⓜ Passeig de Gracia) 🍴 A project in sustainability all round, this is Slow Food done fast, with ingredients, wine and building materials all sourced from Catalonia. Designed by Alfons Tost, there are air-purifying plants, energy-efficient LED lighting, and a water and food recycling system.

Cremeria Toscana   Gelateria €

Map p136 (☎ 93 539 38 25; www.cremeria-tos-cana.es; Carrer de Muntaner 161; ice cream from €2.80; ☺ 1pm-midnight Tue-Sun; ⓜ Hospital Clínic) Yes, you can stumble across quite reasonable ice cream in Barcelona, but close your eyes and imagine yourself across the Mediterranean with the real ice-cream wizards. Creamy *stracciatella*

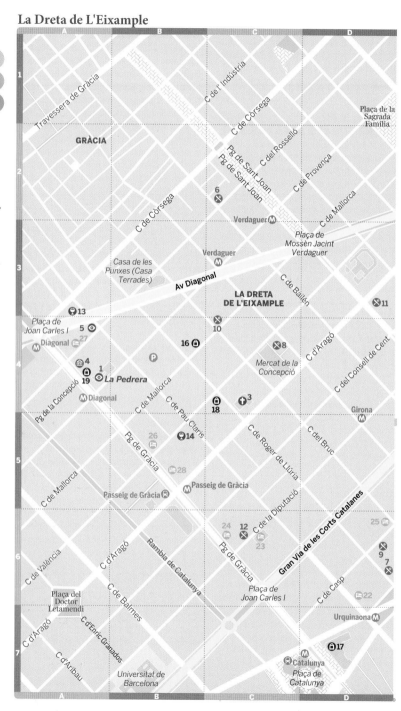

La Dreta de L'Eixample

and wavy *nocciola* and myriad other flavours await at the most authentic gelato outlet in town. Buy a cone or a tub.

Mauri Pastelería €

Map p136 (☏ 93 215 10 20; www.pasteleriasmauri.com; Rambla de Catalunya 102; pastries from €3.40; ◷8am-midnight Mon-Sat, 9am-4pm Sun; Ⓜ Diagonal) Ever since it opened in 1929, this grand old pastry shop has had its regular customers salivating over the endless range of sweets, chocolate croissants and gourmet delicatessen items.

Amaltea
Vegetarian €

Map p136 (www.amalteaygovinda.com; Carrer de la Diputació 164; mains €5-9; ⏰1-4pm & 8-11.30pm Mon-Sat; ✎; MUrgell) The ceiling fresco of blue sky sets the scene in this popular vegetarian eatery. The *menú del día* (€10.70) offers a series of dishes that change frequently with the seasons. At night, the set two-course dinner (€15) offers good value. The homemade desserts are tempting.

The place is something of an alternative lifestyle centre, with yoga, t'ai chi and belly-dancing classes.

El Rincón Maya
Mexican €

Map p136 (☎93 451 39 46; Carrer de València 183; mains €6-9.50; ⏰9-11.30pm Mon, 1.30-4pm & 8.30-11.30pm Tue-Sat; MPasseig de Gràcia) Getting a seat in this Mexican eatery can be a trial, but it's worth it. The setting is warm, modest and simple. The pocket-sized serves of nachos, guacamole and fajitas all burst with flavour. You'll also discover lesser-known items like *tacos de pibil* (pork tacos) and *tinga* (little pasta pockets of chicken). There are also more substantial dishes. The owner-chef spent much of his life in the restaurant business in Mexico City.

A Casa Portuguesa
Cafe €€

Map p136 (☎93 226 25 77; www.acasaportuguesa.com; Carrer d'Aragó 111; mains €12-18; ⏰1pm-1am Mon-Sat, 1-8pm Sun; MRocafort) A Casa Portuguesa is an attractive, colourful space where you can try Barcelona's best *pastéis de Belém (*Portuguese custard tarts). You can also sample the vast variety of food from the region, much of it chargrilled meat and fish.

In addition, there are well over 150 different Portuguese wines available, and a *menú del día* offering typical dishes from chicken piri piri to octopus.

Cata 1.81
Tapas €€

Map p136 (☎93 323 68 18; www.cata181.com; Carrer de València 181; tapas €6-8; ⏰7pm-midnight Mon-Sat; MPasseig de Gràcia) A beautifully designed venue (with lots of small lights, some trapped in birdcages), this is the place to come for fine wines and dainty gourmet dishes like *raviolis amb bacallà* (salt-cod dumplings) or *truita de patates i tòfona negre* (thick potato tortilla with a delicate trace of black truffle). The best option is to choose from one of several tasting-menu options ranging from €29 to €45.

Taktika Berri
Basque, Tapas €€

Map p136 (☎93 453 47 59; Carrer de València 169; tapas from €3; ⏰1-4pm & 8.30-11pm Mon-Fri, 1-4pm Sat; MHospital Clínic) Get in early because the bar teems with punters from far and wide, anxious to wrap their mouths around some of the best Basque tapas in town. The hot morsels are all snapped up as soon as they arrive from the kitchen, so keep your eyes peeled. The seated dining area out the back is also good. In the evening, it's all over by about 10.30pm.

Alba Granados
Spanish, Mediterranean €€

Map p136 (☎93 454 61 16; www.albagranados.cat; Carrer d'Enric Granados 34; mains €14-28; ⏰1-4pm & 8pm-midnight; ⓇFGC Provença) In summer ask for one of the romantic tables for two on the 1st-floor balcony. Overlooking the trees, it is a unique spot, with little traffic.

Inside, the ground- and 1st-floor dining areas are huge, featuring exposed brick and dark parquet. The menu offers a little of everything but the best dishes revolve around meat, such as *solomillo a la mantequilla de trufa con tarrina de patata y beicon* (sirloin in truffle butter, potato and bacon terrine).

Cerveseria Brasseria Gallega
Tapas €€

Map p136 (☎93 439 41 28; Carrer de Casanova 238; mains €8.50-19; ⏰1.30-3.30pm & 8.30-11.30pm Mon-Sat, closed Aug; MHospital Clínic) You could walk right by this modest establishment without giving it a second glance. If you did stop to look, you'd soon notice it was chock-full of locals immersed in animated banter and surrounded by plates of abundant Galician

DMITRI KHREBTUKOV/GETTY IMAGES ©

⭐ Don't Miss
Casa Batlló

One of the strangest residential buildings in Europe, this is Gaudí at his hallucinogenic best. The facade, sprinkled with bits of blue, mauve and green tiles and studded with wave-shaped window frames and balconies, rises to an uneven blue-tiled roof with a solitary tower.

It is one of the three houses on the block between Carrer del Consell de Cent and Carrer d'Aragó that gave it the playful name Manzana de la Discordia, meaning 'Apple (Block) of Discord'. The others are Puig i Cadafalch's Casa Amatller and Domènech i Montaner's Casa Lleó Morera. They were all renovated between 1898 and 1906 and show how eclectic a 'style' Modernisme was.

Locals know Casa Batlló variously as the *casa dels ossos* (house of bones) or *casa del drac* (house of the dragon). It's easy enough to see why. The balconies look like the bony jaws of some strange beast and the roof represents Sant Jordi (St George) and the dragon. Even the roof was built to look like the shape of an animal's back, with shiny scales – the 'spine' changes colour as you walk around. If you stare long enough at the building, it seems almost to be a living being. Before going inside, take a look at the pavement. Each paving piece carries stylised images of an octopus and a starfish, Gaudí designs originally cooked up for Casa Batlló.

NEED TO KNOW

Map p136; ☎93 216 03 06; www.casabatllo.es; Passeig de Gràcia 43; adult/concessions/child under 7yr €21.50/€18.50/free; ⊗9am-9pm daily; Ⓜ Passeig de Gràcia

classics. The fresh *pulpo a la gallega* (spicy octopus chunks with potatoes) as starter confirms this place is a cut above the competition.

La Bodegueta
Provença   Tapas €€

Map p136 (📞 93 215 17 25; Carrer de Provença 233; mains €11-25; ⏰8am-4pm & 8-11.30pm; 🅼Diagonal) The 'Little Wine Cellar' offers classic tapas presented with a touch of class, from *calamares a la andaluza* (lightly battered squid rings) to *cecina* (dried cured veal meat). The house speciality is *ous estrellats* (literally 'smashed eggs') – a mix of scrambled egg, potato and other ingredients ranging from foie gras to *morcilla* (black pudding). Wash it all down with a good Ribera del Duero or *caña* (little glass) of beer. Staff can be a bit curt.

Koyuki   Japanese €€

Map p136 (📞 93 237 84 90; Carrer de Còrsega 242; mains €15-20; ⏰1-3.30pm & 8-11pm Tue-Sat, 8-11pm Sun; 🅼Diagonal) This unas-suming basement Japanese diner is one of those rough-edged diamonds that it pays to revisit. Sit at a long table and order from the cheesy menu complete with pictures courtesy of the Japanese owner – you won't be disappointed. The variety of *sashimi moriawase* (sliced raw fish) is generous and constantly fresh. The *tempura udon* is a particularly hearty noodle option. Splash it all down with Sapporo beer.

Cinc Sentits   International €€€

Map p136 (📞 93 323 94 90; www.cincsentits. com; Carrer d'Aribau 58; tasting menus €65-109; ⏰1.30-3pm & 8.30-10pm Tue-Sat; 🅼Passeig de Gràcia) Enter the realm of the 'Five Senses' to indulge in a jaw-dropping tasting menu (there is no à la carte, although dishes can be tweaked to suit diners' requests), consisting of a series of small, experimental dishes.

A key element here is the use of fresh local produce, such as fish landed on the Costa Brava and top-quality suckling

Left: Cider bottles at a bar; **Below:** A bartender at Dry Martini
(LEFT) MATT MUNRO/LONELY PLANET ©; (BELOW) MATT MUNRO/LONELY PLANET ©

pig from Extremadura,
along with the kind of creative
genius that has earned chef Jordi
Artal a Michelin star.

Speakeasy   International €€€

Map p136 (☎ 93 217 50 80; www.speakeasy-bcn.
com; Carrer d'Aribau 162-166; mains €19-28;
⏰1-4pm & 8pm-midnight Mon-Fri, 8pm-midnight
Sat, closed Aug; Ⓜ Diagonal) This appropriately named clandestine restaurant lurks
behind the Dry Martini bar. You will be
shown a door through the open kitchen
area to the 'storeroom', which is lined with
hundreds of bottles of backlit, quality tip-
ples. Dark decorative tones, a few works
of art, low lighting, light jazz music and
smooth service complete the setting.

The menu includes tempting options
such as wild mushroom ravioli with
langoustine or venison with puréed sweet
potato. If you're after a serious drink
with dinner, consider the pairing menu,
in which a series of courses are matched
with cocktails.

🍷 Drinking & Nightlife

Much of middle-class L'Eixample is dead
at night, but several streets are excep-
tions. Noisy Carrer de Balmes is lined
with a rowdy adolescent set. Much more
interesting is the cluster of locales lining Carrer d'Aribau between Avinguda
Diagonal and Carrer de Mallorca. They
range from quiet cocktail bars to '60s
retro joints. Lower down, on and around
Carrer del Consell de Cent and Carrer de
la Diputació, is the heart of Gaixample,
with several gay bars and clubs.

L'Esquerra de L'Eixample

Dry Martini   Bar

Map p136 (☎ 93 217 50 72; www.javierdelasmue-
las.com; Carrer d'Aribau 162-166; ⏰1pm-2.30am
Mon-Thu, 6pm-3am Fri & Sat; Ⓜ Diagonal)
Waiters with a discreetly knowing smile

will attend to your cocktail needs here. The house drink, taken at the bar or in one of the plush green leather lounges, is a safe bet. The gin and tonic comes in an enormous mug-sized glass – a couple of these and you're well on the way. Out the back is a restaurant, Speakeasy.

Monvínic
Wine Bar

Map p136 (932 72 61 87; www.monvinic.com; Carrer de la Diputació 249; wine bar 1.30-11pm Mon-Sat; Passeig de Gracia) Proclaimed as 'possibly the best wine bar in the world' by the *Wall Street Journal*, and apparently considered unmissable by El Bulli's sommelier, Monvínic is an ode, a rhapsody even, to wine loving. The interactive wine list sits on the bar for you to browse on a digital tablet similar to an iPad and boasts more than 3000 varieties.

La Fira
Bar

Map p136 (682 323 714; Carrer de Provença 171; admission €5 (incl 1 drink); 11pm-5am Fri & Sat; FGC Provença) A designer bar with a difference. Wander in past distorting mirrors and ancient fairground attractions from Germany. Put in coins and listen to hens squawk. Speaking of squawking, the

music swings wildly from whiffs of house through '90s hits to Spanish pop classics. You can spend the earlier part of the night trying some of the bar's shots – it claims to have 500 varieties (but we haven't counted them up).

Cosmo
Cafe

Map p136 (www.galeriacosmo.com; Carrer d'Enric Granados 3; 10am-10pm Mon-Thu, 10am-midnight Fri & Sat, 11am-10pm Sun; Universitat) This groovy space – featuring psychedelic colouring in the tables and bar stools, high white walls out the back for exhibitions and events, a nice selection of teas, pastries and snacks – is perfect for a morning session on your laptop or a civilised evening tipple while admiring the art. It's set on a pleasant pedestrian strip just behind the university

Mediterráneo
Live Music

Map p136 (678 211253; www.elmedi.net; Carrer de Balmes 129; 11pm-3am; Diagonal) This studenty jam joint is a great hangout that attracts a mostly casual student set. Order a beer, enjoy the free nuts and chat at one of the tiny tables while waiting for the next act to tune up at the back.

Summer-time jazz concert atop La Pedrera (p142)

ELAN FLEISHER/LOOK/ROBERT HARDING ©

Sometimes the young performers are surprisingly good.

Premier
Bar

Map p136 (☎93 532 16 50; www.barpremier. com; Carrer de Provença 236; ⏰6pm-2.30am Mon-Thu, 7am-3am Fri & Sat; 🚉FGC Provença) A little cross-pollination has happened in this funky French-run wine bar. The rather short wine list is mostly French – or you can opt for a Moritz beer or a mojito. Hug the bar, sink into a lounge or hide up on the mezzanine. Later in the evening, a DJ adds to the ambience.

Quilombo
Bar

Map p136 (☎93 439 54 06; Carrer d'Aribau 149; ⏰9.30pm-2.30am Tue-Sat; 🚉FGC Provença) Some formulas just work, and this place has been working since the 1970s. Set up a few guitars in the back room, which you pack with tables and chairs, add some cheapish pre-prepared mojitos and plastic tubs of nuts, and let the punters do the rest. They pour in, creating plenty of *quilombo* (fuss).

City Hall
Club

Map p136 (☎652 176272; www.cityhallbarcelona. com; Rambla de Catalunya 2-4; admission €15 (incl 1 drink); ⏰12.30-5am Mon-Thu, to 6am Fri & Sat; Ⓜ Catalunya) A corridor leads to the dance floor of this place, located in a former theatre. House and other electric sounds dominate, including a rather forward-sounding session of cutting-edge funk called Get Funkd! on Tuesdays. Wednesday night is electro-house, while different guest DJs pop up on Thursdays. Out the back from the dance floor is a soothing terrace.

Astoria
Club

Map p136 (☎93 414 47 99; www.astoriabarcelona.com; Carrer de París 193-197; ⏰9pm-2.30am Wed, Thu & Sun, to 3am Fri & Sat; Ⓜ Diagonal) FREE Reds, roses and yellows dominate the colour scheme in this wonderful former cinema. Barcelona's beautiful people, from a broad range of ages, gather to drink around the central rectangular bar, dance a little and eye one another up.

Some come earlier for a bite. At 9pm from Thursday to Saturday there is a 'Circus Cabaret' show with dinner (around €40).

La Dreta de L'Eixample

Les Gens Que J'Aime
Bar

Map p144 (☎93 215 68 79; www.lesgensque-jaime.com; Carrer de València 286; ⏰6pm-2.30am Sun-Thu, 7pm-3am Fri & Sat; Ⓜ Passeig de Gràcia) This intimate basement relic of the 1960s follows a deceptively simple formula: chilled jazz music in the background, minimal lighting from an assortment of flea-market lamps and a cosy, cramped scattering of red velvet-backed lounges around tiny dark tables.

Garaje Hermético
Bar

Map p144 (☎670 253318; Avinguda Diagonal 440; ⏰11pm-4am; Ⓜ Diagonal) It's a pool-playing, rock and roll kinda world in this popular late-night haunt, where those without disco desire but in search of one (or two) more drinkies converge when most of the other bars in Barcelona have closed. It's a no-nonsense place and full of beans after 3am.

☆ Entertainment

Dietrich Café
Cabaret

Map p136 (☎93 451 77 07; Carrer del Consell de Cent 255; ⏰10.30pm-3am; Ⓜ Universitat) It's show time at 1am, with at least one drag-queen gala each night in this cabaret-style locale dedicated to Marlene Dietrich. Soft house is the main musical motif and the place has an interior garden. In between performances, go-go boys heat up the ambience.

 Shopping

Most of the city's classy shopping spreads across the heart of L'Eixample, in particular along Passeig de Gràcia, Rambla de Catalunya and adjacent streets. All about are dotted a surprising array

The Gaixample

Epicenter of Barcelona's gay district is the so-called Gaixample, an area just above Gran Via de les Corts Catalanes and to the left of Rambla de Catalunya. Here are a few favourites:

Mat Bar Map p136 (☎93 453 77 22; www.matbar.es; Carrer de Consell de Cent 245; ◷5pm-2am Tue-Thu & Sun, until 3am Fri & Sat; MUniversitat) A high-design gay bar run by two Aussies, with a retro sporting theme (antique racquets and so on adorn the walls) and some superior bar food, along with craft beers. Those hoping for handbag house and go-go boys will be disappointed – while it gets animated at night, Mat is still a very civilised affair.

Arena Madre Map p136 (☎93 487 83 42; www.grupoarena.com; Carrer de Balmes 32; admission Sun-Fri €6, Sat €12; ◷12.30am-5am Sun-Thu, until 5.30am Fri & Sat; MPasseig de Gràcia) Popular with a hot young crowd, Arena Madre is one of the top clubs in town for boys seeking boys. Keep an eye out for the striptease shows on Mondays and drag queens on Wednesdays, along with the usual combination of disco and Latin music to get those butts moving. Heteros are welcome but a minority.

Pervert Club Map p144 (☎93 453 05 10; Ronda de Sant Pere 19-21; admission €12 (incl 1 drink); ◷midnight-6am Sat; MUrquinaona) With pink laser lights and dense crowds of fit young lads, this is one of the big dance-club locations on a Saturday night. Electronic music dominates the dance nights here and, in spite of the 6am finish, for many this is only the start of the 'evening'. You need to look your gorgeous best to get in past the selective doormen.

Aire Map p136 (☎93 487 83 42; www.arenadisco.com; Carrer de València 236; admission free Thu, €5 Fri, €6 Sat; ◷11pm-2.30am Thu-Sat; MPasseig de Gràcia) A popular locale for lesbians, the dance floor is spacious and there is usually a DJ in command of the tunes, which range from hits of the '80s and '90s to techno. As a rule, only male friends of the girls are allowed entry, although in practise the crowd tends to be fairly mixed. Things can heat up on Thursday nights with live music.

---

of specialty stores, selling anything from gloves to glues.

Vinçon
Homewares

Map p144 (☎93 215 60 50; www.vincon.com; Passeig de Gràcia 96; ◷10am-8.30pm Mon-Fri, 10.30am-9pm Sat; MDiagonal) An icon of the Barcelona design scene, Vinçon has the slickest furniture and household goods (particularly lighting), both local and imported. Not surprising, really, since the building, raised in 1899, belonged to the Modernista artist Ramon Casas. Head upstairs to the furniture area – from the windows and terrace you get close side views of La Pedrera.

El Bulevard dels Antiquaris
Antiques

Map p136 (☎93 215 44 99; www.bulevarddelsan-tiquaris.com; Passeig de Gràcia 55; ◷9am-6pm Mon-Thu, to 2pm Fri & Sat; MPasseig de Gràcia) More than 70 stores (most are open from 11am to 2pm and 5pm to 8.30pm) are gathered under one roof (on the floor above the more general Bulevard Rosa arcade) to offer the most varied selection of collector's pieces, ranging from old porcelain dolls through to fine crystal, from Asian antique furniture to old French goods, and from African and other ethnic art to jewellery.

El Corte Inglés Department Store

Map p144 (📞93 306 38 00; www.elcorteingles.es; Plaça de Catalunya 14; 🕙9.30am-9.30pm Mon-Sat; Ⓜ️Catalunya) This is now the city's only department store, with everything you'd expect to find, from computers to cushions, and high fashion to homewares. It's famous for its decent customer service (not always the case in Spain). The top floor is occupied by a so-so restaurant with fabulous city views.

El Corte Inglés has other branches across the city, including at Portal de l'Àngel 19-21 (Map p60; Ⓜ️Catalunya), Avinguda Diagonal 617 (Map p186; Ⓜ️Maria Cristina) and Avinguda Diagonal 471-473 (Map p136; Ⓜ️Hospital Clínic), near Plaça de Francesc Macià.

Cubiña Homewares

Map p144 (📞93 476 57 21; www.cubinya.es; Carrer de Mallorca 291; 🕙10am-2pm & 4.30-8.30pm Mon-Sat; Ⓜ️Verdaguer) Even if interior design doesn't ring your bell, it's worth a visit to this extensive temple to furniture, lamps and just about any other home accessory your heart might desire just to see this remarkable Domènech i Montaner building.

Admire the enormous and whimsical wrought-iron decoration at street level before heading inside to marvel at the ceiling, timber work, brick columns and windows. Oh, and don't forget the furniture.

Joan Múrria Food

Map p144 (📞93 215 57 89; www.murria.cat; Carrer de Roger de Llúria 85; 🕙9am-2pm & 5-9pm Tue-Thu, 9am-9pm Fri, 10am-2pm & 5-9pm Sat; Ⓜ️Passeig de Gràcia) Ramon Casas designed the century-old Modernista shopfront advertisements featured at this culinary temple. For a century the gluttonous have trembled at this altar of speciality food goods from around Catalonia and beyond.

Cacao Sampaka Food

Map p136 (📞93 272 08 33; www.cacaosampaka.com; Carrer del Consell de Cent 292; 🕙9am-9pm Mon-Sat; Ⓜ️Passeig de Gràcia) Chocoholics will be convinced they have died and passed on to a better place. Load up in the shop or head for the bar out the back where you can have a classic *xocolata* (hot chocolate) and munch on exquisite chocolate cakes, tarts, ice cream, sweets and sandwiches.

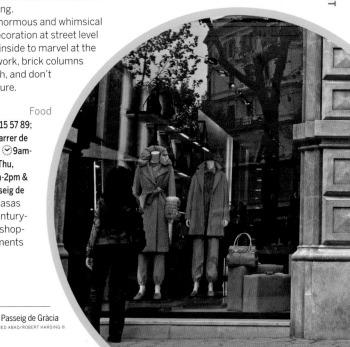

Passeig de Gràcia
ALFRED ABAD/ROBERT HARDING ©

Montjuïc, Poble Sec & Sant Antoni

Montjuïc is home to some of the city's finest art collections – Museu Nacional d'Art de Catalunya, CaixaForum and Fundació Joan Miró. It also hosts several lesser museums, curious sights like the Poble Espanyol, the sinister Castell de Montjuïc and the beautiful remake of Mies van der Rohe's 1920s German pavilion Pavelló Mies van der Rohe. The bulk of the Olympic installations of the 1992 games are also here. Come at night and witness the spectacle of Font Màgica, several busy theatres and a couple of nightclubs. Throw in various parks and gardens and you have the makings of an extremely full couple of days.

You can approach the hill from Plaça d'Espanya on foot and take advantage of a series of escalators up to Avinguda de l'Estadi. Alternatively, and spectacularly, you can get onto a cable car from Barceloneta and take in the beautiful aerial views of the verdant hill.

Font Màgica (p166) **155**

Montjuïc, Poble Sec & Sant Antoni Highlights

Museu Nacional d'Art de Catalunya (p160)

Rising from its stately perch in Montjuïc, the building itself, an imposing neobaroque palace known as the Palau Nacional, is the first and most impressive exhibit of this popular art museum. It was built for the 1929 International Exhibition and converted into a museum in 1995. Once inside, decipher the details of one of the best ensembles of Romanesque painting in Europe.

1

2 ### Fundació Joan Miró (p167)

Contrarian, surrealist, experimentalist and, above all, Catalan, Miró was a local boy who went global with cutting-edge art that provoked and inspired. Barcelona can't claim Picasso as a native but it can gloat about Miró, a talented artistic conjurer who, along with Dalí, dragged surrealism into the mainstream. Fundació Joan Miró is the world's largest single collection of his work. Left: *The caress of a bird,* Joan Miró, 1967

RAFAEL CAMPILLO/AGE FOTOSTOCK/ROBERT HARDING ©

Poble Espanyol (p163)

This microcosmic Spanish 'village' was the brainchild of Modernista architect Josep Puig i Cadafalch and is a bit like an all-Castilian Disneyland. Every region of Spain is architecturally represented, from Andalucía to the Basque Country. Village-like streets and plazas, full-scale replicas of famous buildings, craft workshops (pottery, glassmaking, textiles) and half a dozen restaurants (and a popular nightclub) mean you won't run out of things to do.

Font Màgica (p166)

If you take the dictionary definition of 'magic' as 'something that seems to cast a spell', Font Màgica is aptly named. A grandiose aquatic feature built for the 1929 International Exhibition, the fountain forms the centrepiece of a series of terraces and waterfalls cascading from the Palau Nacional. For full psychedelic effect, catch a nightly sound and light show.

Gardens of Montjuïc (p168)

Montjuïc is also home to large pockets of greenery. These lush environs harbour everything from fragrant botanical gardens planted with exotic species to manicured parks, dotted with sculptures, gurgling fountains and terraced lawns. The views are superb. To make the most of your time, bring a picnic (the Mercat de la Boqueria makes a fine stop before heading uphill).

Above: Jardins de Mossèn Cinto de Verdaguer

Montjuïc Walk

Montjuïc's pretty gardens and scenic views seem a world away from the bustle of downtown Barcelona. This leisurely stroll takes you from the Castell de Montjuïc on a winding (generally downhill) route toward the Font Màgica, passing by manicured flower-filled gardens. Bring along a picnic.

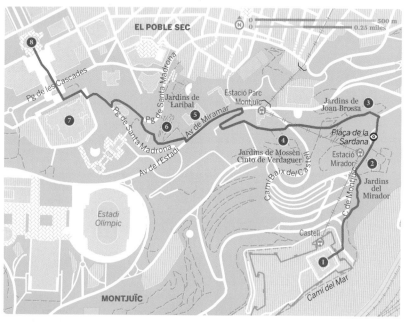

WALK FACTS

- **Start** Castell de Montjuïc
- **Finish** Font Màgica
- **Distance** 2.5km
- **Duration** 90 minutes

① Castell de Montjuïc

Long synonymous with oppression, the dark history of **Castell de Montjuïc** (p162) is today overshadowed by the fine views it commands over the city and sea. The Telefèric is the perfect way to get up and from there on it's all refreshingly downhill through amassing greenery.

② Jardins del Mirador

A short stroll down the road or the parallel Camí del Mar pedestrian trail leads to another fine viewpoint over the city and sea, the **Jardins del Mirador** (p168). Take the weight off your feet on one of the park benches, or pick up a snack and grab some reflection time.

③ Jardins de Joan Brossa

Further downhill is the multitiered **Jardins de Joan Brossa** (p168). The entrance is on the left just beyond Plaça de la Sardana, with the sculpture of people engaged in the classic Catalan folk dance. More fine city views can be had from among the many Mediterranean trees and plants.

4 Jardins de Mossèn Cinto de Verdaguer

Exiting the Jardins de Joan Brossa at the other (west) side, cross Camí Baix del Castell to the painstakingly laid-out **Jardins de Mossèn Cinto de Verdaguer** (p168). This is a beautiful setting for a slow meander among the tulip beds and water lilies, which act as both relaxing and inspiration.

5 Fundació Joan Miró

Joan Miró left a broad collection of his works to the city in his specially designed hillside **foundation** (p167). You can discover his earliest, tentative artistic attempts and continue right through to the characteristic broad canvases for which he is known. Get close-up views of sculptures in the adjacent garden.

6 Jardins de Laribal

Dropping away behind the Fundació Joan Miró, the **Jardins de Laribal** are a combination of terraced gardens linked by paths and stairways. The pretty sculpted watercourses along some of the stairways were inspired by Granada's Muslim-era palace of El Alhambra. Stop for a snack and contemplate a Moorish paradise.

7 Museu Nacional d'Art de Catalunya

Whichever direction you are coming from, it is worth making the effort to reach this huge ochre beast of a **museum** (p160) to see one of Europe's finest collections of Romanesque art, salvaged from countless churches and chapels sprinkled over northern Catalonia. Further collections range from Gothic to Modernista.

8 Font Màgica

Descending from the museum past the Plaça de les Cascades to the **Font Màgica** (p166) is as magic as the name suggests, particularly if you've stretched this walk long enough (easily done) to arrive here after dark – in time for the rather splendid sound and light show.

 The Best…

PLACES TO EAT

Tickets Molecular gastronomy in all its glory. (p170)

Quimet i Quimet An old-time favourite with superb tapas. (p169)

Bodega 1900 Enticing tapas bar with refreshing vermouths. (p169)

Federal Excellent brunches and a small roof terrace. (p169)

Taverna Can Margarit Great old-fashioned ambience and classic Catalan fare. (p168)

PLACES TO DRINK

La Caseta del Migdia An open-air charmer hidden in the thickets of Montjuïc. (p170)

Tinta Roja A bohemian, cabaret-like atmosphere prevails at this Poble Sec bar. (p171)

La Terrazza Lovely summertime dance spot in Poble Espanyol. (p171)

VIEWS

Castell de Montjuïc The castle offers commanding views. (p162)

Miramar The first-rate cuisine is only slightly upstaged by the view. (p168)

Jardins de Mossèn Cinto de Verdaguer (p168)
DIEGO LEZAMA / GETTY IMAGES ©

Don't Miss
Museu Nacional d'Art de Catalunya

From across the city, the bombastic neobaroque silhouette of the Palau Nacional can be seen rising up from the slopes of Montjuïc. Built for the 1929 World Exhibition and restored in 2005, it houses a vast collection of mostly Catalan art spanning the early Middle Ages to the early 20th century. The high point is the collection of extraordinary Romanesque frescoes, which is considered the most important concentration of early medieval art in the world.

MNAC

Map p164

☎ 93 622 03 76

www.mnac.es

Mirador del Palau Nacional

adult/senior & child under 15yr/student €10/free/7, 1st Sun of month free

⊙10am-7pm Tue-Sat, 10am-2.30pm Sun & holidays, library 10am-6pm Mon-Fri, to 2.30pm Sat

Ⓜ Espanya

Romanesque Masterpieces

Rescued from neglected country churches across northern Catalonia in the early 20th century, the Romanesque collection consists of 21 frescoes, woodcarvings and painted altar frontals (low-relief wooden panels that were the forerunners of the elaborate altarpieces that adorned later churches). The insides of several churches have been recreated and the frescoes – in some cases fragmentary, in others extraordinarily complete and alive with colour – have been placed as they were when in situ.

Gothic Collection

Opposite the Romanesque collection is the museum's Gothic art section with Catalan works and paintings from other Spanish and Mediterranean regions. Look out for the work of Bernat Martorell and Jaume Huguet. Images of the martyrdom of St Vincent and St Llúcia feature among Martorell's works. Huguet's *Consagració de Sant Agustí*, in which St Augustine is depicted as a bishop, is dazzling.

Cambò Bequest & Thyssen-Bornemisza Collection

As the Gothic collection draws to a close, you pass through two eclectic collections, which span the history of European painting between the 14th century and the beginning of the 19th century.

Modern Catalan Art

Up on the next floor, after a series of rooms devoted to mostly minor works by a variety of 17th-century Spanish Old Masters, the collection turns to modern Catalan art. The collection is an uneven affair, but it's worth looking out for Modernista painters Ramon Casas and Santiago Rusiñol, as well as the recently deceased Antoni Tàpies.

Also on show are items of Modernista furniture and decoration, including a mural by Ramon Casas of himself and Pere Romeu on a tandem bicycle. The furniture collection comes from the original Modernista houses and includes a great display of decorative objects.

> **Local Knowledge**

Don't Miss List

BY NÚRIA ROCAMORA, CULTURAL MANAGER AND MNAC GUIDE.

1 **PALAU NACIONAL**
The building itself was conceived as the main pavilion for the 1929 Barcelona International Exposition and was designed in a mannerist style, inspired in part by the Spanish Renaissance.

2 **CENTRAL APSE OF SANT CLIMENT DE TAÜLL**
Seeing the magnificent Romanesque works is a highlight of any visit to MNAC. One of the masterpieces was taken from the central apse of the 12th-century Catalan church Sant Climent in Taüll. Here you see a Christ in Majesty, inscribed in a mandorla, seated on the arc of Heaven and joined by the four Evangelists, various key saints and the Virgin Mary.

3 **SAINT FRANCIS OF ASSISI AFTER THE VISION OF POPE NICHOLAS V**
One of the great masters of the 17th century was Spanish painter Francisco Zurbarán, whose exquisite, dramatically lit portraits sometimes earn him comparison with Caravaggio. In this evocative painting of Saint Francis, Zurbarán depicts the saint near the moment of rapture, capturing profound religious feeling while avoiding stylistic cliches.

4 **RAMON CASAS AND PERE ROMEU ON A TANDEM**
This simple, funny work is utterly representative of the whole Catalan Modernista style. Its subject: just one of the most important artists of this period and his friend riding a bicycle. Two years later, Ramon Casas painted a second version of this work of art, but with the two driving in a car!

5 **NUMISMATIC CABINET**
The often overlooked Numismatic Cabinet is a staggering collection of rare coins, some of which date back to the 6th century BC. Highlights include the first silver coins minted in the Iberian Peninsula by the Greeks of Emporion, pieces made during the 17th-century Reapers' War and local notes issued during the Spanish Civil War.

Discover Montjuïc, Poble Sec & Sant Antoni

Getting There & Away

○ **Metro** Metro Línia 3 runs down Avinguda del Paral·lel, between Poble Sec and Sant Antoni. The closest stops to Montjuïc are Espanya, Poble Sec and Paral·lel.

○ **Bus** Bus 50 runs to Montjuïc along Gran Via de les Corts Catalanes via Plaça de l'Universitat and Plaça d'Espanya. Bus 61 runs on weekdays along Avinguda del Paral·lel to Montjuïc via Plaça d'Espanya. Bus 55 runs across town via Plaça de Catalunya and Carrer de Lleida, terminating at the Estació Parc Montjuïc funicular station. The 150 (Parc de Montjuïc) line does a circle trip from Plaça d'Espanya to the Castell de Montjuïc.

○ **Funicular** Take the Metro (Línia 2 or 3) to the Paral·lel stop and pick up the funicular railway, part of the Metro fare system, to Estació Parc Montjuïc.

Sights

Museu Nacional d'Art de Catalunya
Museum

See p160

CaixaForum
Gallery

Map p164 (☎ 93 476 86 00; www.fundacio.lacaixa. es; Avinguda de Francesc Ferrer i Guàrdia 6-8; adult/student & child €4/free, 1st Sun of month free; ◷ 10am-8pm Mon-Fri, to 9pm Sat & Sun; Ⓟ; Ⓜ Espanya) The Caixa building society prides itself on its involvement in (and ownership of) art, in particular all that is contemporary. Its premier art expo space in Barcelona hosts part of the bank's extensive collection from around the globe.

The setting is a completely renovated former factory, the Fàbrica Casaramona, an outstanding Modernista brick structure designed by Puig i Cadafalch. From 1940 to 1993 it housed the First Squadron of the police cavalry unit – 120 horses in all.

Now it is home to a major exhibition space. On occasion portions of La Caixa's own collection of 800 works of modern and contemporary art go on display, but more often than not major international exhibitions are the key draw.

In the courtyard where the police horses used to drink is a steel tree designed by the Japanese architect Arata Isozaki. Musical recitals are sometimes held in the museum, especially in the warmer months.

Castell de Montjuïc
Fortress

Map p164 (☎ 93 256 44 45; www.bcn.cat/castell-demontjuic; Carretera de Montjuïc 66; adult/concessions/child €5/€3/free, free Sun pm & 1st Sun of month; ◷ 10am-8pm; ☐ 150, Telefèric de Montjuïc,

Cable car to Montjuïc
JORG GREUE/GETTY IMAGES ©

Castell de Montjuïc) This forbidding *castell* (castle or fort) dominates the southeastern heights of Montjuïc and enjoys commanding views over the Mediterranean. It dates, in its present form, from the late 17th and 18th centuries. For most of its dark history, it has been used to watch over the city and as a political prison and killing ground.

The views from the castle and the surounding area looking over the sea, port and city below are the best part of the trip here.

Poble Espanyol   Cultural Centre

Map p164 (www.poble-espanyol.com; Avinguda de Francesc Ferrer i Guàrdia 13; adult/child €11/6.25; ⏰9am-8pm Mon, to midnight Tue-Thu & Sun, to 3am Fri, to 4am Sat; 🚌13, 23, 150, Ⓜ Espanya) Welcome to Spain! All of it! This 'Spanish Village' is both a cheesy 'souvenir hunters' haunt and an intriguing scrapbook of Spanish architecture built for the Spanish crafts section of the 1929 World Exhibition. You can meander from Andalucía to the Balearic Islands in the space of a couple of hours, visiting surprisingly good copies of Spain's characteristic buildings.

You enter from beneath a towered medieval gate from Ávila. Inside, to the right, is an information office with free maps. Straight ahead from the gate is the Plaza Mayor (Town Sq), surrounded with mainly Castilian and Aragonese buildings. It is sometimes the scene of summer concerts. Elsewhere you'll find an Andalucian *barrio* (district), a Basque street, Galician and Catalan quarters, and even a Dominican monastery (at the eastern end). The buildings house dozens of restaurants, cafes, bars, craft shops and workshops (for glass artists and other artisans), and some souvenir stores.

Spare some time for the **Fundació Fran Daurel** (www.fundaciofrandaurel.com; ⏰10am-7pm) , an eclectic collection of 300 works of art including sculptures, prints, ceramics and tapestries by modern artists ranging from Picasso and Miró to more contemporary figures, including Miquel Barceló. The foundation also has a sculpture garden, boasting 27 pieces,

nearby within the grounds of Poble Espanyol (look for the Montblanc gate). Frequent temporary exhibitions broaden the offerings further.

At night the restaurants, bars and especially the discos become a lively corner of Barcelona's nightlife.

Children's groups can participate in the **Joc del Sarró**. Accompanied by adults, the kids go around the *poble* (village) seeking the answers to various mysteries outlined in a kit distributed to each group. Languages catered for include English.

Pavelló Mies van der Rohe   Architecture

Map p164 (📞93 423 40 16; www.miesbcn.com; Avinguda de Francesc Ferrer i Guàrdia 7; adult/child €5/free; ⏰10am-8pm; Ⓜ Espanya) The Pavelló Mies van der Rohe is not only a work of breathtaking beauty and simplicity, it is a highly influential building emblematic of the modern movement. The structure has been the subject of many studies and interpretations, and it has inspired several generations of architects.

Museu d'Arqueologia de Catalunya   Museum

Map p164 (MAC; 📞93 423 21 49; www.mac.cat; Passeig de Santa Madrona 39-41; adult/student €4.50/3.50; ⏰9.30am-7pm Tue-Sat, 10am-2.30pm Sun; Ⓜ Poble Sec) This archaeology museum, housed in what was the Graphic Arts Palace during the 1929 World Exhibition, covers Catalonia and cultures from elsewhere in Spain. Items range from copies of pre-Neanderthal skulls to lovely Carthaginian necklaces and jewel-studded Visigothic crosses.

Jardí Botànic   Gardens

Map p164 (www.jardibotanic.bcn.cat; Carrer del Doctor Font i Quer 2; adult/child €3.50/free; ⏰10am-7pm; 🚌55, 150) This botanical garden is dedicated to Mediterranean flora and has a collection of some 40,000 plants and 1500 species that thrive in areas with a climate similar to that of the Mediterranean, such as the Eastern Mediterranean, Spain (including the Balearic and Canary Islands), North Africa, Australia, California, Chile and South Africa.

Montjuïc, Poble Sec & Sant Antoni

Ⓜ Sants Estació

Plaça dels Països Catalans

C de València

C d'Aragó

C del Consell de Cent

C de Calàbria

Rocafort Ⓜ

C de la Diputació

SANTS

Ⓡ Estació Sants

Plaça de Joan Peiró

Tarragona

C de Llançà

Gran Via de les Corts Catalanes

C d'Entença

36 C de Béjar

C de Tarragona

C del Rector Triadó

Les Arenes

Av de Mistral

C de Riego

C de Mundadas

Plaça d'Osca

Hostafrancs Ⓜ

C de Sants

C de la Creu Coberta

Ⓟ

Plaça d'Espanya

Av de la Reina Maria Cristina

Av del Paral·lel

Fira de Barcelona

C de Lleida

Espanya

Plaça de l'Univers

C de la Bordeta

C de Mèxic

Av de Rius i Taulet

Gran Via de les Corts Catalanes

C de Gavà

C de Sant Fructuós

Av del Marquès de Comillas

3 🏛

7 ◉

16 ◉

Plaça del Marquès de Foronda

Pg de les Cascades

C de la Dàlia

C de Sant Fructuós

Av de Francesc Ferrer i Guàrdia

17 ◉

29 ◉

Mirador del Palau Nacional

Mirador del Palau Nacional

2 🏛

Magòria La Campana Ⓡ

8 🏛

Av dels Montanyans

Museu Nacional d'Art de Catalunya (MNAC)

Plaça de Sant Jordi

Av de l'Estadi

Antic Jardí Botànic

Antic Jardí d'Aclimatació

Plaça de la Universitat

Inset

Pg de Minici Natal

Pg Olímpic

33 ☆

Plaça d'Europa

Plaça de Terenci Moix

Plaça de Nemesí Ponsati

Ⓜ 19 ✕

Urgell

30 ◉

20 ✕

C de Pierre de Coubertin

Anella Olímpica

0 ————— 200 m
0 ————— 0.1 miles

Pg de la Zona Franca

C dels Jocs de 92

Parc del Migdia

↓ Col·lecció de Carrosses Fúnebres (850m)

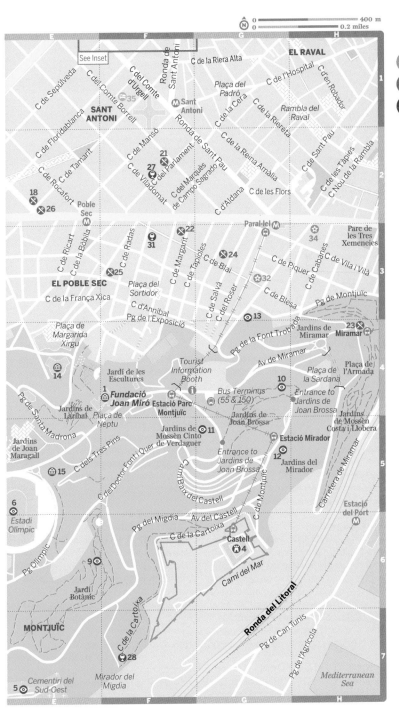

0 —————————— 400 m
0 —————————— 0.2 miles

EL RAVAL

C de la Riera Alta

Plaça del Padró

C de l'Hospital   C en Robador

M Sant Antoni

C del Comte d'Urgell

Ronda de Sant Antoni

C de Sepúlveda

C del Comte Borrell

35

SANT ANTONI

C de Floridablanca

C de Manso

Ronda de Sant Pau

C de la Cera

C de la Riereta

C de la Reina Amàlia

Rambla del Raval

C de Sant Pau

C de les Tàpies

C Nou de la Rambla

C de Tamarit

C de Rocafort

21

27

C del Parlament

C de Viladomat

C del Marquès de Campo Sagrado

C d'Aldana

C de les Flors

18

26

Poble Sec M

Paral·lel M

Parc de les Tres Xemeneies

34

22

31

C de Ricart

C de la Bòbila

C de Radas

25

EL POBLE SEC

C de la França Xica

Plaça del Sortidor

C de Margarit

C de Tàpioles

24

C de Blai

C de Piquer

C de Cabanes

C de Vila i Vila

32

C de Blesa

Pg de Montjuïc

C d'Annibal

Pg de l'Exposició

C de Salvà

C del Roser

13

Plaça de Margarida Xirgu

Jardins de Miramar

23 Miramar

14

Jardí de les Escultures

Tourist Information Booth

Av de Miramar

Plaça de l'Armada

1 **Fundació Joan Miró**

Estació Parc Montjuïc

Bus Terminus (55 & 150)

10

Plaça de la Sardana

Entrance to Jardins de Joan Brossa

Jardins de Mossèn Costa i Llobera

Jardins de Laribal

Plaça de Neptu

Jardins de Joan Brossa

Pg de Santa Madrona

Jardins de Joan Maragall

C dels Tres Pins

Jardins de Mossèn Cinto de Verdaguer

11

Estació Mirador

12

Jardins del Mirador

15

C del Doctor Font i Quer

Entrance to Jardins de Joan Brossa

Camí Baix del Castell

Estació del Port M

6

Estadi Olímpic

Carretera de Miramar

Pg del Migdia

Av del Castell

C de la Cartoixa

Castell

4

C de Montjuïc

Pg Olímpic

9

Jardí Botànic

Camí del Mar

MONTJUÏC

C de la Cartoixa

Ronda del Litoral

28

Pg de Can Tunis

5

Cementiri del Sud-Oest

Mirador del Migdia

Pg de l'Agrícola

Mediterranean Sea

See Inset

Montjuïc, Poble Sec & Sant Antoni

MUHBA Refugi 307   Historic Site

Map p164 (☏93 256 21 22; www.museuhistoria.
bcn.cat; Carrer Nou de la Rambla 169; admission incl tour adult/child under 7yr €3.40/
free; ☾tours 10.30am, 11.30am & 2.30pm Sun;
MParal·lel) Part of the Museu d'Història de
Barcelona (MUHBA), this is a shelter that
dates back to the Spanish Civil War. Barcelona was the city most heavily bombed
from the air during the Spanish Civil War
and had more than 1300 air-raid shelters.
Local citizens started digging this one
under a fold of Montjuïc in March 1937.

Font Màgica   Fountain

Map p164 (☏93 316 10 00; Avinguda de la Reina
Maria Cristina; ☾every 30min 7-9pm Fri & Sat Oct-
Apr, 9.30-11pm Thu-Sun May-Sep; MEspanya) A
huge fountain that crowns the long sweep
of the Avinguda de la Reina Maria Cristina
to the grand facade of the Palau Nacional,
Font Màgica is a unique performance in
which the water can look like seething
fireworks or a mystical cauldron of colour.

Cementiri del Sud-Oest   Cemetery

Map p164 (☏93 484 19 70; www.cbsa.cat; Carrer
de la Mare de Déu de Port 56-58; ☾8am-6pm;

🚌9, 21) FREE On the hill to the south of
the Anella Olímpica stretches this huge
cemetery, the Cementiri del Sud-Oest (or
'Cementiri Nou'), which extends down
the southern side of the hill. Opened
in 1883, it's an odd combination of
elaborate architect-designed tombs for
rich families and small niches for the
rest. It includes the graves of numerous
Catalan artists and politicians, and, at
the entrance, the Col·lecció de Carrosses
Fúnebres.

Col·lecció de
Carrosses Fúnebres   Museum

(☏93 484 19 99; www.cbsa.cat; Carrer de la
Mare de Déu de Port 56-58; ☾10am-2pm Wed-
Sun; 🚌9, 21) FREE If late-18th-century to
mid-20th-century hearses (complete
with period-dressed dummies) are your
thing, then be sure to check out this
collection. It's at the entrance to the
Cementiri del Sud-Oest and is probably
the city's weirdest sight. The museum
is a place to contemplate the pomp and
circumstance of people's last earthly
ride, and the funeral company claims it

ARCHITECT: JOSEP LLUÍS SERT
MAREMAGNUM/GETTY IMAGES ©

⭐ Don't Miss
Fundació Joan Miró

Joan Miró, the city's best-known 20th-century artistic progeny, bequeathed this art foundation to his hometown in 1971. Its light-filled buildings, designed by close friend and architect Josep Lluís Sert (who also built Miró's Mallorca studios), are crammed with seminal works, from Miró's earliest timid sketches to paintings from his last years.

Sert's shimmering white temple to the art of one of the stars of the 20th-century Spanish firmament is considered one of the world's most outstanding museum buildings. The architect designed it after spending much of Franco's dictatorship years in the USA, as the head of the School of Design at Harvard University. The foundation rests amid the greenery of the mountain and holds the greatest single collection of the artist's work, comprising around 220 of his paintings, 180 sculptures, some textiles and more than 8000 drawings spanning his entire career. Only a small portion is ever on display.

NEED TO KNOW
Map p164; ☏93 443 94 70; www.fundaciomiro-bcn.org; Parc de Montjuïc; adult/child €11/free; ⏱10am-8pm Tue-Sat, to 9.30pm Thu, to 2.30pm Sun & holidays; 🚍55, 150, Ⓜ Paral·lel

is the biggest museum of its kind in the world.

Museu Olímpic i de l'Esport
Museum

Map p164 (☏93 292 53 79; www.museu-olimpicbcn.com; Avinguda de l'Estadi 60; adult/student €5.10/3.20; ⏱10am-8pm Tue-Sat, 10am-2.30pm Sun; 🚍55, 150) The Museu Olímpic i de L'Esport is an information-packed interactive museum dedicated to the history of sport and the Olympic Games. After picking up tickets, you wander down a ramp that snakes below

Gardens & Grand Views

The views from the Castell de Montjuïc and the surrounding area looking over the sea, port and city below are the best part of making the trip here. Around the seaward foot of the castle is an airy walking track, the Camí del Mar, which offers breezy views of the city and sea.

From the **Jardins del Mirador** (Map p164; cable car Telefèric de Montjuïc (Mirador)), opposite the Mirador (Telefèric) station, you have fine views over the port of Barcelona. A little further downhill, the **Jardins de Joan Brossa** (Map p164; ⊙10am-sunset; cable car Telefèric de Montjuïc, Mirador) **FREE** are charming, landscaped gardens on the site of a former amusement park near Plaça de la Sardana. These gardens contain many Mediterranean species, from cypresses to pines and a few palms. There are swings, thematic walking trails and some good city views.

Near the Estació Parc Montjuïc funicular/Telefèric station are the ornamental **Jardins de Mossèn Cinto de Verdaguer** (Map p164; www.bcn.cat/parcsijardins; ⊙10am-sunset; ⌑55,150) **FREE**. These sloping, verdant gardens are home to tulips, narcissi, crocuses and dahlias and aquatic plants such as lotus and water lilies.

ground level and is lined with displays on the history of sport, starting with the ancients.

Estadi Olímpic Lluís Companys
Stadium

Map p164 (☏93 426 20 89; Avinguda de l'Estadi; ⊙10am-8pm; ⌑150) **FREE** The Estadi Olímpic was the main stadium of Barcelona's Olympic Games. If you saw the Olympics on TV, the 65,000-capacity stadium may seem surprisingly small. So might the Olympic flame holder into which an archer spectacularly fired a flaming arrow during the opening ceremony. The stadium was opened in 1929 and restored for 1992.

✖ Eating

Montjuïc is largely bereft of notable eating options, for the obvious reason that it is mostly parks and gardens. In gruff old El Poble Sec, however, you'll turn up all sorts of priceless nuggets, from historic taverns offering Catalan classics to a handful of smart, new-wave eateries, while Sant Antoni is the place for new café openings.

Montjuïc

Miramar
Mediterranean, Asian €€

Map p164 (☏93 443 66 27; www.club-miramar. es; Carretera de Miramar 40; mains €16-23, lunchtime 3-course fixed menu €19.50; ⊙1-4pm & 9pm-midnight Tue-Sat, 1-4pm Sun; ⌑D20) With several terraces and a cool designer main-dining area, this restaurant's key draw is the views it offers over Barcelona's waterfront. Hovering just above the Transbordador Aeri cable-car station, you can linger over a coffee or tuck into an elegant meal with a creative Catalan and Mediterranean slant, or opt for an extensive Asian menu.

El Poble Sec

Taverna Can Margarit
Catalan €

Map p164 (☏93 177 07 40; Carrer de la Concòrdia 21; mains €8-12; ⊙9-11.30pm Mon-Sat; Ⓜ Poble Sec) For decades this former wine store has been dishing out dinner to often raucous groups. Traditional Catalan cooking is the name of the game. Surrounded by aged wine barrels, take your place at old tables and benches and perhaps order the *conejo a la jumillana* (fried rabbit served with garlic, onion, bay leaves, rosemary, mint, thyme and oregano).

La Bella Napoli
Pizza €

Map p164 (☎93 442 50 56; Carrer de Margarit 14; pizzas €8-15; ⏱1.30-4pm & 8.30pm-midnight; Ⓜ Paral·lel) There are pizza joints all over Barcelona. And then there's the real thing: the way they make it in Naples. This place even *feels* like Naples. The waiters are mostly from across the Med and have that cheeky southern Italian approach to food, customers and everything else. The pizzas are good, ranging from the simple margherita to a heavenly black-truffle number.

Quimet i Quimet
Tapas €€

Map p164 (☎93 442 31 42; Carrer del Poeta Cabanyes 25; tapas €4-11; ⏱noon-4pm & 7-10.30pm Mon-Fri, noon-4pm Sat & Sun; Ⓜ Paral·lel) Quimet i Quimet is a family-run business that has been passed down from generation to generation. There's barely space to swing a *calamar* (squid) in this bottle-lined, standing-room-only place, but it is a treat for the palate, with *montaditos* (tapas on a slice of bread) made to order. Let the folk behind the bar advise you, and order a drop of fine wine to accompany the food.

Sant Antoni

Escribà
Desserts €

Map p164 (☎93 454 75 35; www.escriba. es; Gran Via de les Corts Catalanes 546; pastries from €2; ⏱8.30am-3pm & 5-9.30pm Mon-Fri, 8.30am-8.30pm Sat & Sun; Ⓜ Urgell) Antoni Escribà carries forward a family tradition (since 1906) of melting *barcelonins'* hearts with remarkable pastries and criminal chocolate creations. Try the Easter *bunyols de xocolata* (little round pastry balls filled with chocolate cream). Escribà has another branch in a Modernista setting at La Rambla de

Sant Josep 83 (www.escriba.es; ⏱8.30am-9pm; Ⓜ Liceu).

Bodega 1900
Tapas €€

Map p164 (☎93 325 26 59; www.bodega1900. com; Carrer de Tamarit 91; tapas from €4.60; ⏱1-10.30pm Tue-Sat; Ⓜ Sant Antoni) The latest venture from the world-famous Adrià brothers, Bodega 1900 mimics an old-school tapas bar – and calls itself a *vermutería* (vermouth bar), though it only stocks Martini – but this is no ordinary spit-and-sawdust joint serving *patatas bravas* and tortilla. Witness, for example, the *mollete de calamars,* probably the best squid sandwich in the world, hot from the pan and served with chipotle mayonnaise, kim chi and lemon zest; or the 'spherified' false olives.

Federal
Cafe €€

Map p164 (☎93 187 36 07; www.federalcafe. es; Carrer del Parlament 39; snacks from €8; ⏱8am-11pm Mon-Thu, 8am-1am Fri, 9am-1am Sat, 9am-5.30pm Sun; Ⓜ Sant Antoni) On a stretch that now teems with cafes,

Paella
DAVID SUTHERLAND/GETTY IMAGES ©

Australian-run Federal was the trailbazer, with its breezy chic and superb brunches. Later in the day there is healthy, tasty cooking from veggie burgers to a ploughman's lunch, and cupcakes and good coffee are available all day. Head to the roof for a small, leafy terrace on which to browse the day's papers.

Fàbrica Moritz
Catalan €€

Map p164 (☎ 93 426 00 50; www.moritz.com; Ronda de Sant Antoni 41; tapas from €3.70; ⏱ 6am-3am; Ⓜ Sant Antoni) With the help of architect Jean Nouvel and chef Jordi Vilà, this microbrewery from the people behind Moritz beer has been rebuilt and opened with great fanfare as a vast food and drink complex, with wine bar and restaurant. The tapas and more substantial dishes comprise all the cornerstones of Catalan cuisine and plenty more, but be prepared to queue.

Tickets
Modern Spanish €€€

Map p164 (www.ticketsbar.es; Avinguda del Paral·lel 164; tapas €6-15; ⏱ 7-11.30pm Tue-Fri, 1.30-3.30pm & 7-11.30pm Sat, closed Aug; Ⓜ Paral·lel) This is, literally, one of the sizzling tickets in the restaurant world, a

tapas bar opened by Ferran Adrià, of the legendary El Bulli, and his brother Albert. And unlike El Bulli, it's an affordable venture – if you can book a table, that is (you can only book online, and two months in advance).

🍷 Drinking & Nightlife

A couple of curious bars in El Poble Sec (literally 'Dry Town'!) make a good prelude to the clubs that hold sway up in the wonderfully weird fantasy world of the Poble Espanyol.

La Caseta del Migdia
Bar

Map p164 (☎ 617 956572; www.lacaseta.org; Mirador del Migdia; ⏱ 8pm-1am Wed & Thu, 8pm-2am Fri, noon-2am Sat, noon-1am Sun, weekends only in winter; Ⓜ Paral·lel, funicular) The effort of getting to what is, for all intents and purposes, a simple *chiringuito* (makeshift cafe-bar) is well worth it. Stare out to sea over a beer or coffee by day. As sunset approaches the atmosphere changes,

Bar Calders

and lounge music (from samba to funk) wafts out over the hammocks.

Walk below the walls of the Castell de Montjuïc along the dirt track or follow Passeig del Migdia – watch out for signs for the Mirador del Migdia.

La Terrrazza Club

Map p164 (www.laterrrazza.com; Avinguda de Francesc Ferrer i Guàrdia; admission €15-20; ⊗midnight-5am Thu, to 6am Fri & Sat, closed Oct-Apr; Ⓜ Espanya) One of the city's top summertime dance locations, La Terrrazza attracts squadrons of the beautiful people, locals and foreigners alike, for a full-on night of music and cocktails partly under the stars inside the Poble Espanyol complex.

Tinta Roja Bar

Map p164 (✆93 443 32 43; www.tintaroja.cat; Carrer de la Creu dels Molers 17; ⊗8.30pm-1am Wed, to 2am Thu, to 3am Fri & Sat; Ⓜ Poble Sec) A succession of nooks and crannies, dotted with flea market finds and dimly lit in violets, reds and yellows, makes Tinta Roja an intimate spot for a drink and the occasional show in the back – with anything from actors to acrobats. This was once a *vaqueria* (small dairy farm), where they kept cows out the back and sold fresh milk at the front.

Bar Calders Wine Bar

Map p164 (✆93 329 93 49; Carrer del Parlament 25; ⊗5pm-1.30am Mon-Thu, to 2.30am Fri, 11am-2.30am Sat, 11am-midnight Sun; Ⓜ Sant Antoni) It bills itself as a wine bar, but actually the wine selection at Bar Calders is its weak point. As an all-day cafe and tapas bar, however, it's unbeatable, with a few tables outside on a tiny pedestrian side street, and has become the favoured meeting point for the neighbourhood's boho element.

Museum Gay

Map p164 (Carrer de Sepúlveda 178; ⊗11pm-3am Fri & Sat; Ⓜ Universitat) Explosion in the kitsch factory is the artistic theme here, where chandeliers meet mock Renaissance sculpture and light pop. Drinks are

served behind a stage-lit bar and can be hard to come by from 1.30am. Twinks and muscle builders mix happily in this self-styled 'Video Bar'.

Entertainment

Sala Apolo Live Music

Map p164 (✆93 441 40 01; www.sala-apolo.com; Carrer Nou de la Rambla 113; admission club €13-18, concerts vary; ⊗midnight-5am Sun-Thu, 12.30am-6am Fri & Sat; Ⓜ Paral·lel) This is a fine old theatre, where red velvet dominates and you feel as though you're in a movie-set dancehall scene featuring Eliot Ness. 'Nasty Mondays' and 'Crappy Tuesdays' are aimed at a diehard, we-never-stop-dancing crowd. Earlier in the evening, concerts generally take place, here and in 'La 2', a smaller auditorium downstairs. Tastes are as eclectic as possible, from local bands and burlesque shows to big-name international acts.

Metro Gay

Map p164 (✆93 323 52 27; www.metrodiscobcn.com; Carrer de Sepúlveda 185; admission €19, incl 1 drink; ⊗12.15am-5am Sun-Thu, until 6am Fri & Sat; Ⓜ Universitat) Metro attracts a casual gay crowd with its two dance floors, three bars and very dark room. Keep an eye out for shows and parties, which can range from parades of models to bingo nights (on Thursday nights, with sometimes-interesting prizes). On Wednesday nights there's a live sex show.

Gran Bodega Saltó Live Music

Map p164 (www.bodegasalto.net; Carrer de Blesa 36; ⊗7pm-2am Mon-Wed, noon-2am Thu, noon-3am Fri & Sat, noon-midnight Sun; Ⓜ Paral·lel) The ranks of barrels give away the bar's history as a traditional bodega. Now, after a little homemade psychedelic redecoration with odd lamps, figurines and old Chinese beer ads, it's a magnet for an eclectic barfly crowd. Mohicans and tatts abound, but the crowd is mixed and friendly, and gets pretty lively on nights when there is live music.

Park Güell, Camp Nou & La Zona Alta

The undulating terrain north of L'Eixample is dominated by the fairy-tale setting of Park Güell, one of Gaudí's most extraordinary creations. From its hillside perch, it has stellar views over Barcelona.

South of here is Gràcia, a separate village until 1897. It still has a distinct vibe and is home to artists, hipsters, expats and young families. Its pretty plazas are ringed with bars and cafes, and there's a plethora of restaurants, vintage shops and drinking dens in its narrow lanes.

West of Gràcia lies the vast Zona Alta, the affluent 'High Zone'. Scattered here are a handful of worthwhile sites, including the serene Pedralbes monastery and the charming neighbourhood of Sarria. Further north is Tibidabo, the city's high point, with acres of green space, fine views and an amusement park. Further south, near the Sants neighbourhood is Camp Nou, the hallowed home stadium of FC Barcelona.

Park Güell (p178)

Park Güell, Camp Nou & La Zona Alta Highlights

Park Güell (p178)

Imagine a Disney fairy tale, scripted by Tolkien and filmed by Fellini, and you've conjured a picture of Park Güell. The park's construction was initiated in 1900 when Count Eusebi Güel bought a scrubby hillside and hired Antoni Gaudí to create a miniature city of posh houses in landscaped grounds. The project was a commercial flop, but the abandoned site was saved in the 1920s and soon garnered a dedicated following.

Camp Nou (p182)

Spanish soccer is a sometimes bitter tale of two teams, Real Madrid and FC Barcelona, with the latter currently enjoying a spell as one of the best in the world, courtesy of such living legends as Lionel Messi and Xavi Hernández. The team's home stadium is the largest in Europe and its on-site museum is a manifestation of fervour, football and intense Catalan pride.

KRZYSZTOF DYDYNSKI/GETTY IMAGES ©

CosmoCaixa (p180)

This sprawling science museum, one of the largest in Europe, is packed with fascinating exhibits exploring the wonders of the natural world. You can wander through a mocked-up Amazonian rainforest, peer back in time at geologic formations and journey to the outer limits of the solar system. Interactive hands-on exhibits make CosmoCaixa a perennial kid-pleaser. It's easy to spend a half-day or more here.

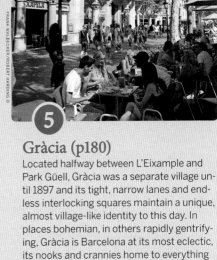

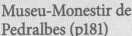

Museu-Monestir de Pedralbes (p181)

The city's periphery hides occasional oases of peace, including this impressive and beautifully preserved 14th-century Catalan-Gothic monastery. Highlights include the three-story cloister, a mural-filled chapel and a fascinating series of rooms that help conjure up life among the Poor Clares. The former sleeping quarters have been transformed into a gallery of religious art dating back to the 1500s.

Gràcia (p180)

Located halfway between L'Eixample and Park Güell, Gràcia was a separate village until 1897 and its tight, narrow lanes and endless interlocking squares maintain a unique, almost village-like identity to this day. In places bohemian, in others rapidly gentrifying, Gràcia is Barcelona at its most eclectic, its nooks and crannies home to everything from sushi bars to badly lit old taverns.

Park Güell, Camp Nou & La Zona Alta Walk

This walk offers a window into centuries past when the Zona Alta was home to lavish summer estates, manicured gardens and sleepy age-old villages.

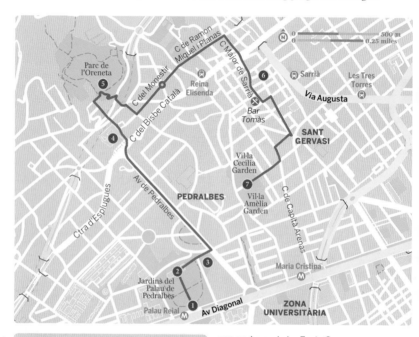

WALK FACTS

- **Start** Jardins del Palau de Pedralbes
- **Finish** Vil·la Amèlia & Vil·la Cecilia Gardens
- **Distance** 5km
- **Duration** Two hours

1 Jardins del Palau de Pedralbes

Although it's located on busy Avinguda Diagonal, this elegant little **park** (p181) feels like a peaceful escape from the bustling city beyond its gates. Pathways lead past manicured shrubbery, cedar and cypress trees, and a vine-covered pergola designed by Antoni Gaudí. A few sculptures dot the pathways, including a 17th-century urn and a nude by Enric Casanovas – one of the pivotal sculptors of the Noucentisme movement of the early 20th century.

2 Palau Reial de Pedralbes

At the north end of the park stands the **Palau Reial de Pedralbes**, an Italian neoclassical design built between 1926 and 1929. The estate belonged to the family of Eusebi Güell (Gaudí's patron) until it was handed over to the city to serve as a royal residence. King Alfonso XIII stayed here when visiting the city and in 1936 the *palau* became the official residence of Manuel Azaña, the last president of the Spanish Republic.

③ Pavellons Güell

Over by Avinguda de Pedralbes are the stables and porter's lodge designed by Gaudí for the Finca Güell, as the Güell estate here was called. Known also as the **Pavellons Güell**, they were built in the mid-1880s, when Gaudí was strongly impressed by Islamic architecture. A magnificent wrought-iron dragon guards the gate.

④ Museu-Monestir de Pedralbes

A stroll uphill along tree-lined Avinguda de Pedralbes leads to an oasis of another time, the peaceful **Museu-Monestir de Pedralbes** (p181). This Gothic convent with its enchanting cloister provides a tantalising glimpse into the life of nuns down the centuries.

⑤ Parc de l'Oreneta

Just behind the Museu-Monestir de Pedralbes rise the green slopes of this somewhat scrubby **woodland**. You can walk amid eucalypts, pines and oaks in a park that attracts few visitors on weekdays. Weekend activities bring out families with pony rides and train rides on a miniature locomotive. Various lookouts provide views over Barcelona.

⑥ Sarrià

Go east along the peaceful Carrer del Monestir for a look at some of the elegant mansions dotting the neighbourhood. Turn right at Carrer Major de Sarrià, which leads you into the heart of what was once the medieval village of **Sarrià**. Wander the pleasant streets and squares in the immediate area and try the city's best *patatas bravas* (potato chunks in a slightly spicy tomato sauce) at **Bar Tomàs** (p185).

⑦ Vil·la Amèlia & Vil·la Cecilia Gardens

Further southwest, these two **gardens** were once part of a magnificent summer estate. Shaded pathways meander beneath cypress, date palms and magnolias, with statuary and pools lending an elegance to the greenery. The 19th-century Vil·la Amèlia today houses the Sarrià civic centre.

 The Best…

PLACES TO EAT

Vivanda Magnficent Catalan cooking with year-round garden dining. (p185)

El Glop A buzzing neighbourhood spot in Gràcia. (p183)

Les Tres a la Cuina Gràcia gem serving unique, Slow Food–minded dishes. (p183)

PLACES TO DRINK

Raïm A slice of old Havana with expert mojitos. (p188)

La Nena One of Gràcia's best-loved neighbourhood cafes. (p183)

Viblioteca A charming little nook for wine and cheese. (p188)

VIEWPOINTS

Parc de Collserola An 8000-hectare park in the hills. (p190)

Mirablau Fun crowd and panoramic views from its Tibidabo perch. (p189)

Temple del Sagrat Cor Giant Christ statue with lift to the top. (p190)

Torre de Collserola A 288m tower with a glass elevator to an observation deck. (p190)

Park Güell Architectural intrigue and breezy views over city and sea. (p178)

Torre de Collserola (p190)

Don't Miss
Park Güell

One of Antoni Gaudí's best-loved creations, Park Güell – a fantasy public park that was designed as a gated playground for Barcelona's rich – climbs a hillside north of the centre. This is where the master architect turned his hand to landscape gardening and the result is an expansive and playful stand of greenery interspersed with otherworldly structures that glitter with ceramic tiles. The lasting impression is of a place where the artificial almost seems more natural than the natural.

Map p184

☏93 413 24 00

Carrer d'Olot 7

admission free

⊗10am-9pm Jun-Sep, 10am-8pm Apr, May & Oct, 10am-7pm Mar & Nov, 10am-6pm Dec-Feb

🚌24, Ⓜ Lesseps or Vallcarca

Background

Park Güell originated in 1900, when Count Eusebi Güell bought a tree-covered hillside (then outside Barcelona) and hired Gaudí to create a miniature city of houses for the wealthy in landscaped grounds. The project was a commercial flop and was abandoned in 1914 – but not before Gaudí had created 3km of roads and walks, steps, a plaza and two gatehouses in his inimitable manner. In 1922 the city bought the estate for use as a public park.

Much of the park is still wooded, but it's laced with pathways. The best views are from the cross-topped Turó del Calvari in the southwest corner.

Sala Hipóstila

The steps up from the entrance, guarded by a mosaic dragon/lizard, lead to the Sala Hipóstila (the Doric Temple). This forest of 88 stone columns – some of which lean like mighty trees bent by the weight of time – was originally intended as a market. To the left curves a gallery whose twisted stonework columns and roof give the effect of a cloister beneath tree roots – a motif repeated in several places in the park.

Banc de Trencadís

On top of the Sala Hipóstila is a broad open space whose centrepiece is the Banc de Trencadís, a tiled bench curving sinuously around its perimeter and designed by one of Gaudí's closest colleagues, architect Josep Maria Jujol (1879–1949). With Gaudí, however, there is always more than meets the eye. This giant platform was designed as a kind of catchment area for rainwater washing down the hillside. The water is filtered through a layer of stone and sand, and it drains down through the columns to an underground cistern.

Casa-Museu Gaudí

The spired house to the right is the Casa-Museu Gaudí, where Gaudí lived for most of his last 20 years (1906–26). It contains furniture he designed (including items that were once at home in La Pedrera, Casa Batlló and Casa Calvet) and other memorabilia.

Local Knowledge

Don't Miss List

BY GONZALO SALAYA VENTURA, TOURIST GUIDE AT ICONO SERVEIS CULTURALS

1 ENTRANCE PAVILIONS
The entrance to Park Güell is flanked by two pavilions, best viewed from the public square up above. Here you'll see classic Gaudí features – hyperbolic shapes, the use of brick and ceramic and cross-topped towers, plus the incredible decoration.

2 SALAMANDER
The most famous creation in the park is this striking, mosaic-covered creature – perhaps a depiction of the legendary salamander associated with medieval alchemy. Like so much of Gaudí's works, this sculpture serves both aesthetic and practical purposes by linking water from an underground reservoir to the (mostly unbuilt) homes.

3 SALA HIPÓSTILA
Located underneath the (planned) main public square, the One Hundred Columns' Room, aka Sala Hipóstila, has an incredible ceiling composed of broken bits of ceramic and glass, including bottles. Here Gaudí created organic forms – suns, waves and other nature-inspired shapes – while employing the innovative technique of *trencadis* (p217).

4 CARYATID COLUMN
Descending from the right stairs leading off the public square to the salamander, you can access a 'diagonal' porch. Here you see dramatically slanting columns, one of Gaudí's trademarks. Nearly concealed amid the columns is a caryatid (a sculpted female figure which serves as a support). It harks back to Ancient Greece, but Gaudí has given the figure the more contemporary appearance of a washerwoman.

5 TURÓ DEL CALVARI
Christian symbols figure heavily in Gaudí's work and Park Güell is no exception. Most obvious are the three crosses atop the Turó del Calvari, evoking the crucifixion of Christ and two thieves atop Mt Calvary. When you find the right perspective, you can appreciate the clever design as the three crosses become one.

Discover Park Güell, Camp Nou & La Zona Alta

Getting There & Away

- **Metro** Take Metro Línia 3 toward Canyelles for Gràcia (Fontana stop) and Park Güell (Vallcarca stop). Take Línia 3 toward Zona Universitària to reach Palau Reial de Pedralbes or Camp Nou (Palau Rail stop).

- **Train** FGC trains are handy for getting near Tibidabo (Tibidabo stop), Sarrià (Sarrià stop) and Museu-Monestir de Pedralbes (Reina Elisenda stop).

- **Tram** Outside Avinguda de Tibidabo station, the tramvia blau runs to Plaça del Doctor Andreu, where you can catch an onward funicular up to Tibidabo.

Sights

Gràcia

Park Güell   Park
See p178

Mercat de la Llibertat   Market
Map p182 (📞93 217 09 95; www.mercatllibertat. com; Plaça de la Llibertat 27; ◷8am-8pm Mon-Fri, 8am-3pm Sat; ℝFGC Gràcia) **FREE** Built in the 1870s, the 'Market of Liberty' was covered over in 1893 in typically fizzy Modernista style, employing generous whirls of wrought iron. It got a considerable facelift in 2009 and has lost some of its aged charm, but the market remains emblematic of the Gràcia district: full of life and all kinds of fresh produce. The man behind the 1893 remake was Francesc Berenguer i Mestres (1866–1914), Gaudí's long-time assistant.

La Zona Alta

CosmoCaixa   Museum
Map p186 (Museu de la Ciència; 📞93 212 60 50; www.fundacio. lacaixa.es; Carrer de Isaac Newton 26; adult/child €4/free; ◷10am-8pm Tue-Sun; 🚌60, ℝFGC Avinguda Tibidabo) Kids (and kids at heart) are fascinated by displays here and this science museum has become one of the city's most popular attractions. The single greatest highlight is the recreation over 1 sq km of a chunk of flooded Amazon rainforest (Bosc Inundat). More than 100 species of Amazon flora and fauna (including anacondas, colourful poisonous frogs and caymans) prosper in this unique, living diorama in which you can even experience a tropical downpour.

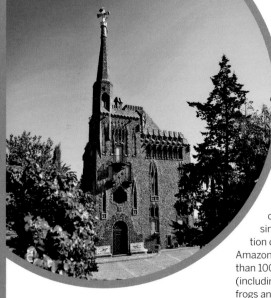

Bellesguard

Bellesguard
Architecture

Map p186 (☎ 93 250 40 93; www.bellesguard-gaudi.com; Carrer de Bellesguard 16; admission €7; ☉10am-7pm Mon-Sat Apr-Oct, 10am-3pm Mon-Sat Nov-Mar; ☒FGC Avinguda Tibidabo) This Gaudí masterpiece was recently rescued from obscurity, and opened to the public in 2013. Built between 1900 and 1909, the private residence (still owned by the original Guilera family) has a castle-like appearance with crenellated walls of stone and brick, narrow stained-glass windows, elaborate ironwork and a soaring turret mounted by a Gaudian cross. It's a fascinating work that combines both Gothic and Modernista elements.

Jardins del Palau de Pedralbes
Park

Map p186 (Avinguda Diagonal 686; ☉10am-8pm Apr-Oct, to 6pm Nov-Mar; Ⓜ Palau Reial) FREE A few steps from busy Avinguda Diagonal lies this small enchanting green space. Sculptures, fountains, citrus trees, bamboo groves, fragrant eucalyptus, towering cypresses and bougainvillea-covered nooks lie scattered along the paths crisscrossing these peaceful gardens. Among the little-known treasures here are a vine-covered parabolic pergola and a gurgling fountain of Hercules, both designed by Antoni Gaudí.

Observatori Fabra
Observatory

Map p186 (☎ 93 431 21 39; www.fabra.cat; Carretera del Observatori; admission €10; ☒tramvia blau, ☒FGC Avinguda Tibidabo then) Inaugurated in 1904, this Modernista observatory is still a functioning scientific foundation. It can be visited on certain evenings to allow people to observe the stars through its grand old telescope. Visits, generally in Catalan or Spanish (Castilian), have to be booked. From mid-June to mid-September an option is to join in the nightly **Sopars amb Estrelles** (Dinner under the Stars; ☎ 93 327 01 21; www.soparsambestrelles.com).

Museu-Monestir de Pedralbes
Monastery

Map p186 (☎ 93 256 34 34; www.bcn.cat/monestirpedralbes; Baixada del Monestir 9; adult/child €7/5, free 3-8pm Sun; ☉10am-5pm Tue-Fri, to 7pm Sat, to 8pm Sun; ☒22, 63, 64 or 75, ☒FGC Reina Elisenda) This peaceful old convent

181

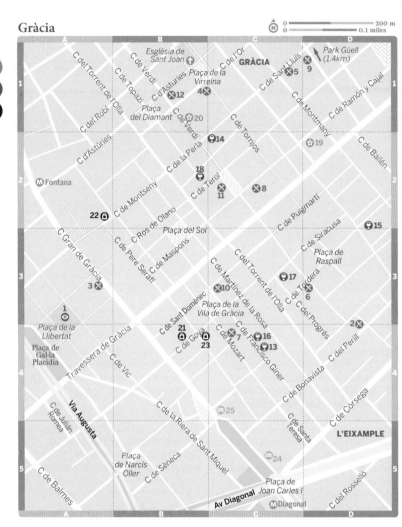

was first opened to the public in 1983 and is now a museum of monastic life (the few remaining nuns have moved into more modern neighbouring buildings). It stands at the top of Avinguda de Pedralbes in a residential area that was countryside until the 20th century, but which remains a divinely quiet corner of Barcelona.

Camp Nou
Stadium

Map p186 (☎902 189900; www.fcbarcelona.com; Carrer d'Aristides Maillol; adult/child €23/17; ⏱10am-7.30pm Mon-Sat, to 2.30pm Sun; ⓜPalau Reial) Among Barcelona's most-visited sites is the massive stadium of Camp Nou (which means New Field in Catalan), home to the legendary Futbol Club Barcelona. Attending a game amid the roar of the crowd is an unforgettable experience. Football fans who aren't able to see a game can get a taste of all the excitement at the museum, with its multimedia exhibits, and can also go on a self-guided tour of the stadium.

Gràcia

Eating

Gràcia

Spread across this busy *barri* (district) are all sorts of enticing options, from simple tapas bars to top-class seafood. Gràcia is loaded with Middle Eastern and, to a lesser extent, Greek restaurants, which are chirpy and good value. Several classic Catalan taverns tick along nicely with a strong local following. There's little of interest, however, around Park Güell.

Les Tres a la Cuina International €
Map p182 (☎ 93 105 49 47; Carrer de Sant Lluis 35; menú del día €9, brunch menú €10; ☺ 10am-6pm Mon-Fri, 11.30am-4.30pm Sat & Sun; Ⓜ Joanic) Colourful, Instagrammable food that tastes superb and uses ingredients you won't find in most other restaurants around town. The menu changes daily but you can choose from the likes of chicken with apricots, prunes and tamarind sauce, or quinoa salad with baked fennel and avocado, and finish up with pistachio and lemon drizzle cake. All this is prepared with love and Slow Food principles for an unbeatable price. There are few tables, so arrive early.

El Glop Catalan €
Map p182 (☎ 93 213 70 58; www.tavern-aelglop.com; Carrer de Sant Lluís 24; mains €8-12; ☺ 1pm-1am; Ⓜ Joanic) This raucous eatery is decked out in country Catalan fashion, with gingham tablecloths and no-nonsense, slap-up meals. The secret is hearty serves of simple dishes, such as *bistec a la brasa* (grilled steak), perhaps preceded by *albergínies farcides* (stuffed aubergines) or *calçots* (spring onions) in winter. To finish try the *tocinillo,* a caramel dessert. Open until 1am, El Glop is a useful place to have up your sleeve for a late bite.

La Nena Cafe €
Map p182 (☎ 93 285 14 76; Carrer de Ramon i Cajal 36; snacks from €3; ☺ 9am-10.30pm; 👶; Ⓜ Fontana) A French team has created this delightfully chaotic space for indulging in cups of *suïssos* (rich hot chocolate) served with a plate of heavy homemade whipped cream and *melindros* (spongy sweet biscuits), fine desserts and even a few savoury dishes (including crêpes). The place is strewn with books and the area out the back is designed to keep kids busy, with toys, books and a blackboard with chalk, making it an ideal family rest stop.

Nou Candanchú Tapas €
Map p182 (☎ 93 237 73 62; Plaça de la Vila de Gràcia 9; mains €7-10; ☺ 7am-1am Mon, Wed & Sun, 7am-3am Fri & Sat; Ⓜ Fontana) The liveliest locale on the square, Nou Candanchú is a long-time favourite for various reasons. Many flock to its sunny terrace

just for a few drinks. Accompany the liquid refreshment with one of the giant *entrepans* (filled rolls) for which this place is famous. Otherwise, it offers a limited range of tapas and reasonable grilled-meat dishes.

Sol i Lluna French €€

Map p182 (☎93 237 10 52; Carrer de Verdi 50; mains €10.50-16.50; ⏰7.30-11pm Mon-Fri, 1-4pm & 7.30pm-midnight Sat & Sun; M Fontana) Bright and sunny by day, softly lit at night, Sol i Lluna is a peaceful, elegant place that has as its distinguishing feature a giant wooden hippo (frequently topped with a small child) in the window. The food is mostly French, but draws on influences from around the globe, such as the 'lasagne' of ratatouille with goat's cheese or the vegetarian Puy lentil 'meatballs'.

El Tossal Spanish €€

Map p182 (☎93 457 63 82; www.eltossalbcn.com; Carrer de Tordera 12; mains €10-16; ⏰1.30-4pm & 8.30-11pm Tue-Sat; M Joanic) A proper old-fashioned, no-frills Catalan restaurant, of the sort in which Gràcia excels, with tables arranged around a central bar area and in a low-ceilinged dining annexe. The speciality is game and similarly hearty fare – the oxtail stew is excellent, as is the duck magret with caramelised onions and a port reduction – and there is a short but well-chosen list of suitably robust wines.

O'Gràcia! Mediterranean €€

Map p182 (www.ogracia.es; Plaça de la Revolució de Setembre de 1868 15; mains €10-12; ⏰1.30-3.30pm & 8-10.30pm Tue-Sat, 1.30-3.30pm Sun; M Fontana) This is an especially popular lunch option, with the *menú del día* good value at €12.90. The *arròs negre de sepia* (black rice with cuttlefish) makes a good first course, followed by a limited set of meat and fish options with vegetable sides. Serves are decent, presentation is careful and service is attentive. There's a more elaborate menu at night for €17.

Bilbao Spanish €€

Map p182 (☎93 458 96 24; Carrer del Perill 33; mains €16-22; ⏰1-4pm & 9-11pm Mon-Sat; M Diagonal) It doesn't look much from the outside, but Bilbao is a timeless classic, where reservations for dinner are imperative. The back dining room, with bottle-lined walls, stout timber tables

Tortilla

MATT MUNRO/LONELY PLANET ©

and a yellow light evocative of a country tavern, will appeal to carnivores especially, although some fish dishes are also on offer. Consider opting for a *chuletón* (T-bone steak), accompanied by a good Spanish red wine.

Cantina Machito   Mexican €€

Map p182 (📞93 217 34 14; www.cantinamachito.com; Carrer de Torrijos 47; mains €12-14; ⏰11am-2am; Ⓜ Fontana or Joanic) On the leafy Torrijos street, the colourful Machito – which seems devoted to the image of Frida Kahlo – gets busy with locals, and the outside tables are a great place to eat and drink until late. You'll find all the standard Mexican delights like quesadillas, tacos, enchiladas and so on, and some wonderfully refreshing iced water flavoured with honey and lime, mint and fruit.

Ipar-Txoko   Basque €€€

Map p182 (📞93 218 19 54; www.ipar-txoko.com; Carrer de Mozart 22; mains €20-25; ⏰1-3.30pm Mon, 1-3.30pm & 9-10.30pm Tue-Sat, closed Aug; Ⓜ Diagonal) Inside this Basque eatery the atmosphere is warm and traditional. Hefty wooden beams hold up the Catalan vaulted ceiling, and the bar (with tapas available) has a garish green-columned front. Getxo-born Mikel turns out traditional cooking from northern Spain, including a sumptuous *chuletón* (T-bone steak) for two – look at the size of that thing – or a less gargantuan *tortilla de bacalao* (a thick salt-cod omelette).

Botafumeiro   Seafood €€€

Map p182 (📞93 218 42 30; www.botafumeiro.es; Carrer Gran de Gràcia 81; mains €16-28; ⏰noon-1am; Ⓜ Fontana) It is hard not to mention this classic temple of Galician shellfish and other briny delights, long a magnet for VIPs visiting Barcelona. You can share a few *medias raciones* (large tapas plates) to taste a range of marine offerings, or share the *safata especial del Mar Cantàbric* (seafood platter) between two. Try the *percebes*, the strangely twisted goose barnacles harvested along Galicia's north Atlantic coast, which many Spaniards consider the ultimate seafood delicacy.

La Zona Alta

Some of the grandest kitchens in the city are scattered across La Zona Alta, from Tibidabo across Sant Gervasi (as far down as Avinguda Diagonal, west of Gràcia) to Pedralbes.

Bar Tomàs   Tapas €

Map p186 (📞93 203 10 77; Carrer Major de Sarrià 49; tapas €3-5; ⏰noon-4pm & 6-10pm Mon-Sat; 🚆 FGC Sarrià) Many *barcelonins* have long claimed that Bar Tomàs is by far the best place in the city for *patatas bravas* (potato chunks in a slightly spicy tomato sauce), prepared here with a special variation on the traditional sauce. The place is a rough-edged bar, but that doesn't stop the well-off citizens of Sarrià piling in, particularly for lunch on weekends.

Foix De Sarrià   Pastelería €

Map p186 (📞93 203 04 73; www.foixdesarria.com; Plaça de Sarrià 12-13; desserts €2-5; ⏰8am-8pm; 🚆 FGC Reina Elisenda) Since 1886 this exclusive pastry shop has been selling the most exquisite cakes and sweets. You can take them away or head out the back to sip tea, coffee or hot chocolate while sampling the little cakes and other wizardry.

Ajoblanco   Tapas €€

Map p186 (📞93 667 87 66; Carrer de Tuset 20; sharing plates €8-20; ⏰noon-3am; 🚆 FGC Gràcia) New in 2014, this beautifully designed space serves up a mix of classic and creative tapas plates that go nicely with the imaginative cocktail menu. Sip the house vermouth while feasting on oxtail tacos, jumbo prawns with avocado and cherry tomato, or arugula salad with goat cheese, strawberries and toasted almonds.

Vivanda   Catalan €€

Map p186 (📞93 203 19 18; www.vivanda.cat; Carrer Major de Sarrià 134; sharing plates €9-15; ⏰1.30-3.30pm Tue-Sun, 9-11pm Tue-Sat; 🚆 FGC Reina Elisenda) With a menu designed by celebrated Catalan chef Jordi Vilà, diners are in for a treat at this Sarrià classic. The changing menu showcases seasonal fare (recent selections include

0 500 m
0 0.25 miles

Parc de la Collserola

A To Tibidabo

Parc d'Atraccions (500m);
Temple del Sagrat Cor (500m)

VALLVIDRERA

Carretera del Vallvidrera al Tibidabo

Funicular de Vallvidrera

Túnel de Vallvidrera

Túnel de Vallvidrera

Peu del Funicular

Parc de l'Oreneta

8

9

Funicular del Tibidabo

Plaça del Doctor Andreu

Ronda de Dalt

7

17

C d'Estève Terradas

Penitents

Parc de la Creueta del Coll

Pg de la Mare de Déu del Coll

VALLCARCA

Vallcarca

Av de l'Hospital Militar

Park Güell

1

EL CARMEL

Travessera de Dalt

Plaça de Lesseps

Lesseps

Av del Príncep d'Astúries

GRÀCIA

Fontana

C de Lincoln   19

Jardins del Turó del Putget

SANT GERVASI DE CASSOLES

Ronda del General Mitre

C de Vallirana

C de Saragossa

Molina

C de Balmes

Pàdua

Sant Gervasi

Via Augusta

Gràcia

C de Freixa

C Copèrnic

Plaça de Adrià

C de Muntaner

C de Mandri

El Putxet

C de Ganduxer

C de les Escoles Pies

C d'Iradier

22

Pg de la Bonanova

Pg de la Bonanova

C de Sant Joan de la Salle

12

Av de Tibidabo

Av Tibidabo

C de Balmes

C de la Infanta Isabel

4

C del Bellesguard

2

SARRIÀ – SANT GERVASI

C d'Iradier

C d'Anglí

Sarrià

SARRIÀ

C Major de Sarrià

Reina Elisenda

Plaça de Sarrià

14 13

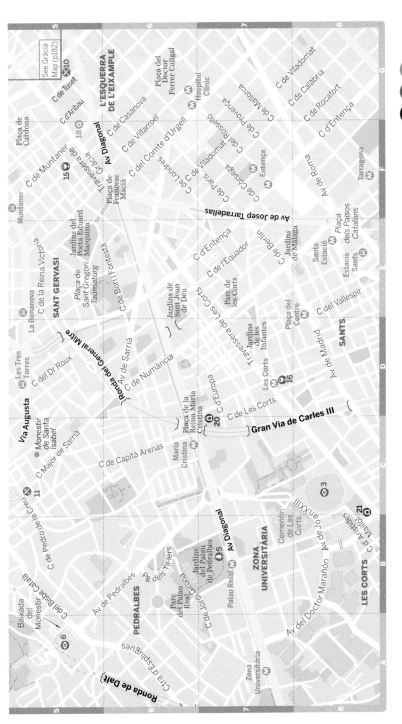

PARK GÜELL, CAMP NOU & LA ZONA ALTA

See Gràcia
Map (p182) ✕10

L'ESQUERRA
DE L'EIXAMPLE

Plaça del
Doctor
Ferrer Cajigal

Hospital
Clínic

C de Tuset

C d'Aribau

18

Av Diagonal

C de Casanova

C de Villarroel

C del Comte d'Urgell

C del Rosselló

C de Provença

C de Viladomat

C de Calàbria

C de Rocafort

C d'Entença

Plaça de
Cardona

Muntaner

C de Muntaner

15

Travessera de Gràcia

SANT GERVASI

La Bonanova

Les Tres
Torres

C de la Reina Victòria

Jardins del
Poeta Eduard
Marquina

Plaça de
Sant Gregori
Taumaturg

C de Borí i Fontestà

C de Londres

C de Viladomat

C de París

C de Còrsega

Entença

C de Mallorca

Av de Roma

Tarragona

Plaça de
Francesc
Macià

Av de Josep Tarradellas

C d'Entença

C de l'Equador

C de Berlín

Jardins
de Màlaga

Plaça
dels Països
Catalans

Sants
Estació

Estació
Sants

C del Dr Roux

Ronda del General Mitre

Av de Sarrià

C de Numància

Jardins de
Sant Joan
de Déu

Parc de
les Corts

Travessera de Les Corts

Jardins
de les
Infantes

Plaça del
Centre

C del Vallespir

SANTS

Av de Madrid

Via Augusta

Monestir
de Santa
Isabel

11

C de Pedro de la Creu

C Major de Sarrià

Plaça de la
Reina Maria
Cristina

C d'Europa

20

C de Les Corts

Gran Via de Carles III

Les Corts

16

Maria
Cristina

C de Capità Arenas

Baixada
del
Monestir

C del Bisbe Català

6

Av de Pedralbes

PEDRALBES

Parc
del Palau
Reial

Jardins
del Palau
de Pedralbes

Pg dels Tillers

C de Joan de Borbó

Av Diagonal

5

Palau Reial

ZONA
UNIVERSITÀRIA

Cementiri
de Les
Corts

Av de Jooo XXIII

3

Av del Doctor Marañón

C d'Arístides Maillol

21

LES CORTS

Av del Doctor Marañón

Cra d'Esplugues

Ronda de Dalt

Zona
Universitària

187

La Zona Alta

eggs with truffles, rice with cuttlefish, and artichokes with romesco sauce). One of Vivanda's best features is the garden-like terrace hidden behind the restaurant.

With heat lamps, it's open year-round – blankets and hot broth are distributed to diners in winter.

El Asador de Aranda   Spanish €€€

Map p186 (☎93 417 01 15; www.asadordearanda. com; Av del Tibidabo 31; mains €20-22; ◎1-4pm daily & 8-11pm Mon-Sat; 🚋Av Tibidabo) A great place for a meal after visiting Tibidabo, El Asador de Aranda is set in a striking art nouveau building, complete with stained-glass windows, Moorish-style brick arches and elaborate ceilings. You'll find a fine assortment of tapas plates for sharing, though the speciality is the meat (roast lamb, spare ribs, beef), beautifully prepared in a wood oven.

🍷 Drinking & Nightlife

Gràcia is a quirky place. In many ways the distrcit its own world, with a mix of rowdy young beer swillers and beaming young parents that fill its bars and cafés.

Gràcia

Viblioteca   Wine Bar

Map p182 (☎93 284 42 02; www.viblioteca.com; Carrer de Vallfogona 12; ◎7pm-1am; Ⓜ Fontana) If the smell of ripe cheese doesn't rock your boat, this is not the place for you – a glass cabinet piled high with the stuff assaults your olfactory nerves as you walk into the small, white, cleverly designed space. The real speciality at Viblioteca, however, is wine, and you can choose from 150 mostly local labels, many of them available by the glass.

Raïm   Bar

Map p182 (Carrer del Progrés 48; ◎7pm-2.30am; Ⓜ Diagonal) The walls in Raïm are alive with black-and-white photos of Cubans and Cuba. Tired wooden chairs of another epoch huddle around marble tables, while grand old wood-framed mirrors hang from the walls. They just don't make Spanish taverns like this anymore.

La Baignoire   Bar

Map p182 (☎93 284 39 67; Carrer de Verdi 6; ◎7pm-2am Mon-Sat, to 1pm Sun; Ⓜ Fontana) This inviting, tiny wine bar is always packed. Grab a stool and high table and order fine wines by the glass (beer and cocktails available too). It's perfect before and after a movie at the nearby Verdi cinema.

La Cigale   Bar

Map p182 (☎93 457 58 23; Carrer de Tordera 50; ◎6pm-2.30am Mon-Thu, 6pm-3am Fri & Sat; Ⓜ Joanic) This is a very civilised place for a cocktail (or, in summer, two for €8 if you order before 10pm) and to hear some poetry readings. Prop up the zinc bar, sink into a secondhand lounge chair around a teeny table or head upstairs. Music is chilled, conversation lively, and you're likely to see Charlie Chaplin in action on the silent flat-screen TV. You can also snack on wok-fried dishes.

Le Journal
Bar

Map p182 (📞93 368 41 37; Carrer de Francisco Giner 36; ⏰6pm-2.30am Sun-Thu, 6pm-3am Fri & Sat; Ⓜ Fontana) Students love the conspiratorial basement air of this narrow bar, whose walls and ceiling are plastered with newspapers (hence the name). Read the headlines of yesteryear while reclining in an old lounge. For a slightly more intimate feel, head upstairs to the rear gallery.

El Sabor
Bar

Map p182 (📞654 849975; Carrer de Francisco Giner 32; ⏰10pm-3am Tue-Sun; Ⓜ Diagonal) Ruled since 1992 by the charismatic Havana-born Angelito is this home of *ron y son* (rum and sound). A mixed crowd of Cubans and fans of the Caribbean island come to drink mojitos and shake their stuff in this diminutive, good-humoured hang-out.

La Zona Alta

North of Avinguda Diagonal, the *pijos* (cashed-up mamma's boys and papa's girls) are in charge. Whether you sample the bars around Carrer de Marià Cubí (and surrounding streets) or try the clubs around Carrer d'Aribau or Tibidabo, expect to be confronted by perma-tanned Audi- and 4WD-driving folks in designer threads.

Mirablau
Bar

Map p186 (Plaça del Doctor Andreu; ⏰11am-4.30am; 🚃Avinguda Tibidabo then 🚃tramvia blau) Gaze out over the entire city from this privileged balcony restaurant on the way up to Tibidabo. Wander downstairs to join the folk in the tiny dance space. In summer

you can step out onto the even smaller terrace for a breather.

Dō Bar
Bar

Map p186 (📞93 209 18 88; www.do-bcn.com; Carrer de Santaló 30; ⏰7pm-1am Mon-Sat; 🚇FGC Muntaner) This neighbourhood charmer has a warm and inviting interior, where friends gather over tall wooden tables to enjoy excellent gin and tonics, wines by the glass, craft beer and satisfying small plates (anchovies, mussels, tacos, charcuterie). On warm nights, arrive early for one of the terrace tables out the front.

Lizarran
Bar

Map p186 (Carrer de Can Bruixa 6; ⏰8am-midnight Sun-Thu, to 2am Fri & Sat; Ⓜ Les Corts) This is a fine pre- or post-game drinking spot if you're catching an FC Barça game at Camp Nou. The beer is plentiful and cheap, there's a decent tapas selection, and on warm days you can sit on the pleasant terrace at the front. From here it's about a 15-minute walk to the stadium.

Alfresco dining, Gràcia
ANDONI CANELA/GETTY IMAGES ©

Tibidabo

Framing the north end of the city, the forest-covered mountain of Tibidabo, which tops out at 512m, is the highest peak in Serra de Collserola. Aside from the superb views from the top, the highlights of Tibidabo include an 8000-hectare park, an old-fashioned amusement park, a telecommunications tower with viewing platform and a looming church that's visible from many parts of the city.

Parc de Collserola (Map p186; ☎93 280 35 52; www.parcnaturalcollserola.cat; Carretera de l'Església 92; ⊗Centre d'Informació 9.30am-3pm, Can Coll 9.30am-3pm Sun & holidays, closed Jul & Aug; ☒FGC Peu del Funicular, funicular Baixador de Vallvidrera) *Barcelonins* (people of Barcelona) needing an escape from the city without heading too far into the countryside seek out this vast park in the hills. It is a great place to hike and bike and bristles with eateries and snack bars. Pick up a map from the Centre d'Informació.

Temple del Sagrat Cor (Church of the Sacred Heart; ☎93 417 56 86; Plaça de Tibidabo; admission free, lift €2; ⊗7am-8pm, lift 10am-8pm), looming above the top funicular station, was built from 1902 to 1961 in a mix of styles with some Modernista influence, and is as visible as its Parisian namesake, Sacre Cœur.

Parc d'Atraccions (☎93 211 79 42; www.tibidabo.cat; Plaça de Tibidabo 3-4; adult/child €29/10.30; ⊗closed Jan & Feb), The reason most *barcelonins* come up to Tibidabo is for some thrills in this amusement park, close to the top funicular station.

Torre de Collserola (Map p186; ☎93 406 93 54; www.torredecollserola.com; Carretera de Vallvidrera al Tibidabo; adult/child €6/4; ⊗noon-2pm & 3.30-8pm Wed-Sun Jul & Aug, noon-2pm & 3.15-6pm Sat, Sun & holidays Sep-Jun, closed Jan & Feb; ▣111, Funicular de Vallvidrera) Sir Norman Foster designed this 288m-high telecommunications tower, which was completed in 1992. The visitors' observation area, 115m up, offers magnificent views – up to 70km on a clear day.

Otto Zutz   Club

Map p186 (www.ottozutz.com; Carrer de Lincoln 15; admission €10-15; ⊗midnight-6am Tue-Sat; ☒FGC Gràcia) Beautiful people only need apply for entry to this three-floor dance den. Shake it all up to house on the ground floor, or head upstairs for funk and soul. DJs come from the Ibiza rave mould and the top floor is for VIPs (although at some ill-defined point in the evening the barriers all seem to come down).

Luz de Gas   Live Music

Map p186 (☎93 209 77 11; www.luzdegas.com; Carrer de Muntaner 246; admission up to €20; ⊗Wed-Sun; ▣6, 7, 15, 27, 32, 33, 34, 58 or 64, ⓂDiagonal) Several nights a week this club, set in a grand former theatre, stages concerts ranging through rock, soul, salsa, jazz and pop. From about 2am, the place turns into a club that attracts a well-dressed crowd with varying musical tastes, depending on the night.

★ Entertainment

Heliogàbal   Live Music

Map p182 (www.heliogabal.com; Carrer de Ramón i Cajal 80; ⊗9.30pm-3am Wed-Sat; ⓂJoanic) This compact bar is a veritable hive of cultural activity where you never quite know what to expect. Aside from art exhibitions and poetry readings, you will be pleasantly surprised by the eclectic live-music program. Jazz groups are often followed by open jam sessions, and experimental music of all kinds gets a run. While many performers are local, international acts also get a look in.

Verdi
Cinema

Map p182 (☎93 238 79 90; www.cines-verdi.com; Carrer de Verdi 32; Ⓜ Fontana) A popular original-language movie house in the heart of Gràcia, handy to lots of eateries and bars for pre- and post-film enjoyment.

🛍 Shopping

Gràcia

A wander along the narrow lanes of Gràcia turns up all sorts of surprises, mostly tiny enterprises producing a variety of pretty garments and trinkets. Carrer de Verdi has plenty of interesting clothes shops.

Nostàlgic
Photography

Map p182 (☎93 368 57 57; www.nostalgic.es; Carrer de Goya 18; ☺5-8.30pm Mon, 11am-2.30pm & 5-8.30pm Tue-Sat; Ⓜ Fontana) A beautiful space with exposed brick walls and wooden furniture specialising in all kinds of modern and vintage photography equipment – you'll find camera bags and tripods for the digital snappers, and the inevitable collection of Lomo cameras, with their quirky variations. There is also a decent collection of photography books.

Hibernian
Books

Map p182 (☎93 217 47 96; www.hibernian-books.com; Carrer de Montseny 17; ☺4-8.30pm Mon, 10.30am-8.30pm Tue-Sat; Ⓜ Fontana) The biggest secondhand English bookshop in Barcelona stocks thousands of titles covering all sorts of subjects, from cookery

to children's classics. There is a smaller collection of new books in English, too.

Érase una Vez
Fashion

Map p182 (☎697 805409; www.eraseunavez.info; Carrer de Goya 7; ☺11am-2pm Mon, 11am-2pm & 5-9pm Tue-Sat; Ⓜ Fontana) 'Once Upon a Time' is the name of this fanciful boutique. It offers ethereal, delicate women's clothes, almost exclusively evening wear, as well as wedding dresses. Local designers such as Llamazares y de Delgado and Zazo & Brull are behind these sometimes sumptuous creations.

La Zona Alta

FC Botiga
Souvenirs

Map p186 (☎93 492 31 11; http://shop.fcbarcelona.com; Carrer de Arístides Maillol; ☺10am-7pm Mon-Sat; Ⓜ Collblanc) Here you will find footballs, shirts, scarves, socks, wallets, bags, sneakers, iPhone covers – pretty much anything you can think of, all featuring FC Barça's famous red-and-blue insignia.

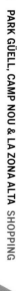

A shop in Gràcia
ALFREDO MAIQUEZ/GETTY IMAGES ©

Day Trips

Girona (p194)

A splendid cathedral, a maze of narrow cobbled streets and Catalonia's finest medieval Jewish quarter are part of this riverside town's charms.

Montserrat (p196)

Catalonia's most important shrine is set in a mountain monastery, complete with Europe's oldest choir and superb scenic walks.

Sitges (p198)

A string of beaches, great nightlife and a hedonistic carnival await visitors at Costa Daurada's premier seaside town.

Monestir de Montserrat (p196)
CULTURA/INGOLF HATZ/GETTY IMAGES

Girona

Girona's big draw is its Old Town, a tight huddle of ancient arcaded houses, grand churches and climbing cobbled streets, so head first for the star attraction – the Catedral – either by strolling along the lazy Río Onyar or by taking the high road along the medieval walls. Follow this with a visit to the Call (medieval Jewish quarter) and the excellent Museu d'Història dels Jueus de Girona before taking your pick of the restaurants in the nearby streets.

After lunch, continue your exploration of other Old Town sights, such as the wonderfully intact Banys Àrabs or the attractive cloisters and verdant grounds of the Monestir de Sant Pere de Galligants, before finding a bar around the Plaça Independencia to while away the evening.

Getting There & Away

Car Take the AP-7 freeway via Granollers.

Train At least 20 trains per day run from Barcelona's Sants Estació (from €8.40, up to 1½ hours).

Need to Know

○ **Area code** 972

○ **Location** 85km northeast of Barcelona

○ **Tourist office** (972 22 65 75; www.girona. cat/turisme; Rambla de la Llibertat 1; 9am-8pm Mon-Fri, 9am-2pm & 4-8pm Sat, 9am-2pm Sun)

◉ Sights

Catedral   Church
(www.catedraldegirona.org; Plaça de la Catedral; adult/student incl Basílica de Sant Feliu €7/5, Sun free; 10am-7.30pm Apr-Oct, 10am-6.30pm Nov-Mar) The billowing baroque facade of the cathedral towers over a flight of 86 steps rising from Plaça de la Catedral. Though the beautiful double-columned Romanesque cloister dates to the 12th century, most of the building is Gothic, with the second-widest nave (23m) in Christendom. The 14th-century gilt-and-silver altarpiece and canopy are memorable, as are the bishop's throne and the

Girona

STEFANO POLITI MARKOVINA/AWL IMAGES LTD/GETTY IMAGES ©

Sleeping in Girona

Casa Cúndaro (☎ 972 22 35 83; www.casacundaro.com; Pujada de la Catedral 9; s/d €88/110; ❄ ⓦ) The understated exterior of this medieval Jewish house hides five sumptuous rooms and four self-catering apartments – all combining original exposed stone walls and antique doors with modern luxuries. You couldn't wish for a more characterful base; the location right next to the cathedral is either a boon or a bane, depending on whether you enjoy the sound of church bells. Reception is at the Hotel Historic, a short stroll up the hill.

Bells Oficis (☎ 972 22 81 70; www.bellsoficis.com; Carrer dels Germans Busquets 2; r incl breakfast €55-85; ❄ ⓦ) A lovingly restored, 19th-century flat just by the Rambla in the heart of Girona makes a stylish and ultra-welcoming place to stop. Period details combine with modern styling most effectively: the whole package is immaculate. There are just five beautiful, light rooms. Some share bathrooms – those with en suite have no bathroom door – while the largest (€105) has ample room for four people.

museum, which holds the masterly Romanesque *Tapís de la creació* (Tapestry of the Creation) and a Mozarabic illuminated *Beatus* manuscript, dating from 975.

Museu d'Història dels Jueus de Girona
Museum

(www.girona.cat/call; Carrer de la Força 8; adult/child €4/free; ⏰10am-8pm Mon-Sat, to 2pm Sun) Until 1492 Girona was home to Catalonia's second-most important medieval Jewish community (after Barcelona), and one of the finest Jewish quarters in the country. The Call (Catalan for 'ghetto'), was centred on the narrow Carrer de la Força for 600 years, until relentless persecution forced the Jews out of Spain. This excellent museum shows genuine pride in Girona's Jewish heritage without shying away from the less salubrious aspects, such as persecution by the Inquisition and forced conversions.

Banys Àrabs
Bathhouse

(www.banysarabs.cat; Carrer de Ferràn el Catòlic; adult/child €2/1; ⏰10am-7pm Mon-Sat, to 2pm Sun Apr-Sep, 10am-2pm daily Oct-Mar) Although modelled on earlier Muslim and Roman bathhouses, the Banys Àrabs are a finely preserved, 12th-century Christian affair in Romanesque style. This is the only public bathhouse discovered from medieval Christian Spain, where, in reaction to the Muslim obsession with water and cleanliness, washing almost came to be regarded as ungodly. The baths contain an *apodyterium* (changing room), followed by a *frigidarium* and *tepidarium* (with respectively cold and warm water) and a *caldarium* (a kind of sauna) heated by an underfloor furnace.

Monestir de Sant Pere de Galligants
Monastery

(www.mac.cat; Carrer de Santa Llúcia; adult/child €2.30/free; ⏰10.30am-1.30pm & 4-7pm Tue-Sat, 10am-2pm Sun) This beautiful 11th- and 12th-century Romanesque Benedectine monastery has a sublime bell tower and a lovely cloister, featuring otherworldly animals and mythical creatures on the capitals of its double columns – there are some great ones in the church too. It's also home to the **Museu Arqueològic**, with exhibits that range from prehistoric to Roman times. Opening hours vary.

Museu d'Història de Girona
Museum

(www.girona.cat/museuciutat; Carrer de la Força 27; adult/student/child €4/2/free; ⏰10.30am-5.30pm Tue-Sat, to 1.30pm Sun) The engaging and well-presented city history museum does Girona's long and impressive story justice. Its displays cover everything from the city's Roman origins, through the siege of the city by Napoleonic troops to the *sardana* (Catalonia's national folk dance) tradition. A separate gallery houses cutting-edge temporary art and photography exhibits.

Basílica de Sant Feliu Church

(Plaça de Sant Feliu; adult/student incl Catedral €7/5, Sun free; ⏲10am-5.30pm Mon-Sat, 1-5.30pm Sun) Girona's second great church, with its landmark truncated bell tower, is downhill from the cathedral and entered on a combined ticket. The nave is majestic with Gothic ribbed vaulting, while St Narcissus, the patron of the city, is venerated in an enormous marble-and-jasper, late-Baroque side chapel. His remains were formerly held in a glorious 14th-century sepulchre displayed alongside. A decent audioguide tour is included with admission.

Eating

+Cub Cafe €

(www.mescub.cat; Carrer de l'Albereda 15; 3 tapas €10.40; ⏲8am-9pm Mon-Thu, 8am-midnight Fri, 9am-midnight Sat; 🛜📶) This übercentral cafe is great at any time of day and distinguished by friendly service, innovative tapas – from black pudding with pistachio to salad with black-fig sorbet – fresh fruit-juice combos, shakes and Girona's own La Moska microbrew. There's a great terrace overlooking Plaça de Catalunya.

L'Alqueria Catalan €€

(☎972 22 18 82; www.restaurantalqueria.com; Carrer de la Ginesta 8; mains €14-20; ⏲1-4pm & 9-11pm Wed-Sat, 1-4pm Tue & Sun) This smart minimalist *arrocería* (restaurant specialising in rice dishes) serves the finest *arròs negre* (rice cooked in cuttlefish ink) and *arròs a la Catalan* (Catalan rice) in the city, as well as around 20 other superbly executed rice dishes, including paellas. Eat your heart out, Valencia! It's wise to book ahead for dinner.

Montserrat

Though the monastery complex itself is compact, allow a whole day for the visit if you want to take advantage of the many splendid mountain walks. Take the earliest *cremallera* (rack-and-pinion train) or cable car up the mountain to beat the crowds and begin with the exploration of the monastery complex, paying a visit to the Virgin and then the worthwhile Museu de Montserrat before grabbing an early lunch at the cafeteria. Season permitting, you might be able to catch a choir performance inside the basilica.

Afterwards, ride the funiculars, or else take a walk down to the Santa Cova – the spot where the Virgin was originally found – or up to the Sant Jeroni peak for a splendid view of the valley below.

Getting There & Away

Train, rack railway & cable car The R5 line trains operated by FGC (www.fgc.net) run hourly from Plaça d'Espanya station, starting at 8.36am (52 to 56 minutes). They connect with the cable car (www.aeridemontserrat.com) at the Montserrat Aeri stop (oneway/return €7/10, 17 minutes, 9.40am to 7pm, closed mid-Jan–Feb) and the *cremallera* (www.cremalleradomontserrat.com) at the following stop, Monistrol de Montserrat (one way/return €6/9, five minutes).

Need to Know

○ **Area code** ☎938

○ **Location** 50km northwest of Barcelona

○ **Information office** (☎938 77 77 01; www.montserratvisita.com; ⏲9am-5.45pm)

◎ Sights

Monestir de Montserrat Monastery

(www.abadiamontserrat.net; ⏲7am-8pm) This monastery was founded in 1025 to commemorate a vision of the Virgin Mary on the mountain. Today it houses a community of a few dozen monks, and pilgrims come to venerate La Moreneta (the Black Madonna), a 12th-century Romanesque wooden sculpture of Mary with the baby Jesus; La Moreneta has been Catalonia's official patron since 1881.

Museu de Montserrat   Museum
(www.museudemontserrat.com; Plaça de Santa Maria; adult/student €7/6; ⊙10am-5.45pm, to 6.45pm Jul-Aug) This museum has an excellent collection, ranging from an Egyptian mummy and Gothic altarpieces to fine canvases by Caravaggio, El Greco, Picasso and several Impressionists, as well as a comprehensive collection of 20th-century classic Catalan art and some fantastic Orthodox icons.

Basilica   Church
(www.abadiamontserrat.net; ⊙7am-8pm) FREE The 16th-century church's facade, with carvings of Christ and the 12 Apostles, dates from 1901, despite its plateresque style. The stairs to the narrow **Cambril de la Mare de Déu** (⊙7-10.30am & 12.15-6.30pm), housing La Moreneta, are to the right of the main basilica entrance; expect queues. The room across the courtyard

Sleeping in Montserrat

Hotel Abat Cisneros (☎938 77 77 01; www.montserratvisita.com; s/d €63/108; P 🛜) The only hotel in the monastery complex has a super location next to the basilica, and tasteful, spacious rooms, some of which look over Plaça de Santa Maria. There are also inexpensive basic apartments and family packages available. Its restaurant serves imaginative Catalonian dishes (mains €17–20).

from the basilica entrance is filled with offbeat ex-voto gifts and thank-you messages to the Virgin from people crediting her for all manner of happy events. FC Barcelona dedicate victories to her.

Montserrat Mountain   Mountain
You can explore the mountain above the monastery on a web of paths leading to some of the peaks and to 13 empty

The Basilica's facade

and rather dilapidated hermitages. The **Funicular de Sant Joan** (one way/return €5.85/9; ⊘every 20min 10am-6.50pm, closed mid-Jan–Feb) will carry you up the first 250m from the monastery. If you prefer to walk, which takes about 45 minutes, the road past the funicular's bottom station leads to its top station.

From the top station, it's a 20-minute stroll (signposted) to the **Sant Joan chapel**, with fine westward views. More exciting is the one-hour walk northwest, along a path marked with some blobs of yellow paint, to Montserrat's highest peak, **Sant Jeroni**, from where there's an awesome sheer drop on the north face. The walk takes you across the upper part of the mountain, with a close-up experience of some of the weird rock pillars, all named.

Santa Cova   Chapel
To see the chapel on the spot where the holy image of the Virgin was discovered, you can drop down the **Funicular de Santa Cova** (one way/return €2.20/3.50; ⊘every 20min, closed mid-Jan–Feb), or else it's an easy walk down, followed by a stroll along a precipitous mountain path with fabulous views of the valley below.

Sitges

Sitges is perfect for seafront promenading and sun worshipping, so in warmer weather you'll find the most central beaches quite crowded. Luckily, there are quite a few to choose from, so pick your spot for a morning of sunbathing (or skinny dipping off the nudist beach) before choosing a seafood restaurant nearby.

But it's not all about the sea here; if you have an interest in contemporary art and in the Modernisme movement, the classy old centre's array of elegant buildings, many housing museums, is well worth some of your time. The gay scene in Sitges – and its vibrant party atmosphere

in general – is legendary, so many a day-trip ends up the morning after...

Getting There & Away

Car The best road from Barcelona is the C-32 tollway. More scenic is the C-31, which hooks up with the C-32 after Castelldefels, but it is often busy and slow.

Train Four R2 *rodalies* trains an hour, from about 6am to 10pm, run from Barcelona's Passeig de Gràcia and Estació Sants to Sitges (€4.10, 27 to 46 minutes depending on stops).

Need to Know

⊙ **Area code** ☑938

⊙ **Location** 32km southwest of Barcelona

⊙ **Tourist office** (☑938 94 42 51 ; www.sitgestur.cat; Plaça de E Maristany 2; ⊘10am-2pm & 4-6.30pm or 8pm Mon-Sat, 10am-2pm Sun)

◎ Sights

Beaches   Beaches
The main beach is flanked by the attractive seafront Passeig Maritim, dotted with *chiringuitos* (beachside bars) and divided into nine sections with different names by a series of breakwaters. The **Sant Sebastià**, **Balmins** and **D'aiguadolç** beaches run east of the headland. Though **Bassa Rodona** used to be the unofficial 'gay beach', gay sunbathers are now spread out pretty evenly, while Balmins is the sheltered bay favoured by nudists.

Museu Romàntic   Museum
(www.museusdesitges.cat; Carrer de Sant Gaudenci 1; adult/student €3.50/2; ⊘10am-2pm & 3.30-7pm Tue-Sat, 11am-3pm Sun) Housed in a late-18th-century Can Llopis mansion, this faded museum recreates with its furnishings and dioramas the lifestyle of a 19th-century Catalan landowning family, the likes of which would often have made their money in South America, and were commonly dubbed *indianos* on their return. Upstairs is an entertaining collection of several hundred antique dolls, some downright creepy. Hours vary seasonally.

Eating & Drinking

El Pou
Tapas €€

(www.elpoudesitges.com; Carrer de Sant Pau 5; dishes €4-10; ⏰noon-4pm & 8-11.30pm Wed-Mon; 📶) The tiny Wagyu beef burgers at this friendly gourmet tapas place are an absolute delight, and the rest doesn't lag far behind; the traditional *patatas bravas* (potatoes in a spicy tomato sauce) sit alongside the likes of *mojama* (salted dried tuna) with almonds, fried aubergine and *xató;* the presentation delights the eye as much as the flavours delight the palate.

La Nansa
Seafood €€

(www.restaurantlanansa.com; Carrer de la Carreta 24; mains €14-22; ⏰1.30-3.30pm & 8.30-11pm Thu-Sat & Mon, 1.30-3.30pm Sun, closed Jan) Cast just back from the town's waterfront and up a little lane in a fine old house is this seafood specialist, appropriately named after a fishing net. It does a great line in paella and other rice dishes, including a local speciality, *arròs a la sitgetana.*

eF & Gi
Fusion €€€

(www.efgirestaurant.com; Carrer Major 33; mains €18-25; ⏰1-4pm & 7.30-11.30pm Wed-Mon Mar-Jan; 📶) Fabio and Greg (eF & Gi) are not afraid to experiment and the results are startlingly good: the mostly Mediterranean menu, with touches of Asian inspiration, throws out such delights as chargrilled beef infused with lemongrass and kaffir lime and tuna loin encrusted with peanuts and kalamata olives with mango chutney. Don't skip the dessert, either.

Bar Voramar
Bar

(www.pub-voramar.com; Carrer del Port Alegre 55; ⏰4.30pm-1am Thu-Tue) On Platja de Sant Sebastià, this is a fabulous old-time bar decked out like a ship. It plays flamenco, jazz and more and offers brilliant caipirinhas, mojitos, and other drinkable delights. The chummy booth seating is a Sitges classic.

Beach volleyball, Sitges

BETHUNE CARMICHAEL/GETTY IMAGES ©

Barcelona
In Focus

Rambla de Mar (p110)
KRZYSZTOF DYDYNSKI/GETTY IMAGES ©

Barcelona Today

Homenage a la Natacion by Alfredo Lanz, Plaça del Mar, Port Vell

> *Recent polls indicate 60% of Catalans support the region becoming a new European state*

belief systems
(% of population)

90 — Roman Catholic

10 — Other

if Barcelona were 100 people

62 would be Catalan
24 would be other Spanish
14 would be non-Spanish

population per sq km

= 90 people

Spain

Barcelona

A Nation in Crisis

Spain's ongoing economic woes showed mild signs of improvement at the end of 2013 and the beginning of 2014, with a projected annual growth rate of 1.2% for the year. This was some small relief for a country that had been mostly in recession since the global financial crisis erupted in 2007. Like many other Spaniards, Catalans have yet to break out the cava. Unemployment remains startlingly high, particularly among young workers (above 40% for those under the age of 25). Meanwhile, hardship measures prescribed by bureaucrats – slashing budgets, raising taxes and freezing public sector pay – have done nothing to alleviate the hardship for those struggling to pay their bills.

A Bid for Independence

Spain's ongoing financial turmoil has been a catalyst for Catalan independence. Ever since the days of Franco – when Catalan was banned in schools and in the media – Catalonia has felt

centre of Camp Nou, home stadium of FC Barça, long a symbol of pride among Catalans. Recent polls indicate 60% of Catalans support the region becoming a new European state. Madrid, however, has clamped down, with Spanish judges ruling that a vote on independence is illegal, and in clear violation of the Spanish constitution. Many financial analysts and outside observers (such as Moody's Investors Service) believe independence is unlikely for Catalonia.

MATT MUNRO/LONELY PLANET

stymied by the sometimes heavy-handed policies of the central government. These days anger revolves around the topic of taxation. Catalonia's economy, one of the best performing in the country, is estimated at $275 billion, accounting for 20% of Spain's GDP. But it suffers a heavy tax burden, which some see as a penalty for Madrid's financial struggles. Not surprisingly, talk of independence has rattled not only Spain but the EU. Catalonia is home to some of the nation's biggest industries, including textiles, car manufacturing and banking, and its secession could cause much turmoil – and more bailouts – in an already troubled Europe.

The fervour has only grown in the last few years. In 2013, on the Catalan National Day (11 September), hundreds of thousands of separatist supporters formed a 400km human chain across Catalonia. It even passed through the

Redesigning the City

Poblenou, once a centre of industrial activity during the 19th century, went through a time of decay before a slow period of revitalisation that kicked off with the 1992 Olympics. Today Poblenou is once again a hive of activity, and Barcelona's new focal point in the realm of urban renewal. Wild new buildings have arrived in the form of Els Encants Vells market and the monolithic Disseny Hub, which houses the city's newest museum (dedicated to decorative arts, textiles and graphic design). Jean Nouvel's cucumber-like Torre Agbar lies just beyond, adding to the ultramodern architectural landscape. City officials believe the tower, which will be transformed into a hotel in years to come, and other attractions will help make the area a new destination for visitors to Barcelona.

Also part of Poblenou is the zone known as 22@ (vint-i-dos arroba), a 200-hectare district with a staggering number of media, high-tech and design firms. Over 4000 firms have arrived since the turn of the millennium, helping make 22@ Barcelona's leading centre of innovation. Some 47% of the newly opened businesses have been start-ups.

History

Parlament de Catalunya (p94)

GUY HEITMANN/DESIGN PICS/GETTY IMAGE

The storied settlement of Barcelona has seen waves of immigrants and conquerors over its 2000-plus years of existence, including Romans, Visigoths, Franks and later Catalans. Barcelona has seen its fortunes rise and fall over the years – from the golden era of princely power in the 14th century to dark days of civil war and the Franco era. Throughout, a fierce independent streak has always run through Barcelona.

Wilfred the Hairy & Mediterranean Expansion

It was the Romans who first etched Barcino onto Europe's map in the 3rd century BC, though the nascent settlement long played second fiddle to their provincial capital in Tarragona. The Visigoths came next, followed by the Moors, whose relatively brief occupation was usurped when the Franks put the city under the control of local counts in 801

circa AD 15

Settlement of Barcino first mentioned in Roman chronicles under control of Tarraco (Tarragona).

as a buffer zone against the still Muslim-dominated caliphate to the south.

Eccentrically named Wilfred the Hairy (Count Guifré el Pelós) moulded the entity we now know as Catalonia in the 9th century by wresting control over several neighbouring territories and establishing Barcelona as its key city. The hirsute one founded a dynasty that lasted nearly five centuries and developed almost independently from the Reconquista wars that were playing out in the rest of Iberia.

The counts of Barcelona gradually expanded their territory south and, in 1137, Ramon Berenguer IV, the Count of Barcelona, married Petronilla, heir to the throne of neighbouring Aragón. Thus, the combined Crown of Aragón was created.

In the following centuries the regime became a flourishing merchant empire, seizing Valencia and the Balearic Islands from the Muslims, and later taking territories as far flung as Sardinia, Sicily and parts of Greece.

Santa Eulàlia

Barcelona's first patron saint, Santa Eulàlia (290–304) was martyred for her faith during the persecutory reign of Diocletian. Her death involved 13 tortures (one for each year of her life), including being rolled in a glass-filled barrel, having her breasts cut off and crucifixion. Some artwork (such as a sculpture inside the Museu Frederic Marès) depicts Eulàlia holding a tray containing her excised breasts. The cathedral (p56), which is dedicated to her, holds her remains, as well as a cloister with 13 lily-white geese – also symbolic of Eulàlia's tender age at martyrdom.

Castilian Dominance

Overstretched, racked by civil disobedience and decimated by the Black Death, Catalonia began to wobble by the 14th century. When the last count of Wilfred the Hairy's dynasty expired without leaving an heir, the Crown of Aragón was passed to a noble of Castile. Soon these two Spanish kingdoms merged, with Catalonia left as a very junior partner. As business shifted from the Mediterranean to the Atlantic after the discovery of the Americas in 1492, Catalans were increasingly marginalised from trade.

Decline & Fall

The region, which had retained some autonomy in the running of its own affairs, was dealt a crushing blow when it supported the wrong side in the War of the Spanish

717

Barcelona captured by the Moors, who rule until the arrival of the Franks in 801.

1137

Barcelona's power increases as it allies with the Kingdom of Aragon through royal marriage.

1380s

Catalonia's Mediterranean empire extends as far as Sardinia, Sicily and Greece.

Succession (1702–14). Barcelona, under the auspices of British-backed archduke Charles of Austria, fell after a stubborn siege on 11 September 1714 (now celebrated as National Catalan Day) to the forces of Bourbon king Philip V, who established a unitary Castilian state. Barcelona now faced a long backlash as the new king banned the writing and teaching of Catalan, swept away the remnants of local legal systems and tore down a whole district of medieval Barcelona in order to construct an immense fort (on the site of the present-day Parc de la Ciutadella), whose sole purpose was to watch over Barcelona's troublemakers.

The Renaixença & the Road Back

Buoyed by the lifting of the ban on its trade with the Americas in 1778, Barcelona embarked on the road to industrial revolution, based initially on textiles but spreading to wine, cork and iron in the mid-19th century.

It soon became Spain's leading city. As the economy prospered, Barcelona outgrew its medieval walls, which were demolished in 1854–56. Work on the grid-plan L'Eixample (the Extension) district began soon after. The so-called Renaixença (Renaissance) brought a revival of Catalan culture, as well as political activism. It sowed the seeds of growing political tension in the early 20th century, as demands for autonomy from the central state became more insistent.

The Masses Against the Classes

Adding to the fiery mix was growing discontent among the working class. The grand Catalan merchant-bourgeois families grew richer, displaying their wealth in a slew of whimsical private mansions built with verve and flair by Modernista architects such as Antoni Gaudí. At the same time, the industrial working class, housed in cramped quarters such as Barceloneta and El Raval, and oppressed by poverty and disease, became organised and, on occasion, violent. Spain's neutrality during WWI had boosted Barcelona's economy, and from 1900 to 1930 the population doubled to one million, but the postwar global slump hit the city hard. Waves of strikes, organised principally by the anarchists' Confederación Nacional del Trabajo, brought tough responses. Left- and right-wing gangs took their ideological conflict to the streets. Tit-for-tat assassinations became common currency and the death toll mounted.

When the Second Spanish Republic was created under a left-wing government in 1931, Catalonia declared independence. Later, under pressure, its leaders settled for devolution, which it then lost in 1934, when a right-wing government won power in Madrid. The election of a left-wing popular front in 1936 again sparked Catalan autonomy claims but also led General Franco to launch the Spanish Civil War (1936–39), from which he emerged the victor.

1714

Under siege, Barcelona falls to King Philip V in the War of the Spanish Succession. King Philip V

1860s

Barcelona outgrows its medieval city walls and work begins on L'Eixample (the Extension).

THE ART ARCHIVE / ALAMY ©

Revolutionary Fervour

The acting capital of Spain for much of the civil war, Barcelona was run by anarchists and the Partido Obrero de Unificación Marxista (Marxist Unification Workers' Party) Trotskyist militia until mid-1937. Unions took over factories and public services, hotels and mansions became hospitals and schools, everyone wore workers' clothes, bars and cafes were collectivised, trams and taxis were painted red and black (the colours of the anarchists), and one-way streets were ignored as they were seen to be part of the old system.

The more radical anarchists were behind the burning of most of the city's churches and the shooting of more than 1200 priests, monks and nuns. The anarchists in turn were shunted aside by the communists (directed by Stalin from Moscow) after a bloody internecine battle in Barcelona that left 1500 dead in May 1937. Later that year the Spanish Republican government fled Valencia and made Barcelona the official capital (the government had left besieged Madrid early in the war).

The Republican defeat at the hands of the Nationalists in the Battle of the Ebro in southern Catalonia in the summer of 1938 left Barcelona undefended. It fell to the Nationalists on 25 January 1939, triggering a mass exodus of refugees to France, where most were long interned in makeshift camps. Purges and executions under Franco continued until well into the 1950s. Former Catalan president Lluís Companys was arrested in France by the Gestapo in August 1940, handed over to Franco, and shot on 15 October on Montjuïc. He is reputed to have died with the words 'Visca Catalunya!' ('Long live Catalonia!') on his lips.

The Best...
Places to Discover Barcelona's Past

1 Museu d'Història de Barcelona (p67)

2 Museu d'Història de Catalunya (p112)

3 Basílica de Santa Maria del Mar (p99)

4 Via Sepulcral Romana (p63)

5 Temple Romà d'August (p63)

6 Sinagoga Major (p62)

The City Reborn

The Francoist Josep Maria de Porcioles was mayor from 1957 until his death in 1973, a grey time for Barcelona, marked by regular demonstrations against the regime, always brutally put down. When Franco himself died two years later, the city rejoiced. In 1977 Catalonia was granted regional autonomy.

1888

The first International Exposition in Barcelona paves the way for two decades of Modernisme architecture.

1936-39

Thousands die from bloody fighting in the Civil War before the city falls to Franco's fascist forces.

1977

After one million demonstrate peacefully on Barcelona's streets, Catalonia is granted regional autonomy.

The 1992 Olympics marked the beginning of a long process of urban renewal. The waterfront, beaches and Montjuïc were in the first wave, but the momentum hasn't been lost since. The Ciutat Vella (Old City) has seen dramatic improvement with a host of museums and cultural spaces transforming the once down-and-out Raval district into a budding arts district. Out in Poblenou, the city envisions a new centre of activity, with the building of a new design museum and abundant green space. Nearby, the rechristened district of 22@ (vint-i-dos arroba) continues to be a centre for innovation and design, with some of the city's best new architecture – like Zaha Hadid's wild Torre Espiral (Spiral Tower) – happening here.

1992
Barcelona hosts a highly lauded Summer Olympics, ushering in another prolonged period of urban renewal.

2000s
Fresh immigration and slick modern buildings along the waterfront bring Barcelona into the 21st century.

2013
Successionists form a 400km human chain across Catalonia in support of Catalan independence.

Family Travel

ADINA TOVY/GETTY IMAGES ©

*Barcelona offers abundant re-
wards to stimulate young minds.
The city has running-around
space in the parks and gardens
of Montjuïc and Tibidabo, and
the ample beaches near Barceloneta. It has quirks: fairy-tale
Modernista architecture and the
ever-revolving street theatre that
is La Rambla. There are also
activities aimed specifically at
children, including a dreamlike
aquarium, a hands-on science
museum and an amusement
park with panoramic views.*

Catalan-Style

Going out to eat or sipping a beer on a
late summer evening at a *terraza* (terrace) needn't mean leaving children with
minders. Locals take their kids out all the
time and don't worry about keeping them
up late.

To make the most of your visit, try
to adjust your child's sleeping habits
to 'Spanish time' early on, or else you'll
miss out on much of Barcelona. Also,
be prepared to look for things 'outside
the box': there's the childlike creativity of
Picasso and Miró (give your children paper
and crayons and take them around the
museums), the Harry-Potter-meets-Tolkien
fantasy of Park Güell and La Pedrera, and
the wild costumes, human castle-building
and street food at festivals.

Babysitters

Most of the midrange and top-end hotels in Barcelona can organise babysitting services. A company that many hotels use and that you can also contact directly is **Tender Loving Canguros** (☎647 605989; www.tlcanguros.com), which has English-speaking babysitters for a minimum of three hours (from €9 an hour).

Kids & Bikes

Barcelona has excellent bike hire facilities, with some companies offering special kids' bicycles. Barcelonabiking.com (p237) rents bikes as well as baby seats.

Getting Around

The metro provides speedy access around town, and most stations have elevators. Sometimes getting from point A to point B can be the best part of the experience. If heading up to Tibidabo's amusement park (p190), the kids will love the old tram (tramvia blau) that rattles through the mansion-lined streets, followed by a ride on a funicular up the steep wooded hillside. Likewise, the aerial gondola ride from Barceloneta up to Montjuïc is another crowd-pleaser, with fantastic views of city and sea.

Eating with Kids

Barcelona – and Spain in general – is super friendly when it comes to eating with children. Spanish kids tend to eat the Mediterranean offerings enjoyed by their parents, but some restaurants have children's menus that serve up burgers, pizzas, tomato-sauce pasta and the like. Good local – and child-proof – food commonly found on tapas menus is *tortilla de patatas* (potato omelet) or *croquetas de jamon* (ham croquettes).

Need to Know

- **Changing facilities** Not as ubiquitous as in North America, but generally good and clean.
- **Cots** Usually available in hotels; reserve ahead.
- **Health** High health-care standards. Make sure you have your child's **EHIC card** (www.applyehic.org) before you travel within the EU.
- **Highchairs** Many restaurants have at least one; bring your own crayons.
- **Nappies (diapers)** Nappies, dummies, creams and formula can be had at any of the city's many pharmacies. Nappies are cheaper in supermarkets.
- **Strollers** Bring your own (preferably a fold-away).
- **Transport** Barcelona's metro is accessible and great for families with strollers – just be mindful of your bags around the pickpockets who often target distracted parents.

Top Kid-Friendly Eateries

Fastvínic (p143)is a good choice for an off-peak lunch or quick dinner while the kids entertain themselves drawing on the glass wall. At Le Cucine Mandarosso (p102), the incredible food means even the fussiest eaters will surrender – it's best for older kids since it can feel a bit cramped, but the little ones will be made to feel welcome too.

If you're after something sweet, La Nena (p183) is fantastic for chocolate and all manner of sweet things. There's also a play area and toys and books in a corner. And don't miss Granja M Viader (p83). No kid will be left unimpressed – and without a buzz! – by the thick hot chocolate here.

The Best...
Kid-Friendly Sights

1 CosmoCaixa (p180)

2 Museu d'Idees i Invents de Barcelona (p59)

3 Zoo de Barcelona (p95)

4 L'Aquàrium (p112)

5 Poble Espanyol (p163)

6 Parc d'Attracions (p190)

Food & Drink

Fideuà, a seafood dish

JORDI RUIZ/GETTY IMAGES

Barcelona has a celebrated food scene fueled by a combination of world-class chefs, imaginative recipes and magnificent ingredients fresh from farm and sea. Catalan culinary masterminds like Ferran Adrià and Carles Abellán have become international icons, reinventing the world of haute cuisine, while classic old-world Catalan recipes continue to earn accolades in dining rooms and tapas bars across the city.

New Catalan Cuisine

The Adrià brothers have brought culinary fame to Barcelona with a growing empire of restaurants. Their tapas restaurant Tickets (p170) is a delectable showcase of whimsy and imagination, with deconstructed dishes like liquid olives, 'air baguettes' (made with Iberian ham) and cotton-candy-covered trees with edible dark chocolate 'soil'.

Other great chefs who've followed on the heels of Adrià continue to redefine contemporary cuisine. Michelin-starred chef Carles Abellán at Comerç 24 reinterprets traditional tapas with dishes like the bite-sized mini-pizza sashimi with tuna; *melón con jamón*, a millefeuille of layered caramelised Iberian ham and thinly sliced melon; oxtail with cauliflower puree; and a changing parade of other mouth-watering bites.

Other stars of the Catalan cooking scene include Jordi Vilà, who continues to wow diners with reinvented classics at Alkímia (p143), and Jordi Artal who has earned rave reviews for his cooking at Cinc Sentits.

Classic Catalan

Traditional Catalan recipes showcase the great produce of the Mediterranean: fish, prawns, cuttlefish, clams, pork, rabbit, game, first-rate olive oil, peppers and loads of garlic. Classic dishes also feature unusual pairings (seafood with meat, fruit with fowl): cuttlefish with chickpeas, cured pork with caviar, rabbit and prawns, goose with pears.

Sauces

The essence of Catalan food lies in its sauces for meat and fish. There are five main types: *sofregit* (fried onion, tomato and garlic), *samfaina* or *chanfaina* (*sofregit* plus red pepper and aubergine or courgette), *picada* (based on ground almonds, usually with garlic, parsley, pine nuts or hazelnuts, and sometimes breadcrumbs), *allioli* (a mayonnaise-style sauce of pounded garlic with olive oil) and *romesco* (an almond, red pepper, tomato, olive oil, garlic and vinegar sauce, used especially with *calçots*).

Paella & Fideuà

Arròs a la cassola or *arròs a la catalana* is the moniker given to Catalan paella. It's cooked in an earthenware pot without saffron, whereas *arròs negre* is rice cooked in squid ink – much tastier than it sounds. *Fideuà* is similar to paella, but uses vermicelli noodles rather than rice. It usually comes with a little side dish of *allioli* to mix in.

Seafood

Apart from more standard approaches such as serving up steamed, baked or fried fish, the Catalans like to mix it up a little, by way of fish soups and stews. *Suquet*, which combines several types of fish with potatoes, is the best known, while *sarsuela*

Need to Know

○ **Price Ranges** In our listings, the following price codes represent the cost of a main course:

€	less than €10
€€	€10 to €20
€€€	over €20

○ **Opening Hours** Most restaurants open 1pm to 4pm, and 8.30pm to midnight.

○ **Reservations** At high-end restaurants, reserve ahead, especially for Thursday to Saturday nights.

○ **Tipping** A service charge is often included in the bill. If you are particularly happy, add 5% to 10% on top.

○ **Menú del Día** The *menú del día*, a multicourse set meal with water and wine, is a great way to cap prices at lunchtime. They range from €8 to €25.

The Best...
Tapas

includes a richer variety of fish ingredients. Other themed stews often go by the name of *caldereta*, where one item (usually lobster) is the star ingredient.

Calçots

Catalans are passionate about *calçots* (large, sweet spring onions), which are barbecued over hot coals, dipped in tangy *romesco* sauce and eaten voraciously when in season (between January and March). *Calçots* are usually the first course followed by copious meat and sausage dishes.

Tapas

Although tapas, Spain's quintessential bar snacks, were invented in Andalucía and weren't originally part of the Catalan eating tradition, they have been enthusiastically imported. Particularly popular are the Basque Country tapas known as *pintxos,* most of which come in the form of canapés. On slices of baguette are perched anything from *bacalao* (cod) to *morcilla* (black pudding). These are most refreshingly washed down with a slightly tart Basque white wine, *txacoli,* which is served like cider to give it a few (temporary) bubbles. Each *pintxo* comes with a toothpick, and payment is by the honour system – keep your toothpicks and present them for the final count when you ask for the bill.

In some gourmet spots, tapas have become something of an art form, while in many straightforward, beery bars you might just get a saucer of olives to accompany your tipple.

Cava

Welcome to *cava* country. That's sparkling wine to the uninitiated, or wine with significant levels of carbon dioxide either added after fermentation or produced during a second process of fermentation. Catalonia produces 95% of Spain's *cava* and the grapes are grown almost exclusively in the grape-rich Penedès region, most notably in the village of Sant Sadurni d'Anoia. Cava goes brilliantly with tapas. A couple of lively eat-drink *cava* spots where you can experience the magic include Can Paixano (p121) and El Xampanyet (p104).

Architecture

Casa Batlló (p147)

ALLE RECHTE VORBEHALTEN/GETTY IMAGES ©

Barcelona's architectural gift to the world was Modernisme, a flamboyant Catalan creation that erupted in the late 19th century. Barcelona's other great architectural epoch was during the Middle Ages, when mercantile wealth fuelled the creation of magnificent Gothic buildings. More recently, the city has continued to host cutting-edge designs and dramatic urban renewal projects that all began in the makeover before and after the 1992 Olympics.

Catalan Gothic

Barcelona's first great moment of creative electricity came when the city, grown rich on its Mediterranean trade and empire-building, transformed what is now the old city centre into the pageant of Gothic building that has survived in great part to this day.

Historically, Gothic sits between the Romanesque and Renaissance periods of medieval construction. It was an architectural style that emerged in France in the 1100s, but gradually spread throughout Europe, spawning numerous regional variations. The overlying themes, best exemplified in the ecclesial buildings of the day, were humungous scale (Gothic churches were the skyscrapers of their era), well-lit interiors, large windows, pointed arches, lofty pinnacles and spires, and majestic decoration.

The Best... Gothic Masterpieces

Most of these themes were employed in medieval Barcelona in a raft of buildings that spanned the whole era and later inspired a small neo-Gothic revival in the mid-19th century. The Basílica de Santa Maria del Mar is a fairly unembellished example of Levantino (14th-century) Gothic style at its height and is usually considered the city's greatest Gothic achievement. The more decorative Catedral is the synthesis of a Levantino Gothic base overlaid with a neo-Gothic facade.

The Modernistas

The second wave of Catalan creativity, also carried on the wind of boom times, came around the turn of the 20th century. The urban expansion program known as L'Eixample (the Extension), designed to free the choking population from the city's bursting medieval confines, coincided with a blossoming of unfettered thinking in architecture that arrived in the back-draft of the 1888 International Exposition of Barcelona.

The vitality and rebelliousness of the Modernistas is best summed up in the epithets modern, new, liberty, youth and secession. A key uniting element was the sensuous curve, implying movement, lightness and vitality. But the movement never stood still. Gaudí, in particular, repeatedly forged his own path. As he became more adventurous he appeared a lone wolf. With age he became almost exclusively motivated by stark religious conviction and devoted much of the latter part of his life to what remains Barcelona's call sign – the unfinished La Sagrada Família.

Paradoxically, Modernista architects often looked to the past for inspiration. Gothic, Islamic and Renaissance design all had something to offer. At its most playful, Modernisme was able to intelligently flout the rule books of these styles and create exciting new cocktails.

Antoni Gaudí

Leading the way was Antoni Gaudí. Born in Reus to a long line of coppersmiths, Gaudí was initially trained in metalwork. In childhood he suffered from poor health, including rheumatism, and became an early adopter of a vegetarian diet. He was not a promising student. In 1878, when he obtained his architecture degree the school's headmaster is reputed to have said: 'Who knows if we have given a diploma to a nutcase or a genius. Time will tell.'

As a young man, what most delighted Gaudí was being outdoors, and he became fascinated by the plants, animals and geology beyond his door. This deep admiration for the natural world would heavily influence his designs. 'This tree is my teacher,' he once said. 'Everything comes from the book of nature.' Throughout his work, he sought to emulate the harmony he observed in the natural world, eschewing the straight line and favouring curvaceous forms and more organic shapes.

The spiral of a nautilus shell can be seen in staircases and ceiling details, tight buds of flowers in chimney pots and roof ornamentation. Meanwhile undulating arches evoke a cavern, overlapping roof tiles mimic the scales of an armadillo and flowing walls resemble waves on the sea. Tree branches, spider webs, stalactites, honeycombs, starfish, mushrooms, shimmering beetle wings and many other elements from nature – all were part of the Gaudían vernacular.

Gaudí was a devout Catholic and a Catalan nationalist. In addition to nature, he drew inspiration from Catalonia's great medieval churches and took pride in utilising the building materials of the countryside: clay, stone and timber. In contrast to his architecture, Gaudí lived a simple life, and was not averse to knocking on doors, literally begging for money to help fund construction on the cathedral.

His masterpiece was La Sagrada Família (begun in 1882), and in it you can see the culminating vision of many ideas developed over the years. Its massive scale evokes the grandeur of Catalonia's Gothic cathedrals, while organic elements foreground its harmony with nature. As Gaudí became more adventurous he appeared as a lone wolf. With age he became almost exclusively motivated by stark religious conviction and devoted much of the latter part of his life to what remains Barcelona's call sign – the unfinished La Sagrada Família. He died in 1926, struck down by a streetcar while taking his daily walk to the Sant Felip Neri church. Wearing ragged clothes with empty pockets – save for an orange peel – Gaudí was initially taken for a beggar and taken to a nearby hospital where he was left in a pauper's ward. He died two days later. Thousands attended his funeral, in a half-mile procession to Sagrada Família where he was buried in the crypt.

Domènech i Montaner

Although overshadowed by Gaudí, Domènech i Montaner (1849–1923) was one of the great masters of Modernisme. He was a widely travelled man of prodigious intellect, with knowledge in everything from mineralogy to medieval heraldry, and he was an architectural professor, a prolific writer and a nationalist politician. The question of Catalan identity and how to create a national architecture consumed Domènech i Montaner, who designed over a dozen large-scale works in his lifetime.

The exuberant, steel-framed Palau de la Música Catalana is one of his masterpieces. Adorning the facade are elaborate Gothic-style windows, floral designs (Domènech i Montaner also studied botany) and sculptures depicting characters from Catalan folklore and the music world as well as everyday citizens of Barcelona. Inside, the hall leaves visitors dazzled with delicate floral-covered colonnades, radiant stained-glass walls and ceiling and a rolling, sculpture-packed proscenium referencing the epics of musical lore.

Puig i Cadafalch

Like Domènech, Puig i Cadafalch (1867–1956) was a polymath; he was an archaeologist, an expert in Romanesque art and one of Catalonia's most prolific architects. As a politician – and later president of the Mancomunitat de Catalunya (Commonwealth of Catalonia) – he was instrumental in shaping the Catalan nationalist movement.

One of his many Modernista gems is the Casa Amatller, a rather dramatic contrast to Gaudí's Casa Batlló next door. Here the straight line is very much in evidence, as is the foreign influence (the gables are borrowed from the Dutch). Puig i Cadafalch has designed a house of startling beauty and invention blended with playful Gothic-style sculpture.

Trencadís

The Arabs invented the ancient technique of *trencadís*, but Gaudí was the first architect to revive it. The procedure involves taking ceramic tiles or fragments of broken pottery or glass and creating a mosaic-like sheath on roofs, ceilings, chimneys, benches, sculptures or any other surface. Noted art critic Robert Hughes even suggested that Gaudí's *trencadís* was undoubtedly influential on the development of Picasso's fragmented forms in his Cubist period.

The Best...
Modernista Creations

Other important works by Puig i Cadafalch include the Casa Martí (better known as Els Quatre Gats), which was one of Barcelona's first Modernista-style buildings (from 1896), with Gothic window details and whimsical wrought-iron sculpture.

Barcelona Since the Olympic Games

Barcelona's latest architectural revolution began in the 1980s, when in the run up to the 1992 Olympics the city set about its biggest phase of renewal since the heady days of L'Eixample.

The Olympic makeover included the transformation of the Port Vell waterfront, the long road to resurrecting the 1929 International Exhibition sites in Montjuïc (including the refurbishment of the Olympic stadium) and the creation of landmarks such as Santiago Calatrava's (b 1951) Torre Calatrava.

Post-1992, landmark buildings still went up in strategic spots, usually with the ulterior motive of trying to pull the surrounding area up by its bootstraps.

One of the most emblematic of these projects was the gleaming white Museu d'Art Contemporani de Barcelona (MACBA), opened in 1995. The museum was designed by Richard Meier and incorporates the characteristic elements for which the American architect is so well known – the geometric minimalism, the pervasive use of all-white with glass and steel – and remains much debated in architectural circles.

Another big recent project (mostly completed in 2004) is Diagonal Mar, a whole district built in the northeast coastal corner of the city where before there was a void. Striking additions include high-rise apartments, waterfront office towers and a gigantic photovoltaic panel that provides some of the area's electricity.

The most visible addition to the skyline came in 2005. The shimmering, cucumber-shaped Torre Agbar is emblematic of the city's desire to make the developing hi-tech zone of 22@ (*vint-i-dos arroba*; www.22barcelona.com) a reality. The centerpiece is the new Disseny Hub (design museum), a building completed in 2013 that incorporates sustainable features in its cantilevered, metal-sheathed building. Vaguely futuristic (though some say it looks like a stapler), it has a rather imposing, anvil-shaped presence over the neighbourhood.

Nearby, stands the Els Encants Vells ('the Old Charms' flea market), which was given a dramatic new look by local architecture firm b720 Fermín Vázquez Arquitectos. Traders now sell their wares beneath a giant, mirrored canopy, arrayed a geometric angles and held aloft with long, slender poles. It opened to much acclaim in 2013.

In a rather thoughtful bit of recycling, British architect Lord Richard Rogers transformed the former Les Arenes bullring on Plaça d'Espanya into a singular, circular leisure complex, with shops, cinemas and more, which opened in 2011. He did so while still maintaining its red-brick, 19th-century Moorish-looking facade. Perhaps its best feature is the rooftop with 360-degree views from the open-air promenade and cafes and restaurants.

In the *ciutata vela* (old city), El Raval continues to be the focal point for urban renewal. The Filmoteca de Catalunya is a hulking rather brutalist building of concrete and glass, with sharp angles. It was designed by Catalan architect Josep Lluís Mateo and completed in 2011. It sits near the Richard Meier-designed MACBA, which opened in 1995.

Modern Art

Fundació Antoni Tàpies (p135)

DAMIEN SIMONIS/GETTY IMAGES©

Barcelona is to modern art what Greece is to ruined temples. Three of the figures at the vanguard of 20th-century avant-gardism – Picasso, Miró and Dalí – were either born or spent their formative years here. Their powerful legacy is stamped all over Barcelona in museums and public installations. In the contemporary art world, Catalonia continues to be an incubator for innovative works, with instrumental figures like Antoni Tàpies leading the way.

The Crucial Three

Spain has been a giant in world art ever since Velázquez etched his haunting *Las Meninas* and ushered in the glittery Siglo de Oro (c 1492–1680), though Catalonia was a little late to the ball.

Picasso

It wasn't until the late 19th century that truly great artists began to emerge in Barcelona and its hinterland, led by dandy portraitist Ramón Casas (1866–1932). Casas, an early Modernista, founded a Barcelona bar known as Els Quatre Gats, which became the nucleus for the city's growing art movement, holding numerous shows and expositions. An early host was a young then unknown Malagueño named Pablo Picasso (1881–1973).

Picasso lived sporadically in Barcelona between the innocence-losing ages of 16 and 24, and the city heavily influenced his early painting. This was the period in which he amassed the raw materials for his Blue Period. In 1904 the then-mature Picasso moved to Paris where he found fame, fortune and Cubism, and went on to become one of the greatest artists of the 20th century.

Miró

Continuing the burst of brilliance was the Barcelona-born experimentalist Joan Miró (1893–1983), best remembered for his use of symbolic figures in primary colours. Declaring he was going to 'assassinate art', Miró wanted nothing to do with the constricting labels of the era, although he has often been called a pioneering surrealist, Dadaist and automatist.

Dalí

Rising on Miró's coattails was the extravagant Catalan surrealist and showman, Salvador Dalí (1904–89), from nearby Figueres, who mixed imaginative painting with posing, attention-seeking and shameless self-promotion. Dalí is hard to avoid anywhere in the world, especially Barcelona.

Public Art

The streets, squares and parks of Barcelona are littered with the signatures of artists past and present, famous and unknown. They range from Modernista sculptors, such as Josep Llimona, to international star sculptors, such as Roy Lichtenstein and Fernando Botero. Picasso and Joan Miró both left lasting reminders in the city.

Since the return of democracy in the late 1970s, the town hall has not been shy about encouraging the placement of sometimes grandiose and often incomprehensible contemporary works in the city's public spaces. Reactions range from admiration to perplexity.

Justly proud of its rich street-art heritage, the council has created an extensive archive of it all on the internet at www.bcn.cat (click on Art Públic). The site is rich in description of hundreds of items scattered across the city, and includes commentary on the history of the city through its street art. You can search particular items by district, period and key word.

The best thing about art in the streets is that it is open to all comers.

Art goes Informal

Picasso, Miró and Dalí were hard acts to follow. Few envied the task of Catalan Antoni Tàpies in reviving the red hot Modernista flame. An early admirer of Miró, Tàpies soon began pursuing his own esoteric path embracing 'art informal' (a Jackson Pollack–like use of spontaneity) and inventing painting that utilised clay, string and even bits of rubbish. In April 2010 King Juan Carlos I elevated Tàpies to the Spanish nobility for his contribution to postwar art with the hereditary title the 1st Marquess of Tàpies. He was arguably Spain's greatest living painter during his lifetime.

Contemporary Art

In the wake of the big three, Barcelona has been a minor cauldron of activity, dominated by the figure of Antoni Tàpies (1923–2012). Early in his career (from the mid-1940s onwards) he seemed keen on self-portraits, but also experimented with collage using all sorts of materials, from wood to rice.

A poet, artist and man of theatre, Joan Brossa (1921–98) was a cultural beacon in Barcelona. His 'visual poems', lithographs and other artworks in which letters generally figure, along with all sorts of objects, make his world accessible to those who can't read his Catalan poetry.

Joan Hernández Pijuan (1931–2005), one of Barcelona's most important 20th-century abstract painters, produced work concentrating on natural shapes and figures, often using neutral colours on different surfaces.

Jaume Plensa (b 1955) is possibly Spain's best contemporary sculptor. His work ranges from sketches, through sculpture, to video and other installations that have been shown around the world.

Susana Solano (b 1946), one of Barcelona's best painters and sculptors, also works with video installations, collages and jewellery.

The Best...
Places to See Modern Art

1 Museu Picasso (p92)

2 Fundació Joan Miró (p167)

3 Fundació Antoni Tàpies (p135)

4 MACBA (p81)

IN FOCUS MODERN ART

Football

An FC Barcelona fan

JEAN-PIERRE LESCOURRET/GETTY IMAGES

To understand a country – any country – you must first decipher its sporting rituals. In Barcelona that means football. Challenging the cathedral as the city's primary place of worship is Camp Nou, home of FC Barcelona – football club, international brand and fervent bastion of Catalan identity. Its blue-and-red stripes can be seen on everyone from football-mad Thai schoolkids to goat herders in the African bush.

A Cultural Force

The story starts on 29 November 1899, when Swiss Hans Gamper founded FC Barcelona, four years after English residents had first played the game here. His choice of club colours – the blue and maroon of his home town Winterthur – has stuck. By 1910 FC Barcelona was the premier club in a rapidly growing league and had picked up its first Spanish Cup. When Spain's La Liga was founded in 1929, Barcelona ran away with the first title, though its playing record became patchier as the decades wore on and the Franco regime suppressed all manifestations of Catalan-ness.

FC Barça's reemergence as a footballing and cultural force coincided with the death of Franco and an influx of foreign players, starting with Dutch midfield ace Johann Cruyff in 1973. More legends followed, with

Diego Maradona arriving in 1982, the Brazilian Ronaldo in 1996 and Ronaldinho in 2003. Fortunes went from good to better. FC Barça won La Liga four years in a row in the early '90s, took the Champions League in 2006, and in 2009 won an unprecedented 'treble' of La Liga, Spanish Cup and Champions League. They are led by the formidable talents of vertically challenged Argentine midfielder Lionel Messi, who is the club's all-time highest goal scorer and is widely considered one of the best active players on the planet.

Getting to See a Game

A match at Camp Nou (p182), the largest stadium in Europe, can be breathtaking. Don't pass up a chance to see the magic in person if you're in town when Barça is playing.

You can purchase tickets at the stadium box office, from FNAC and Carrerfour stores and from Servicaixa ATMs.Tickets can cost anything from €35 to upwards of €200, depending on seat and match. The ticket windows are open on Saturday morning and in the afternoon until the game starts. If the match is on Sunday, the ticket windows open Saturday morning only and then on Sunday until the match starts. Usually tickets are *not* available for matches with Real Madrid.

You will almost definitely find scalpers lurking near the ticket windows. They are often club members and can sometimes get you in at a significant reduction. Don't pay until you are safely seated.

If you can't catch a game, it's still worth a trip out to Camp Nou. You can relive the club's great moments over the years at the hi-tech museum, followed by a self-guided tour through the locker rooms and out onto the pitch.

The Other Team

The pub-quiz question pretty much guaranteed to stump all but the most in-the-know football geeks is: what is Barcelona's other team? The answer: Espanyol, the city's perennial underachievers based at the **Estadi RCD Espanyol** (✆93 292 77 00; www.rcdespanyol.com; Avinguda del Baix Llobrega; M Cornellà Centre), which was built in 2009. The Barça–Espanyol rivalry is one of the most one-sided and divisive in football. While FC Barcelona is traditionally associated with Catalan nationalism, Espanyol is usually identified with Spanish immigrants from other parts of the country. Then there's the trophy haul: currently standing at Barcelona 79, Espanyol 4.

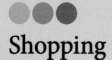

Shopping

Carrer de Ferran, off La Rambla

MANFRED GOTTSCHALK/GETTY IMAGE

Mixing old junk with top name brands, and bohemian ethnicity with a penchant for Euro-chic, Barcelona does quirky shops like novelist Carlos Luís Zafón does Gothic thrillers. Whether you're an extravagant prince or a thrifty pauper matters not a jot. Hit the Passeig de Gràcia to tear metaphoric chunks out of your credit card. For bargain-hunting, ephemera and indie boutiques, gravitate towards shabby-chic El Raval or the ubertrendy La Ribera district.

The Cutting Edge

Prêt-à-porter giant Mango is one of Barcelona's main success stories. Emerging as one of the hippest local names on the world fashion catwalks is the youthful Custo Dalmau (aka Custo Barcelona), with a rapidly growing chain of stores in Spain and abroad. Other local names or Barcelona-based designers include Antonio Miró, Joaquim Verdú, David Valls, Josep Font, Armand Basi, Purificación García, Konrad Muhr, Sita Murt and TCN. All the big names of Spanish couture, from Adolfo Domínguez to Zara, are also present and there's barely an international brand that doesn't have outlets in Barcelona.

Twice a year the exclusive urban fashion salon Bread & Butter attracts hundreds of fashion producers and buyers from around the world to Barcelona. Founded in Berlin, the salon transferred to Barcelona in 2006 and is going from strength to strength.

Neighbourhood by Neighbourhood

In Barcelona, different enclaves offer different shopping experiences.

For high fashion, design, jewellery and many department stores, the main shopping axis starts on Plaça de Catalunya, proceeds up Passeig de Gràcia and turns left (west) into Avinguda Diagonal, along which it proceeds as far as Plaça de la Reina Maria Cristina. The densely packed section between Plaça de Francesc Macià and Plaça de la Reina Maria Cristina is good hunting ground.

The heart of L'Eixample – known as the Quadrat d'Or (Golden Square) – is jammed with all sorts of glittering shops. La Rambla de Catalunya is lined with chic stores, and it's not just about fashion. Carrer del Consell de Cent bursts with art galleries and the nearby streets are also busy with shopping options, from specialist wine purveyors to bookstores.

Shopkeepers in the Barri Gòtic think of their area as 'Barnacentre' (from Barna, slang for Barcelona). Some of the most curious old stores, whether milliners or candle-makers, lurk in the narrow lanes around Plaça de Sant Jaume. The once-seedy Carrer d'Avinyó has become a minor fashion boulevard, with creations by up-and-coming designers for a young (and young at heart) clientele. Antique stores abound on and around Carrer de la Palla and Carrer dels Banys Nous.

Over in La Ribera there are two categories of shops to look out for: some fine old traditional stores dealing in speciality foodstuffs, and a new crop of fashion and design stores (particularly along the stretch of Carrer del Rec between Passeig del Born and Avinguda del Marquès de l'Argentera), catering to the young professionals who have moved into the *barri*. Old-time stores abound in El Raval, where you'll also discover a cluster of preloved-clothes shops on Carrer de la Riera Baixa.

To Market, to Market

One of the greatest sound, smell and colour sensations in Europe is Barcelona's most central produce market, the Mercat de la Boqueria (p82). It spills over with all the rich and varied colour of plentiful fruit and vegetable stands, seemingly limitless varieties of sea critters, sausages, cheeses, meat and sweets. It is also sprinkled with half a dozen or so unassuming places to eat well, at lunchtime stalls. According to some chronicles, there has been a market on this spot since 1217. These days it's no easy task getting past the gawping tourists to get to the slippery slab of sole you're after.

The Urge to Rummage

Lovers of old books, coins, stamps and general bric-a-brac can indulge their habits uninhibited at several markets. They generally get going from 9am and wind down by late afternoon. Els Encants Vells (p123) is the biggest and best flea market in the city with all manner of bric-a-brac.

The Barri Gòtic is enlivened by an **art and crafts market** (Plaça de Sant Josep Oriol; Ⓜ Liceu) on Saturday and Sunday, the antiques-filled **Mercat Gòtic** (Plaça Nova; Ⓜ Liceu or Jaume I) on Thursday, and a **coin and stamp collectors' market** (Plaça Reial; Ⓜ Liceu) on Sunday morning.

On the waterfront on weekends you'll find a few small markets worth checking out. The Port Antic (p123) near the base of La Rambla has old photographs, frames, oil paintings, records, vintage toys and other antiques.

The Best...
Shopping
Secrets

1 El Rey de la Magia (p98)

2 Taller de Marionetas Travi (p69)

3 Holala! Plaza (p85)

4 El Ingenio (p69)

5 La Manual Alpargatera (p69)

6 Loisaida (p104)

Nearby, you can stroll along the pedestrian-only Rambla de Mar to reach the Mercado de Pintores (p123), with a broad selection of paintings both collectable and rather forgettable. Also in the area is the Feria de Artesanía del Palau de Mar (p123) vendors, who sell a range of crafty items, including jewellery, graphic t-shirts, handwoven hats, fragrant candles and soaps, scarves and decorative items. The market runs daily in July and August.

Just beyond the western edge of El Raval, the punters at the Modernista **Mercat de Sant Antoni (Carrer de Mallorca 157; ⊙7am-8.30pm; M Hospital Clínic)** dedicate Sunday morning to old maps, stamps, books and cards.

Once a fortnight, gourmands can poke about the homemade honeys, sweets, cheeses and other edible delights at the **Fira Alimentació (M Liceu)** from Friday to Sunday.

Refunds

Non-EU residents are entitled to a refund of the 21% IVA (the Spanish equivalent of VAT or GST) on purchases of more than €90.16 from any shop if they take the goods out of the EU within three months. Ask the shop for a Cashback (or similar) refund form, which you present (with goods, prior to check-in) at the customs booth for IVA refunds when you leave Spain. At Barcelona airport, look for the customs booth opposite the bar on the ground floor of Terminal A.

Survival
Guide

Transbordador Aeri (p113)
MATT MUNRO/LONELY PLANET

Sleeping

Barcelona has an excellent range of accommodation, with high-end luxury hotels, small-scale boutique lodgings and a varied spread of midrange and budget selections. There is a great choice in settings, from exploring historic districts to facing the seaside or being in the thick of charming neighbourhoods packed with restaurants and nightlife. The continuing economic crisis has slowed price increases, making the city reasonable value overall.

Accommodation Types

Hotels

Hotels cover a broad range. At the bottom end there is often little to distinguish them from better *pensiones* and *hostales* (small private hotels), and from there they run up the scale to five-star luxury. Some of the better features to look out for include rooftop pools and lounges, views (either of the sea or a cityscape such as La Sagrada Família, Montjuïc or the Barri Gòtic) and of course proximity to the important sights.

B&Bs

Barcelona has a growing number of B&B-style accommodation. These tend to be in historic or heritage buildings in the Ciutat Vella (Old City) and L'Eixample, with boutique-style charm. Most have between three and 10 rooms. Attractive common areas and an extensive cooked breakfast are common features. Not all will have private bathrooms.

Pensiones & Hostales

The city has plenty of hostels. If dorm living is not your thing but you are still looking for a budget deal, check out the many *pensiones* and *hostales*. These are family-run, small-scale hotels, often housed in sprawling apartments. Some are fleapits, others immaculately maintained gems.

If your budget is very tight, look at the economical options on www.Barcelona30.com.

Apartment & Room Rentals

A cosier (and sometimes more cost-effective) alternative to hotels can be short-term apartment rental. A plethora of firms organise short lets across town, including **Air BnB** (www.airbnb.com). Typical prices are around €80 to €100 for two people per night. For four people you might be looking at an average of €160 a night. In addition to full apartments, the site also lists rooms available, which can be a good way to meet locals and/or other travellers if you don't mind sharing common areas. Prices for a room range from €30 to €60 on average.

Need to Know

PRICE GUIDE

These € signs indicate the price of a double room per night during high season. Prices include a private bathroom unless otherwise stated.

- €   under €75
- €€   €75 to €200
- €€€   over €200

ROOM TAX

Virtually all accommodation is subject to IVA, the Spanish version of value-added tax, at 10%. The city also levies an additional tax of €1.21 per night.

RESERVATIONS

Booking ahead is recommended, especially during peak periods such as Easter, Christmas/ New Year, trade fairs and throughout much of summer.

CHECK-IN & CHECK-OUT TIMES

Check-in time is around 2pm or 3pm. Check-out time is generally noon.

Costs

Depending on the season and the hostel, you will pay from €16 to €28 for a dorm bed in a youth hostel. In small *pensiones* or *hostales* you are looking at a minimum of around €40/60 for basic *individual/doble* (single/double) rooms, mostly without a private bathroom. It is occasionally possible to find cheaper rooms, but they can be unappealing. For about €100 to €140, there are extensive options for good doubles across a broad range of hotels and areas. The top-end category starts at €200 for a double, and can rise to €500 (and beyond for suites).

Some hotels, particularly at the lower and mid levels, maintain the same prices year round. Others vary the rates for *temporada alta* (high season), *temporada media* (midseason) and *temporada baja* (low season). Low season is roughly November to Easter, except during the Christmas/New Year period.

Whenever there is a major trade fair (they are frequent), high-season prices generally apply. Conversely, business-oriented hotels often consider weekends, holiday periods and other slow business times to be low season. Booking on the web is often cheaper than turning up at the door.

Rooms for Travellers with Disabilities

Many hotels claim to be equipped for guests with disabilities but reality frequently disappoints. Check out www.barcelona-access.com for help with finding genuinely accessible accommodation.

Useful Websites

Lonely Planet (hotels. lonelyplanet.com) A large selection of accommodations at all price levels.

Oh-Barcelona (www.oh-barcelona.com) Well-curated selection of hotels, hostels and apartment rentals, plus helpful profiles and articles on Barcelona.

Air BnB (www.airbnb.com) One of the best options for apartment rentals or shares, with hundreds of listings.

Barcelona 30 (www. barcelona30.com) Top choice for budget-minded travellers.

Where to Stay

NEIGHBOURHOOD	FOR	AGAINST
La Rambla & Barri Gòtic	Great location close to major sights; perfect area for exploring on foot. Good nightlife and dining options.	Very touristy and noisy. Some rooms are small, lack windows.
El Raval	Central option, with good local nightlife and access to sights. Bohemian vibe with few tourists.	Can be noisy, seedy and run-down in parts. Feels unsafe to walk late at night.
La Ribera	Great restaurant scene and neighbourhood exploring. Central with top sights including the Museu Picasso and the Palau de la Música Catalana.	Can be noisy, overly crowded and touristy.
Barceloneta & the Waterfront	Excellent seafood restaurants, local easy-going vibe, handy access to the promenade and beaches.	Very few sleeping options. Outside of Barceloneta, can be far from the action and aimed more at business travellers.
La Sagrada Família & L'Eixample	Wide range of options for all budgets. Close to Modernista sights with good restaurants and nightlife. Prime gay scene (in the Gaixample).	Can be very noisy with lots of traffic. Not a great area for walking. A bit far from the old city.
Montjuïc	Near the museums, gardens and views of Montjuïc. Great local exploring in Poble Sec, which is also convenient to El Raval.	Somewhat out of the way. Can be a bit gritty up by El Sants train station.
Park Güell, Camp Nou & La Zona Alta	Youthful, local scene with lively restaurants and bars.	Far from the old city. Few formal options (but lots of rooms for rent). La Zona Alta is geared more towards business travellers.

Best Places to Stay

NAME	LOCATION	REVIEW
DO €€€	La Rambla & Barri Gòtic	An 18-room property with a great location, lovely rooms and top service, plus first-rate market-to-table restaurants.
HOTEL NERI €€€	La Rambla & Barri Gòtic	Beautifully designed rooms in a centuries-old building next to tranquil Plaça de Sant Felip Neri.
HOTEL COLÓN €€	La Rambla & Barri Gòtic	Rooms range from modest singles to elegant doubles; the best have magical views of La Catedral.
EL JARDÍ €€	La Rambla & Barri Gòtic	Average doubles unless you nab one with a balcony overlooking one of Barcelona's prettiest squares.
CASA CAMPER €€€	El Raval	Vinçon furniture, Camper slippers and hanging gardens outside your window. Sweeping views from the rooftop.
BARCELÓ RAVAL €€	El Raval	Designer hotel with rooftop terrace and a stylish bar-restaurant; has slick gadget-filled rooms.
HOTEL SANT AGUSTÍ €€	El Raval	Opened in 1840, this is the city's oldest hotel. Light-filled rooms overlook a curious square.
CHIC & BASIC TALLERS €	El Raval	Rooms have smart touches that include plasma-screen TVs and iPod docks.
HOTEL PENINSULAR €	El Raval	Former convent with a plant-draped atrium and spacious, well-kept rooms.
PENSIÓN FRANCIA €	La Ribera	This quaint 11-room hostel has simple rooms (some with balconies) in a great location near El Born's nightlife.
GRAND HOTEL CENTRAL €€€	La Ribera	Spacious designer rooms with high ceilings, dark timber floors and subtle lighting. Rooftop pool.
CHIC & BASIC €€	La Ribera	Cool hotel, with 31 spotlessly white rooms and original features, including a marble staircase.
HOTEL BANYS ORIENTALS €€	La Ribera	Magnetically popular boutique hotel with cool blue tones and dark-hued floors.
W BARCELONA €€€	Barceloneta & the Waterfront	A spinnaker-shaped tower with chic rooms. Amenities include a spa, massive pool and top-floor bar.
MELIÁ SKY BARCELONA €€€	Barceloneta & the Waterfront	Offers designer digs, fine views and extensive amenities – bars and terraces, an enticing pool and a 24th-floor Michelin-starred restaurant.
EUROSTARS GRAND MARINA HOTEL €€€	Barceloneta & the Waterfront	Has a maritime flavour that continues into the rooms, with lots of polished timber. Rooftop pool.
AMISTAT BEACH HOSTEL €	Barceloneta & the Waterfront	Small, warm and welcoming hostel, near the beach and restaurants of Poblenou.
HOTEL MARINA FOLCH €	Barceloneta & the Waterfront	Good-value family-run hotel with 10 rooms. The best have small balconies facing out towards the marina.
BED & BEACH €€	Barceloneta & the Waterfront	This pleasant guesthouse is just a five-minute walk to the beach. With rooftop terrace and shared kitchen.
EQUITY POINT SEA HOSTEL €	Barceloneta & the Waterfront	A cramped party hostel (bring earplugs) with fantastic beachfront location.
POBLENOU BED & BREAKFAST €€	Barceloneta & the Waterfront	Classy 1930s house, with high ceilings and beautiful tile floors. Breakfast is served on the rear terrace.
HOTEL ESPAÑA €€	L'Eixample	Clean, straighforward rooms in a Modernista building that still manages to ooze a little history.

PRACTICALITIES	BEST FOR
Map p60; ☎ 93 481 36 66; www.hoteldoreial.com; Plaça Reial 1; s/d from €230/280; ❄ 🛜 ☕; Ⓜ Liceu	Luxury-minded foodies
Map p60; ☎ 93 304 06 55; www.hotelneri.com; Carrer de Sant Sever 5; d from €270; ❄ @ 🛜; Ⓜ Liceu	Superb Barri Gòtic location
Map p60; ☎ 93 301 14 04; www.hotelcolon.es; Avinguda de la Catedral 7; s/d from €130/195; ❄ @ 🛜; Ⓜ Jaume I	Unrivaled cathedral views
Map p60; ☎ 93 301 59 00; www.eljardi-barcelona.com; Plaça de Sant Josep Oriol 1; d €90-120; ❄ 🛜; Ⓜ Liceu	Peaceful location
Map p78; ☎ 93 342 62 80; www.casacamper.com; Carrer d'Elisabets 11; s/d from €238/260; ❄ @ 🛜; Ⓜ Catalunya	A stylish but fun stay
Map p78; ☎ 93 320 14 90; www.barceloraval.com; Rambla del Raval 17-21; r from €128; ❄ @; Ⓜ Liceu	Designer digs
Map p78; ☎ 93 318 16 58; www.hotelsa.com; Plaça de Sant Agustí 3; r from €125; ❄ @ 🛜; Ⓜ Liceu	Good, central location
Map p78; ☎ 93 302 51 83; www.chicandbasic.com; Carrer dels Tallers 82; s/d from €71/84; ❄ @; Ⓜ Universitat	Good-value rooms
Map p78; ☎ 93 302 31 38; www.hotelpeninsular.net; Carrer de Sant Pau 34; s/d €57/80; ❄ @ 🛜; Ⓜ Liceu	Historic penny-pincher
Map p96; ☎ 93 319 03 76; www.pensionfrancia-barcelona.com; Carrer de Rera Palau 4; s/d without bathroom €30/55; 🛜; Ⓜ Barceloneta	Great location
Map p96; ☎ 93 295 79 00; www.grandhotelcentral.com; Via Laietana 30; d €285; ❄ @ 🛜 ☕; Ⓜ Jaume I	Designer style
Map p96; ☎ 93 295 46 52; www.chicandbasic.com; Carrer de la Princesa 50; s €81-87, d €103-150; ❄ @ 🛜; Ⓜ Jaume I	Artful design
Map p96; ☎ 93 268 84 60; www.hotelbanysorientals.com; Carrer de l'Argenteria 37; s €96, d €115.50-143; ❄ 🛜; Ⓜ Jaume I	Superb location
☎ 93 295 28 00; www.w-barcelona.com; Plaça de la Rosa del Vents 1; r from €326; Ⓟ ❄ @ 🛜 ☕; 🚌 17, 39, 57 or 64, Ⓜ Barceloneta	Style & beachside location
Map p120; ☎ 93 367 20 50; www.melia.com; Carrer de Pere IV 272-286; r €152-257; Ⓟ ❄ @ 🛜 ☕; Ⓜ Poblenou	Sea views
Map p116; ☎ 93 603 90 00; www.grandmarinahotel.com; Moll de Barcelona; r from €200; ❄ @ 🛜 ☕; Ⓜ Drassanes	Sea breezes
Map p120 ☎ 93 221 32 81; www.amistatbeachhostel.com; Carrer Amistat 21; dm €21-33; 🛜; Ⓜ Poblenou	Poblenou charm
Map p116; ☎ 93 310 37 09; Carrer del Mar 16; s/d/tr from €45/65/85; ❄ 🛜; Ⓜ Barceloneta	Price & marina location
Map p120; ☎ 630 528156; www.bedandbeachbarcelona.com; Passatge General Bassols 26; d €67-110, s/d without bathroom €39/64; ❄ 🛜; Ⓜ Bogatell	Affordability near the waterfront
Map p116; ☎ 93 231 20 45; www.equity-point.com; Plaça del Mar 1-4; dm €19-34; ❄ @ 🛜; 🚌 17, 39, 57 or 64, Ⓜ Barceloneta	Beachfront on a budget
Map p120; ☎ 93 221 26 01; www.hostalpoblenou.com; Carrer del Taulat 30; s/d from €50/80; ❄ @ 🛜; Ⓜ Llacuna	*Barcelonin* charm
Map p78 ☎ 93 550 00 00; www.hotelespanya.com; Carrer de Sant Pau 9-11; r €164; ❄ @ 🛜 ☕; Ⓜ Liceu	Elegant mid-range option

NAME	LOCATION	REVIEW
HOTEL MAJÈSTIC €€€	L'Eixample	This sprawling, central option has a rooftop pool, a pampering spa and European charm.
HOTEL OMM €€€	L'Eixample	A wild Dalí-esque facade contains ultramodern rooms, a roof terrace and a sprawling minimalist bar.
CONDES DE BARCELONA €€	L'Eixample	Clean, designer lines dominate, with luxurious rooms, hardwood floors and architectural touches.
HOTEL SIXTYTWO €€	L'Eixample	Designer rooms with Bang & Olufsen TVs and expansive beds. Relax in the pretty Japanese garden.
HCC ST MORITZ €€	L'Eixample	Upmarket hotel with fully equipped rooms and an elegant restaurant and terrace bar.
SUITES AVENUE €€	L'Eixample	Apartment-style living with a terrace, gym and pool (plus a mini-museum of Hindu and Buddhist art).
FIVE ROOMS €€	L'Eixample	Features include broad, firm beds, exposed brick walls, restored mosaic tiles and minimalist decor.
HOTEL CONSTANZA €€	L'Eixample	Well-loved boutique stay. The terrace has fine views over the rooftops of the L'Eixample.
HOTEL MARKET €	L'Eixample	An attractively renovated building, around the corner from the grand old Sant Antoni market.
BARCELONA CENTER INN €€	L'Eixample	Rooms have a charming simplicity, with wrought-iron bedsteads and flowing drapes. Some have terraces.
HOTEL PRAKTIK €€	L'Eixample	Modernista gem with high ceilings, original tile floors and art-filled rooms, plus a chilled reading area.
HOSTAL OLIVA €	L'Eixample	This 4th-floor hostal is a terrific, reliable cheapie in one of the city's most expensive neighbourhoods.
FASHION HOUSE €	L'Eixample	Tastefully done rooms with 4.5m-high ceilings, parquet floors and, in some cases, a little balcony onto the street.
URBAN SUITES €€	Montjuïc	Contemporary spot with 16 suites and four apartments. Convenient and comfortable.
HOTEL TURÓ DE VILANA €€	Park Guell, Camp Nou & La Zona Alta	Bright, designer hotel with 20 rooms set in the charming residential hood of Sarrià.
HOTEL CASA FUSTER €€€	Park Guell, Camp Nou & La Zona Alta	Period features and plush rooms (plus a rooftop terrace with pool) in a lovely Modernista mansion.
CASA GRÀCIA €	Park Guell, Camp Nou & La Zona Alta	Stylish hostel with colourful rooms, communal dinners, film screenings and other events.
INOUT HOSTEL €	Park Guell, Camp Nou & La Zona Alta	This welcoming place with panoramic views has a strong social ethos. Over 90% of staff here have disabilities.

PRACTICALITIES	BEST FOR
Map p144; ☎ 93 488 17 17; www.hotelmajestic.es; Passeig de Gràcia 68; d €251-278; P ❄ @ 🛜 🏊; M Passeig de Gràcia	Old-world sophistication
Map p144; ☎ 93 445 40 00; www.hotelomm.es; Carrer de Rosselló 265; s/d from €204/300; P ❄ @ 🛜 🏊; M Diagonal	Artful design
Map p136; ☎ 93 445 00 00; www.condesdebarcelona.com; Passeig de Gràcia 73-75; r €164; P ❄ @ 🛜 🏊; M Passeig de Gràcia	Luxury and Modernista setting
Map p144; ☎ 93 272 41 80; www.sixtytwohotel.com/en; Passeig de Gràcia 62; s/d from €149/164; P ❄ @ 🛜; M Passeig de Gràcia	High-end comfort
Map p144; ☎ 93 412 15 00; www.hcchotels.com; Carrer de la Diputació 264; s/d €137; P ❄ @ 🛜; M Passeig de Gràcia	Central l'Eixample location
Map p136; ☎ 93 487 41 59; www.suitesavenue.com; Passeig de Gràcia 83; apt from €169; P ❄ @ 🛜 🏊; M Diagonal	Serviced apartments in l'Eixample
Map p144; ☎ 93 342 78 80; www.thefiverooms.com; Carrer de Pau Claris 72; s/d from €155/165; ❄ @ 🛜; M Urquinaona	Boutique charm
Map p144; ☎ 93 270 19 10; www.hotelconstanza.com; Carrer del Bruc 33; s/d €80/100; ❄ @ 🛜; M Girona, Urquinaona	A romantic stay
Map p164; ☎ 93 325 12 05; www.forkandpillow.com; Passatge de Sant Antoni Abad 10; s/d from €72/76; ❄ @ 🛜; M Sant Antoni	A colourful getaway
Map p144; ☎ 93 265 25 60; www.hostalcenterinn.com; Gran Via de les Corts Catalanes 688; s/d €75/89; ❄ @ 🛜; M Tetuan	Catalan classic
Map p136; ☎ 93 343 66 90; www.hotelpraktikrambla.com; Rambla de Catalunya 27; r €119-129; ❄ 🛜; M Passeig de Gràcia	Refined setting
Map p144; ☎ 93 488 01 62; www.hostaloliva.com; Passeig de Gràcia 32; d €51-91, s/d without bathroom €41-71; ❄ 🛜; M Passeig de Gràcia	An affordable classic
Map p144; ☎ 637 904044; www.bcnfashionhouse.com; Carrer del Bruc 13; s/d €51/91, without bathroom €41/71; ❄ 🛜; M Urquinaona	Elegance on a budget
Map p164; ☎ 93 201 51 64; www.theurbansuites.com; Carrer de Sant Nicolau 3; ste from €130; P ❄ @ 🛜; M Sants Estació	Self-catering
Map p186; ☎ 93 434 03 63; www.turodevilana.com; Carrer de Vilana 7; s/d €105/120; ❄ @ 🛜; 🚌 64, 🚆 FGC Les Tres Torres	Neighbourhood charm
Map p182; ☎ 93 255 30 00; www.hotelcasafuster.com; Passeig de Gràcia 132; r from €247; P ❄ @ 🛜 🏊; M Diagonal	Modernista allure
Map p182; ☎ 93 187 44 97; www.casagraciabcn.com; Passeig de Gràcia 116; dm from €27, d from €50; ❄ @ 🛜; M Diagonal	Hip, affordable stay
☎ 93 280 09 85; www.inouthostel.com; Major del Rectoret 2; dm €18; ❄ @ 🛜 🏊; 🚆 FGC Baixador de Vallvidrera	Socially minded travellers

Transport

●●●
Arriving in Barcelona

Most travellers enter Barcelona through El Prat airport. Some budget airlines use Girona-Costa Brava airport or Reus airport.

Flights from North America take about eight hours from the east coast (10 to 13 hours with a stopover); from the west coast count on 13 or more hours including a stopover. Flights from London take around two hours; from Western Europe it's about two to three hours.

Travelling by train is a pricier but perhaps more romantic way of reaching Catalonia from other European cities. The new TGV takes around seven hours from Paris to Barcelona. Long-distance trains arrive in Estació Sants, about 2.5km west of La Rambla.

Long-haul buses arrive in Estació del Nord.

Flights, tours and rail tickets can be booked online at lonelyplanet.com.

El Prat Airport

Barcelona's **El Prat airport** (☏ 902 404704; www.aena.es) lies 17km southwest of Plaça de Catalunya at El Prat de Llobregat. The airport has two main terminal buildings: the new T1 terminal and the older T2, itself divided into three terminal areas (A, B and C).

In T1, the main arrivals area is on the 1st floor (with separate areas for EU Schengen Area arrivals, non-EU international arrivals and the Barcelona–Madrid corridor). Boarding gates for departures are on the 1st and 3rd floors.

The main **tourist office** (🕒 8.30am-8.30pm) is on the ground floor of Terminal 2B. Others on the ground floor of Terminal 2A and in Terminal 1 operate the same hours. Lockers (which come in three sizes) can be found on the 1st floor of Terminal 1. Lost-luggage offices can be found by the arrivals belts in Terminal 1 and on the arrivals floor in Terminals 2A and 2B.

Bus

The **A1 Aerobús** (☏ 902 100104; www.aerobusbcn.com; one way/return €5.90/10.20) runs from Terminal 1 to Plaça de Catalunya (30 to 40 minutes depending on traffic) via Plaça d'Espanya, Gran Via de les Corts Catalanes (corner of Carrer del Comte d'Urgell) and Plaça de la Universitat every five to 10 minutes from 6.10am to 1.05am. Departures from Plaça de Catalunya are from 5.30am to 12.30am and stop at the corner of Carrer de Sepúlveda and Carrer del Comte d'Urgell, and at Plaça d'Espanya.

The **A2 Aerobús** from Terminal 2 (stops outside terminal areas A, B and C) runs from 6am to 1am with a frequency of between 10 and 20 minutes and follows the same route as the A1 Aerobús.

Buy tickets on the bus or from agents at the bus stop. Considerably slower local buses (such as the No 46 to/from Plaça d'Espanya and a night bus, the N17, to/from Plaça de Catalunya) also serve Terminals 1 and 2.

Mon-Bus (www.monbus.cat) has regular direct buses (which originate in central Barcelona) between Terminal 1 only and Sitges (€4). In Sitges you can catch it at Avinguda de Vilanova 14. The trip takes about 40 minutes and runs hourly.

Alsa (☏ 902 422242; www.alsa.es) runs the Aerobús Ràpid service several times daily from El Prat airport to various cities including Girona, Figueres, Lleida, Reus and Tarragona. Fares range from €8/15 one way/return to Tarragona and up to €28/50 one way/return to Lleida.

Plana (☏ 977 553680; www.busplana.com) has services between the airport and Reus (one way/return €15/27), stopping at Tarragona, Port Aventura and other nearby southwest coastal destinations along the way.

Train

Train operator Renfe runs the R2 Nord line every half-hour from the airport (from 5.42am to 11.38pm) via several stops to Barcelona's main train station, **Estació Sants** (Plaça dels Països Catalans; Ⓜ Estació Sants), and Passeig de Gràcia in central Barcelona, after which it heads northwest out of the city. The first service from Passeig de Gràcia leaves at 5.08am and the last at 11.07pm, and about five minutes later from Estació Sants. The trip between the airport and Passeig de Gràcia takes 25 minutes. A one-way ticket costs €4.10.

The airport train station is about a five-minute walk from Terminal 2. Regular shuttle buses run from the station and Terminal 2 to Terminal 1 – allow an extra 15 to 20 minutes.

Taxi

A taxi between either terminal and the city centre – about a half-hour ride depending on traffic – costs around €25. Fares and charges are posted inside the passenger side of the taxi – make sure the meter is used.

Girona-Costa Brava Airport

Girona-Costa Brava airport (☎ 902 404704; www.aena.es) is 12km south of Girona and 92km northeast of Barcelona. You'll find a tourist office, ATMs and lost-luggage desks on the ground floor.

Regular **Renfe** (☎ 902 320320; www.renfe.es) train services run between Girona and Barcelona (€8.40 to €11.25, around 1½ hours). Speedier Avant trains get there in 38 minutes (one way €16).

Sagalés (☎ 902 130014; www.sagales.com) runs hourly bus services from Girona-Costa Brava airport to Girona's main bus/train station (€2.75, 30 minutes) in connection with flights. The same company runs direct

Barcelona Bus (☎ 902 130014; www.barcelonabus. com) services to/from Estació del Nord (p45) bus station in Barcelona (one way/return €16/25, 75 minutes).

A taxi ride into Girona from the airport costs €20 to €26. To Barcelona you would pay around €140.

Reus Airport

Reus airport (☎ 902 404704; www.aena.es) is 13km west of Tarragona and 108km southwest of Barcelona. The tourist office and lost-luggage desks are in the main terminal building.

Hispano-Igualadina (☎ 902 292900; www. igualadina.net; Estació Sants) buses run between Reus airport and **Estació d'Autobusos de Sants** (Carrer de Viriat; Ⓜ Estació Sants) to meet flights (one way €16, 1½ hours). Local bus 50 (www. reustransport.cat) serves central Reus (€3, 20 minutes) and other buses run to local coastal destinations.

Estació Sants

The main train station in Barcelona is Estació Sants, located 2.5km west of La Rambla. Direct overnight trains from Paris, Geneva, Milan and Zurich arrive here. From Estació Sants it's a short metro ride to the Ciutat Vella or L'Eixample.

Estació Sants has a tourist office, a telephone and fax office, currency exchange booths open between 8am and 10pm, ATMs and left-luggage lockers.

Climate Change & Travel

Every form of transport that relies on carbon-based fuel generates CO_2, the main cause of human-induced climate change. Modern travel is dependent on aeroplanes, which might use less fuel per kilometre per person than most cars but travel much greater distances. The altitude at which aircraft emit gases (including CO_2) and particles also contributes to their climate change impact. Many websites offer 'carbon calculators' that allow people to estimate the carbon emissions generated by their journey and, for those who wish to do so, to offset the impact of the greenhouse gases emitted with contributions to portfolios of climate-friendly initiatives throughout the world. Lonely Planet offsets the carbon footprint of all staff and author travel.

●●●

Getting Around Barcelona

Barcelona has abundant options for getting around town. The excellent metro can get you most places, with buses and trams filling in the gaps. Taxis are the best option late at night.

Ⓜ Metro

The easy-to-use **TMB Metro** (☎ 010; www.tmb.net) system has 11 numbered and colour-coded lines. It runs from 5am to midnight Sunday to Thursday and holidays, from 5am to 2am on Friday and

Tickets & Targetes

The metro, FGC trains, *rodalies/cercanías* (Renfe-run local trains) and buses come under one zoned-fare regime. Single-ride tickets on all standard transport within Zone 1 cost €2.15.

Targetes are multitrip transport tickets. They are sold at all city-centre metro stations. The prices given here are for travel in Zone 1. Children under four years of age travel free. Options include the following:

o Targeta T-10 (€10.30) – 10 rides (each valid for 1¼ hours) on the metro, buses, FGC trains and *rodalies*. You can change between metro, FGC, *rodalies* and buses.

o Targeta T-DIA (€7.60) – unlimited travel on all transport for one day.

o Two-/three-/four-/ five-day tickets (€14/20/25.50/30.50) – unlimited travel on all transport except the Aerobús; buy them at metro stations and tourist offices.

o T-Mes (€52.75) – 30 days' unlimited use of all public transport.

o Targeta T-50/30 (€42.50) – 50 trips within 30 days, valid on all transport.

o T-Trimestre (€142) – 90 days' unlimited use of all public transport.

routes pass through Plaça de Catalunya and/or Plaça de la Universitat. After 11pm a reduced network of yellow *nitbusos* (night buses) runs until 3am or 5am. All *nitbus* routes pass through Plaça de Catalunya and most run every 30 to 45 minutes.

Taxi

Taxis charge a €2.10 flag fall plus meter charges of €1.03 per kilometre (€1.30 from 8pm to 8am and all day on weekends). A further €3.10 is added for all trips to/from the airport, and €1 for luggage bigger than 55cm x 35cm x 35cm. The trip from Estació Sants to Plaça de Catalunya, about 3km, costs about €11. You can flag a taxi down in the streets or call one:

Radio Taxi BCN (93 225 00 00; www.radiotaxibcn.org)

Fonotaxi (93 300 11 00)

Radio Taxi Barcelona (902 222111, 93 293 31 11)

The call-out charge is €3.40 (€4.20 at night and on weekends). In many taxis it is possible to pay with a credit card and, if you have a local telephone number, you can join the T033 Ràdio taxi service for booking taxis online (www.radiotaxi033.com, in Spanish). You can also book online at www.catalunyataxi.com.

Taxi Amic (93 420 80 88; http://rtljtic. wix.com/taxiamic) is a special taxi service for people with disabilities or difficult situations (such as transporting big objects).

days immediately preceding holidays, and 24 hours on Saturday.

Ongoing work to expand the metro continues on several lines. Lines 9 and 10 will eventually connect with the airport (2016 at the earliest). Suburban trains run by the **Ferrocarrils de la Generalitat de Catalunya** (FGC; 93 205 15 15; www.fgc. net) include a couple of useful city lines. All lines heading north from Plaça de Catalunya stop at Carrer de Provença and Gràcia. One of these lines (L7) goes to Tibidabo and another (L6 to Reina Elisenda) has a stop near the Monestir de Pedralbes. Most trains from Plaça de Catalunya continue beyond Barcelona

to Sant Cugat, Sabadell and Terrassa. Other FGC lines head west from Plaça d'Espanya, including one for Manresa that is handy for the trip to Montserrat.

Depending on the line, these trains run from about 5am (with only one or two services before 6am) to 11pm or midnight Sunday to Thursday, and from 5am to about 1am on Friday and Saturday.

Bus

Transports Metropolitans de Barcelona (TMB; 010; www.tmb.net) buses run along most city routes every few minutes between 5am and 6.30am to between around 10pm and 11pm. Many

Book at least 24 hours in advance if possible.

Women passengers who feel safer with taxis driven by women can order one on the **Línea Rosa** (☎ 93 330 07 00; www.servitaxi.com).

Tram

TMB (☎ 902 193275; www.trambcn.com) runs three tram lines (T1, T2 and T3) from Plaça de Francesc Macià into the suburbs of greater Barcelona, which are of limited interest to visitors. The T4 line runs from behind the zoo (near the Ciutadella Vila Olímpica metro stop) to Sant Adrià via Glòries and the Fòrum. The T5 line runs from Glòries to Badalona (Gorg stop). The T6 runs between Badalona (Gorg) and Sant Adrià. All standard transport passes are valid. A more scenic option is *tram via blau* (blue tram), which runs up to the foot of Tibidabo.

Cable Car

Several aerial cable cars operate in Barcelona and provide excellent views over the city. The Transbordador Aeri (p113) travels between the waterfront southwest of Barceloneta and Montjuïc. The two-stage **Telefèric de Montjuïc** (return €10.80; ⏱10am-9pm) runs between Estació Parc Montjuïc and the Castell de Montjuïc.

🚲 Bicycle

More than 180km of bike lanes have been laid out across the city, so it's possible to commute on two environmentally friendly wheels. A waterfront path runs northeast from Port Olímpic towards Riu Besòs. Scenic itineraries are mapped

for cyclists in the Collserola parkland, and the *ronda verda* is an incomplete 75km cycling path that extends around the city's outskirts. You can cycle a well-signed 22km loop path (part of the *ronda verda*) by following the seaside bike path northeast of Barceloneta.

You can transport your bicycle on the metro on weekdays (except between 7am and 9.30am or 5pm and 8.30pm). On weekends and holidays, and during July and August, there are no restrictions. You can use FGC trains to carry your bike at any time and Renfe's *rodalies* trains from 10am to 3pm on weekdays and all day on weekends and holidays.

Hire

Countless companies around town offer bicycles (and anything remotely resembling one, from tandems to tricycle carts and more). They include the following:

Rent Electric (☎ 902 474474; www.rentelectric.com; Plaça del Mar 1; bike hire per 2/4hr €8/12; ⏱10am-7pm; Ⓜ Barceloneta)

Fat Tire Bike Tours (☎ 93 342 92 75; http://fattirebiketours.com; Carrer Sant Honorat 7; bike hire per hr/half-day €3/8, tour €24; ⏱10am-8pm; Ⓜ Jaume I or Liceu)

BarcelonaBiking.com (☎ 656 356300; www.barcelonabiking.com; Baixada de Sant Miquel 6; bike hire per hr/24hr €5/15, tour €21; ⏱10am-8pm, tour 11am daily; Ⓜ Jaume I or Liceu)

Biciclot (☎ 93 221 97 78; bikinginbarcelona.net; Passeig Marítim de la Barceloneta 33; bike hire per hr/day €5/€17; ⏱11am-6pm Mon-Fri, 10am-8pm Sat & Sun; Ⓜ Ciutadella Vila Olímpica)

My Beautiful Parking (☎ 93 186 73 65; www.mybeautifulparking.com; Carrer Viagatans 2; bike hire per 2hr/24hr €6/15; ⏱10am-9pm Mon-Sat; Ⓜ Jaume I or Liceu)

Un Cotxe Menys (☎ 93 268 21 05; www.bicicletabarcelona.com; Carrer de l'Esparteria 3; bike hire per hr/day/week €5/15/55; ⏱10am-7pm; Ⓜ Jaume I)

🚗 Car & Motorcycle

With the convenience of public transport and the high price of parking in the city, it's unwise to drive in Barcelona. However, if you're planning a road trip outside the city, a car is handy.

Hire

Avis, Europcar, National/Atesa and Hertz have desks at El Prat airport, Estació Sants and Estació del Nord. Rental outlets in Barcelona include the following:

Avis (☎ 902 110275; www.avis.com; Carrer de Còrsega 293-295; Ⓜ Diagonal)

Cooltra (☎ 93 221 40 70; www.cooltra.com; Passeig de Joan de Borbó 80-84; Ⓜ Barceloneta) You can rent scooters here for around €35 (plus insurance). Cooltra also organises scooter tours.

Europcar (☎ 93 302 05 43; www.europcar.com; Gran Via

de les Corts Catalanes 680; Ⓜ Girona)

Hertz (📞 902 998707; www. hertz.com; Carrer del Viriat 45; Ⓜ Sants)

MondoRent (📞 93 295 32 68; www.mondorent.com; Passeig de Joan de Borbó 80-84; Ⓜ Barceloneta) Rents scooters (including stylish Vespas) as well as electric bikes.

National/Atesa (📞 93 323 07 01; www.atesa.es; Carrer de Muntaner 45; Ⓜ Universitat)

Tours

There are many ways to get a more in-depth look at the city, whether on a specialised walking tour through the Ciutat Vella, on a bicycle excursion around the centre or on a hop-on, hop-off bus tour all across town.

Walking Tours

The Oficina d'Informació de Turisme de Barcelona (p243) organises a series of guided walking tours. One explores the Barri Gòtic (adult/child €16/free); another follows in Picasso's footsteps and winds up at the Museu Picasso, entry to which is included in the price (adult/child €22/7); and a third takes in the main jewels of Modernisme (adult/child €16/free). It also runs a 'gourmet' tour of traditional purveyors of fine foodstuffs across the old city (adult/child €22/7). Stop by the tourist office or go online for the latest schedule. Tours

typically last two hours and start at the tourist office.

More specialised tours are also bookable through the tourist office: themes include running, shopping, literary Barcelona, tapas tours, Civil War tours, the Gothic quarter by night, Park Güell and half a dozen other options. Other tours include the following:

Barcelona Metro Walks
Consists of seven self-guided routes across the city, combining travel on the metro and other public transport as well as stretches on foot. Tourist information points at Plaça de Catalunya and Plaça de Sant Jaume sell the €16 package, which includes a walks guide, two-day transport pass and map.

My Favourite Things
(📞 637 265405; www.myft. net; tours from €26) Offers tours for no more than 10 participants based on numerous themes: anything from design to food. Other activities include flamenco and salsa classes and bicycle rides in and out of Barcelona.

Runner Bean Tours
(📞 636 108776; www.runnerbeantours. com; 🕐 tours 11am year-round & 4.30pm Apr-Sep) Has several daily thematic tours. It's a pay-what-you-wish tour, with a collection taken at the end for the guide. The Old City tour explores the Roman and medieval history of Barcelona, visiting highlights in the Ciutat Vella. The Gaudí tour takes in the great works of Modernista Barcelona. It involves two trips on the metro. Runner Beans also has ghostly evening tours and

a Kids and Family Walking Tour; check the website for departure times.

Bicycle Tours
Barcelona is awash with companies offering bicycle tours. Tours typically take two to four hours and generally stick to La Sagrada Família, the Ciutat Vella and the beaches. Operators include Barcelona-Biking.com (p237) and Fat Tire Bike Tours (p237), as well as the following:

Barcelona By Bicycle
(📞 93 268 21 05; www. bicicletabarcelona.com; Carrer de l'Esparteria 3; tour €22)

Barcelona By Bike
(📞 671 307325; www.barcelonabybike. com; Carrer de la Marina 13; tours €22; Ⓜ Cuitadella/Vila Olimpica)

CicloTour
(📞 93 317 19 70; www.barcelonaciclotour.com/ eng; Carrer dels Tallers 45; tours €22; 🕐 11am daily, 4.30pm mid-Apr-Oct, 7.30pm Thu-Sun Jun-Sep)

Terra Diversions
(📞 93 416 08 05; www.terradiversions. com; Carrer de Santa Tecla 1bis) Mostly mountain-bike tours outside the city.

Bus Tours
Bus Turístic (p239) is a hop-on, hop-off service that stops at virtually all of the city's main sights. Audio guides (in 10 languages) provide running commentary on the 44 stops on the three different circuits. The service operates from Plaça de Catalunya and Plaça del Porta de la Pau.

Tickets are available online and on the buses, and cost

€27 (€16 for children from four to 12 years) for one day of unlimited rides, or €35 (€20 for children) for two consecutive days. Buses run from 9am to 8pm (7pm in winter) and the frequency varies from every five to 25 minutes.

The two key routes take about two hours each; the blue route runs past La Pedrera on Passeig de Gràcia and takes in La Sagrada Família, Park Güell and much of the Zona Alta (including Pedralbes and Camp Nou). The red route also runs up Passeig de Gràcia and takes in Port Vell, Port Olímpic and Montjuïc. The third (green route), from Port Olímpic to the Fòrum, runs from April to September and takes 40 minutes. Other private companies run similar services.

Barcelona Guide Bureau (93 315 22 61; www.barcelonaguidebureau. com; Via Laietana 54) places professional guides at the disposal of groups for tailormade tours of the city. Several languages are catered for. It also offers a series of daily tours, from a five-hour highlights of Barcelona tour (adult/child €59/30, departing at 10am) to a trip to Montserrat, leaving Barcelona at 3pm and lasting about four hours (adult/child €47/23).

Boat Tours

Several companies take passengers on short jaunts out on the water. These depart several times daily (with many departures in the summer) from Moll de les Drassanes near the southern end of La Rambla. **Las Golondri-**

nas (📞 93 442 31 06; www. lasgolondrinas.com; Moll de les Drassanes; 35min tour adult/ child €6.80/2.60; **M** Drassanes), **BC Naval Tours** (📞 93 795 85 68; www.barcelonanavaltours.com; Moll de les Drassanes; cruise 40/80min €7.50/12; **M** Drassanes) and other companies offer scenic catamaran trips around the harbour and beyond. Avoid going on a windy day, when the seas can be rough.

A-Z
Directory

●●●
Discount Cards

The **ISIC** (International Student Identity Card; www.isic.org) and the **European Youth Card** (www.euro26.org) are available from most national student organisations and allow discounted access to some sights. Students generally pay a little more than half of adult admission prices, as do children aged under 12 and senior citizens (aged 65 and over) with appropriate ID.

Possession of a **Bus Turístic** ticket (📞 93 285 38 32; www.barcelonabusturistic. cat/en; day ticket adult/child

€27/16; 🕙 9am-8pm) entitles you to discounts at some museums.

Articket (www.articketbcn. org; per person €30) gives admission to six sites – Museu Picasso, Museu Nacional d'Art de Catalunya (MNAC), Museu d'Art Contemporani de Barcelona (MACBA), Fundació Antoni Tàpies, Centre de Cultura Contemporània de Barcelona (CCCB) and Fundació Joan Miró – and is valid for six months. You can pick up the ticket at the tourist offices at Plaça de Catalunya, Plaça de Sant Jaume and Estació Sants train station.

Arqueoticket (€13) is for those with a special interest in archaeology and ancient history. The ticket is available from participating museums and tourist offices and grants free admission to the following sites: Museu Marítim, Museu d'Història de Barcelona, Museu d'Arqueologia de Catalunya (MAC) and Museu Egipci.

Barcelona Card (www. barcelonacard.com; 2/3/4/5 days €34/44/52/58) is handy if you want to see lots in a limited time. You get free transport (and 20% off the Aerobús), and discounted admission prices (up to 30% off) or free entry to many museums and other sights, as well as minor discounts on purchases at a small number of shops, restaurants and bars. The card costs about 50% less for children aged four to 12. You can purchase it at tourist offices and online (buying online saves you 10%).

Ruta del Modernisme (www.rutadelmodernisme. com; €12) This pack is well worth looking into for visiting Modernista sights at discounted rates.

●●● Electricity

Spain uses 220V, 50Hz, like the rest of continental Europe.

220V/230V/50Hz

●●● Emergency

The following are the main emergency numbers:

Ambulance (🕿 061)

Catalan police (Mossos d'Esquadra; 🕿 088)

EU standard emergency number (🕿 112)

Fire brigade (Bombers; 🕿 080, 085)

Guardia Civil (Civil Guard; 🕿 062)

Guàrdia Urbana (Local Police; 🕿 092; La Rambla 43; Ⓜ Liceu)

Policía Nacional (National Police; 🕿 091)

Tourist Police (🕿 93 256 24 30; La Rambla 43; ⏱ 24hr; Ⓜ Liceu)

●●● Internet Access

In an increasingly wired city (where many folks have smartphones or web-enabled devices), internet cafes are a disappearing breed. Aside from an internet cafe, look also for *locutorios* (public phone centres), which often double as internet centres.

Bornet (🕿 93 268 15 07; Carrer Barra de Ferro 3; per 15 min/hr €1/2.80; ⏱ 11am-midnight Mon-Thu, to 2.30am Fri-Sun; Ⓜ Jaume I) is a cool little internet centre and art gallery.

Wi-Fi Access

Most hotels, hostels, guesthouses and apartment rentals offer their guests wi-fi access (not always for free). A growing array of city bars and restaurants are latching on to the service – look for the black-and-white wi-fi signs.

The city also has dozens of free public wi-fi hotspots. Look for the small blue signs with the blue 'W' symbol. You can find a complete list of sites here: www.bcn.cat/barcelonawifi/en.

Places in this guide that offer wi-fi have the symbol 🛜.

●●● Medical Services

All foreigners have the same right as Spaniards to emergency medical treatment in public hospitals. EU citizens are entitled to the full range of health-care services in public hospitals, but must present a European Health Insurance Card (enquire at your national health service) and may have to pay upfront.

Non-EU citizens have to pay for anything other than emergency treatment. Most travel-insurance policies include medical cover.

For minor health problems you can try any *farmàcia* (pharmacy); pharmaceuticals tend to be sold more freely without prescription than in places such as the USA, Australia or the UK.

If your country has a consulate in Barcelona, its staff should be able to refer you to doctors who speak your language.

Hospitals include the following:

Hospital Clínic i Provincial (🕿 93 227 54 00; Carrer de Villarroel 170; Ⓜ Hospital Clínic)

Hospital Dos de Maig (🕿 93 507 27 00; Carrer del Dos de Maig 301; Ⓜ Sant Pau–Dos de Maig)

Some 24-hour pharmacies:

Farmàcia Castells Soler (Passeig de Gràcia 90; ⏱ 24hr; Ⓜ Diagonal)

Farmàcia Clapés (La Rambla 98; ⏱ 24hr; Ⓜ Liceu)

Farmàcia Torres (www.farmaciaabierta24h.com; Carrer d'Aribau 62; ⏱ 24hr; Ⓡ FGC Provença)

Money

ATMS

Barcelona abounds with banks, many of which have ATMs. ATMs are also in plentiful supply around Plaça de Catalunya, Plaça de Sant Jaume (in the Barri Gòtic) and La Rambla.

Changing Money

You can change cash or travellers cheques in most major currencies without problems at virtually any bank or *bureau de change* (usually indicated by the word *canvi/cambio*).

The foreign-exchange offices that you see along La Rambla and elsewhere are open for longer hours than banks, but they generally offer poorer rates. Also, keep a sharp eye open for commissions at *bureaux de change*.

Credit Cards

Major cards such as Visa, MasterCard, Maestro and Cirrus are accepted throughout Spain. They can be used in many hotels, restaurants and shops. If your card is lost, stolen or swallowed by an ATM, you can telephone toll free to immediately stop its use:

Amex (☏ 902 375637)

Diners Club (☏ 900 801331)

MasterCard (☏ 900 971231)

Visa (☏ 900 991124)

Travellers Cheques & Moneycards

Travellers cheques are far less convenient than simply using bank cards at ATMs. If you do opt for this old-school option, Amex and Visa are widely accepted brands. For lost cheques, call a **24-hour freephone number** (for Amex ☏ 900 810029, for Visa ☏ 900 948978).

The **Travelex Cash Passport** (www.travelex.com) and **Thomas Cook Travel Moneycard** (www.thomascookmoney.com) are prepaid cards. You can load funds onto them before you travel and use them like any card in ATMs, restaurants or shops worldwide.

Opening Hours

Standard opening hours are as follows:

Restaurants Lunch 1pm to 4pm, dinner 8.30pm to midnight

Shops 9am or 10am to 1.30pm or 2pm and 4pm or 4.30pm to 8pm or 8.30pm Monday to Saturday

Department stores 10am to 10pm Monday to Saturday

Bars 6pm to 2am (closing at 3am on weekends)

Clubs Midnight to 6am Thursday to Saturday

Banks 8.30am to 2pm Monday to Friday; some also

Practicalities

Currency Euro (€)

Smoking Banned in restaurants and bars

Major Barcelona newspapers *La Vanguardia* and *El Periódico* are available in Spanish and Catalan. *El País* publishes an online English supplement (elpais.com/elpais/inenglish.html).

4pm to 7pm Thursday or 9am to 1pm Saturday

Museums & art galleries Opening hours vary considerably, but generally fall between 10am and 8pm (some shut for lunch from around 2pm to 4pm). Many museums and galleries are closed all day on Monday and from 2pm on Sunday.

Public Holidays

New Year's Day (Any Nou/Año Nuevo) 1 January

Epiphany/Three Kings' Day (Epifanía or El Dia dels Reis/Día de los Reyes Magos) 6 January

Good Friday (Divendres Sant/Viernes Santo) March/April

Easter Monday (Dilluns de Pasqua Florida) March/April

Labour Day (Dia del Treball/Fiesta del Trabajo) 1 May

Day after Pentecost Sunday
(Dilluns de Pasqua Granda)
May/June

Feast of St John the Baptist
(Dia de Sant Joan/Día de San Juan Bautista) 24 June

Feast of the Assumption
(L'Assumpció/La Asunción)
15 August

Catalonia's National Day
(Diada Nacional de Catalunya)
11 September

Festes de la Mercè 24 September

Spanish National Day (Festa de la Hispanitat/Día de la Hispanidad) 12 October

All Saints Day (Dia de Tots Sants/Día de Todos los Santos) 1 November

Constitution Day (Día de la Constitución) 6 December

Feast of the Immaculate Conception (La Immaculada Concepció/La Inmaculada Concepción) 8 December

Christmas (Nadal/Navidad)
25 December

Boxing Day/St Stephen's Day (El Dia de Sant Esteve) 26 December

Safe Travel

It cannot be stressed enough that newcomers to Barcelona must be on their guard. Petty theft is a problem in the city centre, on public transport and around main sights. Report thefts to the tourist police (p240) office on La Rambla. You are unlikely to recover your goods but you will need to make this formal *denuncia* (police report) for insurance purposes. To avoid endless queues at the *comisaría* (police station), you can make the report by phone (☎902 102112) in various languages. The following day you go to the station of your choice to pick up and sign the report (for a list of *comisarías*, go to the website www.policia.es under 'Denuncias').

Taxes & Refunds

Value-added tax (VAT) is also known as IVA (*impuesto sobre el valor añadido;* pronounced 'EE-ba'). IVA is 10% on accommodation and restaurant prices and is usually – but not always – included in quoted prices. On most retail goods the IVA is 21%. IVA-free shopping is available in duty-free shops at all airports for people travelling between EU countries.

Non-EU residents are entitled to a refund of the 21% IVA on purchases costing more than €90 from any shop, if the goods are taken out of the EU within three months. Ask the shop for a Cashback (or similar) refund form showing the price and IVA paid for each item and identifying the vendor and purchaser. Then present the form at the customs booth for IVA refunds when you depart from Spain (or elsewhere in the EU). You will need your passport and a boarding card that shows you are leaving the EU, and your luggage (so do this before checking in bags). The officer will stamp the invoice and you hand it in at a bank at the departure point to receive a reimbursement.

Telephones

To call Barcelona from outside Spain, dial the international access code, followed by the code for Spain (☎34) and the full number (including Barcelona's area code, ☎93, which is an integral part of the number). To make an international call, dial the international access code (☎00), country code, area code and number.

Operator Services

International operator for reverse-charge calls ☎1408

International directory enquiries ☎11825

Domestic operator for a domestic reverse-charge call (*llamada por cobro revertido*) ☎1409

National directory inquiries ☎11818

Mobile Phones

Mobile-phone numbers start with ☎6 or ☎7. Numbers starting with ☎900 are national toll-free numbers, while those starting with numbers between ☎901 and ☎905 come with varying conditions. A common one is ☎902, which is a national standard-rate number. In a similar category are numbers starting with ☎803, ☎806 and ☎807.

Spain uses GSM 900/1800, compatible with the rest of Europe and Australia but not with the North American GSM 1900 or the system used in Japan. If your phone is tri- or quadriband, you will probably be fine. You can buy SIM cards and prepaid call time in Spain for your own national mobile phone (provided what you own is a GSM, dual- or tri-band cellular phone and not code-blocked). You will need your passport to open any kind of mobile-phone account, prepaid or otherwise.

Public Telephones

The blue payphones are easy to use for international and domestic calls. They accept coins, *tarjetas telefónicas* (phonecards) issued by the national phone company Telefónica and, in some cases, credit cards. *Tarjetas telefóni-cas* are sold at post offices and tobacconists.

Call centres

A few *locutorios*, which also double as internet centres, are scattered around El Raval (look around Carrer de Sant Pau and Carrer de l'Hospital). Check rates before making calls.

Time

Spain is one hour ahead of GMT/UTC during winter, and two hours ahead during daylight saving (the last Sunday in March to the last Sunday in October). Most other western European countries are on the same time as Spain year-round. The UK, Ireland and

Portugal are one hour behind. Spaniards use the 24-hour clock for official business (timetables etc) but generally switch to the 12-hour version in daily conversation.

Tourist Information

Several tourist offices operate in Barcelona. A couple of general information telephone numbers worth bearing in mind are ☎ 010 and ☎ 012. The first is for Barcelona and the other is for all Catalonia (run by the Generalitat). You sometimes strike English speakers, although for the most part operators are Catalan/Spanish bilingual. In addition to tourist offices, information booths operate at Estació del Nord bus station and at Portal de la Pau, at the foot of the Mirador de Colom at the port end of La Rambla. Others set up at various points in the city centre in summer.

Plaça de Catalunya (☎ 93 285 38 34; www.barcelonaturisme.com; underground at Plaça de Catalunya 17-S; ⏰ 9.30am-9.30pm; Ⓜ Catalunya)

Plaça Sant Jaume (☎ 93 285 38 32; Carrer de la Ciutat 2; ⏰ 8.30am-8.30pm Mon-Fri, 9am-7pm Sat, 9am-2pm Sun & holidays; Ⓜ Jaume I)

Estació Sants (⏰ 8am-8pm; Ⓡ Estació Sants)

El Prat airport (El Prat Airport, Terminal 1 arrivals,

Terminal 2B arrivals hall; ⏰ 8.30am-8.30pm)

La Rambla Information Booth (www.barcelonaturisme.com; La Rambla dels Estudis 115; ⏰ 8.30am-8.30pm; Ⓜ Liceu)

Palau Robert Regional Tourist Office (☎ 93 238 80 91, from outside Catalonia 902 400012; www.gencat.net/probert; Passeig de Gràcia 107; ⏰ 10am-8pm Mon-Sat, to 2.30pm Sun; Ⓜ Diagonal) A host of material on Catalonia, audiovisual resources, a bookshop and a branch of Turisme Juvenil de Catalunya (for youth travel).

Travellers with Disabilities

Some hotels and public institutions have wheelchair access. All buses in Barcelona are wheelchair accessible and a growing number of metro stations are theoretically wheelchair accessible (generally by lift, although there have been complaints that they are only any good for parents with prams). Lines 2, 9, 10 and 11 are completely adapted, as are the majority of stops on Line 1. In all, about 80% of stops have been adapted (you can check which ones by looking at a network map here: www.tmb.cat/en/transport-accessible). Ticket vending machines in metro stations are adapted for the disabled and have Braille options for the blind.

Several taxi companies have adapted vehicles including Taxi Amic (p236)

and **Gestverd** (📞 93 303 09 09).

Most street crossings in central Barcelona are wheelchair-friendly.

For more information on what the city is doing to improve accessibility check out the council's *Accessible Barcelona Guide* in several languages (www.barcelona-access.com). Other services include the following:

Barcelona Turisme (www.barcelonaturisme.com) Barcelona's official tourism organisation maintains a website devoted to making the city accessible to visitors with a disability (www.barcelona-access.com).

ONCE (📞 93 325 92 00; Carrer de Sepúlveda 1; Ⓜ Plaça d'Espanya) The national organisation for the vision-impaired can help with information, including lists of places such as restaurants where Braille menus are provided.

Visas

Spain is one of 25 member countries of the Schengen Convention, under which 22 EU countries (all but Bulgaria, Cyprus, Ireland, Romania and the UK) plus Iceland, Norway and Switzerland have abolished checks at common borders.

EU nationals require only their ID cards to visit Spain. Nationals of many other countries, including Australia, Canada, Israel, Japan, New Zealand and the USA, do not require visas for tourist visits to Spain of up to 90 days. Non-EU nationals who are legal residents of one Schengen country do not require a visa to visit another Schengen country.

All non-EU nationals entering Spain for any reason other than tourism (such as study or work) should contact a Spanish consulate, as they may need a specific visa and will have to obtain work and/ or residence permits. Citizens of countries not mentioned above should check with their Spanish consulate whether they need a visa.

Women Travellers

Think twice about going by yourself to isolated stretches of beach or down empty city streets at night. It's inadvisable for women to hitchhike, either alone or in pairs.

Topless bathing is OK on beaches in Catalonia and also at swimming pools. While skimpy clothing tends not to attract much attention in Barcelona and the coastal resorts, tastes in inland Catalonia tend to be somewhat conservative.

Ca la Dona (📞 93 412 71 61; www.caladona.org; Carrer de Ripoll 25; Ⓜ Urquinaona) The nerve centre of the region's feminist movement, Ca la Dona (Women's Home) includes many diverse women's groups.

Centre Francesca Bonnemaison (📞 93 268 42 18; www.labonne.org; Carrer de Sant Pere més Baix 7; Ⓜ Urquinaona) A women's cultural centre where groups put on expositions, stage theatre productions and carry out other cultural activities.

Institut Català de les Dones (📞 93 495 16 00; www.gencat.net/icdona; Plaça de Pere Coromines 1; Ⓜ Liceu) It can point you in the right direction for information on marriage, divorce, rape/assault counselling and related issues. The 24-hour hotline for victims of assault is 📞 900 900120.

Language

Catalan and Spanish both have official-language status in Catalonia. In Barcelona, you'll hear as much Spanish as Catalan, so we've provided some Spanish to get you started. Spanish pronunciation is not difficult as most of its sounds are also found in English. You can read our pronunciation guides below as if they were English and you'll be understood just fine. And if you pronounce 'th' in our guides with a lisp and 'kh' as a throaty sound, you'll even sound like a real Spanish person.

To enhance your trip with a phrasebook, visit **lonelyplanet.com**. Lonely Planet iPhone phrasebooks are available through the Apple App store.

BASICS

Hello.
Hola.   *o·*la

How are you?
¿Qué tal?   ke tal

I'm fine, thanks.
Bien, gracias.   byen *gra·*thyas

Excuse me. (to get attention)
Disculpe.   dees·*kool·*pe

Yes./No.
Sí./No.   see/no

Thank you.
Gracias.   *gra·*thyas

You're welcome./That's fine.
De nada.   de *na·*da

Goodbye. /See you later.
Adiós./Hasta luego.   a·*dyos/as·*ta *lwe·*go

Do you speak English?
¿Habla inglés?   a·bla een·*gles*

I don't understand.
No entiendo.   no en·*tyen·*do

How much is this?
¿Cuánto cuesta?   *kwan·*to *kwes·*ta

Can you reduce the price a little?
¿Podría bajar un   po·*dree·*a ba·*khar* oon
poco el precio?   *po·*ko el *pre·*thyo

ACCOMMODATION

I'd like to make a booking.
Quisiera reservar   kee·*sye·*ra re·ser·*var*
una habitación.   *oo·*na a·bee·ta·*thyon*

How much is it per night?
¿Cuánto cuesta por noche?   *kwan·*to *kwes·*ta por *no·*che

EATING & DRINKING

I'd like ..., please.
Quisiera ..., por favor.   kee·*sye·*ra ... por fa·*vor*

That was delicious!
¡Estaba buenísimo!   es·*ta·*ba bwe·*nee·*see·mo

Bring the bill/check, please.
La cuenta, por favor.   la *kwen·*ta por fa·*vor*

I'm allergic to ...
Soy alérgico/a al ... (m/f)   soy a·*ler·*khee·ko/a al ...

I don't eat ...
No como ...   no *ko·*mo ...

chicken	pollo	*po·*lyo
fish	pescado	pes·*ka·*do
meat	carne	*kar·*ne

EMERGENCIES

I'm ill.
Estoy enfermo/a. (m/f)   es·*toy* en·*fer·*mo/a

Help!
¡Socorro!   so·*ko·*ro

Call a doctor!
¡Llame a un médico!   *lya·*me a oon *me·*dee·ko

Call the police!
¡Llame a la policía!   *lya·*me a la po·lee·*thee·*a

DIRECTIONS

I'm looking for a/an/the ...
Estoy buscando ...   es·*toy* boos·*kan·*do ...

ATM
un cajero   oon ka·*khe·*ro
automático   ow·to·*ma·*tee·ko

bank
el banco   el *ban·*ko

... embassy
la embajada de ...   la em·ba·*kha·*da de ...

market
el mercado   el mer·*ka·*do

museum
el museo   el moo·*se·*o

restaurant
un restaurante   oon res·tow·*ran·*te

toilet
los servicios   los ser·*vee·*thyos

tourist office
la oficina de   la o·fee·*thee·*na de
turismo   too·*rees·*mo

Behind the Scenes

Author Thanks

Regis St Louis

I'm grateful to the many friends and acquaintances who provided guidance and tips along the way. Biggest thanks go to co-author Sal Davies for her hard work, Manel Casanovas for gourmet insight at Barcelona Turisme, Sol Polo and friends, Margherita Bergamo, Carine Ferry, Gonzalo Salaya, Anna Aurich, Núria Rocamora, Manel Baena, Malén Gual and Bernardo Laniado-Romero. Thanks also to Alan Waterman for making the trip down from London. Finally big hugs to my family for all their support.

Acknowledgments

Climate map data adapted from Peel MC, Finlayson BL & McMahon TA (2007) 'Updated World Map of the Köppen-Geiger Climate Classification', Hydrology and Earth System Sciences, 11, 1633¬44.

Illustration pp132-3 by Javier Zarracina.

Cover photographs: Front: Park Güell, Sylvain Sonnet/Corbis ©; Back: Font Màgica, Montjuïc, David Noton/Alamy ©

This Book

This 3rd edition of Lonely Planet's *Discover Barcelona* guidebook was coordinated by Regis St Louis, and researched and written by Regis St Louis, Sally Davies and Andy Symington. The previous two editions were written by Anna Kaminski, Vesna Maric, Brendan Sainsbury, Damien Simonis and Regis St Louis. This guidebook was commissioned in Lonely Planet's London office, and produced by the following:

Commissioning Editor Dora Whitaker
Destination Editor Jo Cooke
Product Editor Luna Soo
Senior Cartographers David Kemp, Anthony Phelan
Book Designer Wendy Wright
Assisting Editors Penny Cordner, Kate Mathews
Assisting Book Designer Virginia Moreno
Assisting Cartographer Julie Sheridan
Cover Researcher Naomi Parker
Thanks to Sasha Baskett, Elin Berglund, Ryan Evans, Samantha Forge, Larissa Frost, Jouve India, Kate James, Helle Overbeck, Martine Power, Wibowo Rusli, Samantha Russell-Tulip

SEND US YOUR FEEDBACK

We love to hear from travellers – your comments keep us on our toes and help make our books better. Our well-travelled team reads every word on what you loved or loathed about this book. Although we cannot reply individually to postal submissions, we always guarantee that your feedback goes straight to the appropriate authors, in time for the next edition. Each person who sends us information is thanked in the next edition, the most useful submissions are rewarded with a selection of digital PDF chapters.

Visit **lonelyplanet.com/contact** to submit your updates and suggestions or to ask for help. Our award-winning website also features inspirational travel stories, news and discussions.

Note: We may edit, reproduce and incorporate your comments in Lonely Planet products such as guidebooks, websites and digital products, so let us know if you don't want your comments reproduced or your name acknowledged. For a copy of our privacy policy visit lonelyplanet.com/privacy.

Index

See also separate subindexes for:

 Eating p251

 Drinking & Nightlife p252

 Entertainment p253

 Shopping p253

Sports & Activities p254

Sights 000
Map pages 000

Sights 000
Map pages 000

N

O

P

Sights 000
Map pages 000

Sights 000
Map pages 000

🏃 Sports & Activities

Sights 000
Map pages 000

How to Use This Book

These symbols will help you find the listings you want:

⊙ Sights
🌟 Entertainment
❌ Eating
🅰 Shopping
🍷 Drinking & Nightlife
➕ Sports & Activities

Look out for these icons:

FREE No payment required

 A green or sustainable option

Our authors have nominated these places as demonstrating a strong commitment to sustainability – for example by supporting local communities and producers, operating in an environmentally friendly way, or supporting conservation projects.

These symbols give you the vital information for each listing:

☑ Telephone Numbers	☏ Wi-Fi Access	🚌 Bus
☺ Opening Hours	☒ Swimming Pool	Ferry
Ⓟ Parking	☑ Vegetarian Selection	Ⓜ Metro
⊝ Nonsmoking	⓪ English-Language Menu	Ⓢ Subway
✳ Air-Conditioning	⊞ Family-Friendly	Tram
@ Internet Access	☸ Pet-Friendly	Train

Reviews are organised by author preference.

Map Legend

Note: Not all symbols displayed appear on the maps in this book

Sights
- 🏖 Beach
- 🐦 Bird Sanctuary
- Buddhist
- 🏰 Castle/Palace
- ✝ Christian
- Confucian
- Hindu
- ☪ Islamic
- Jain
- ✡ Jewish
- Monument
- 🏛 Museum/Gallery/Historic Building
- Ruin
- Sento Hot Baths/Onsen
- Shinto
- Sikh
- Taoist
- Winery/Vineyard
- Zoo/Wildlife Sanctuary
- ⊙ Other Sight

Activities, Courses & Tours
- Bodysurfing
- Diving
- Canoeing/Kayaking
- Course/Tour
- Skiing
- Snorkelling
- Surfing
- Swimming/Pool
- Walking
- Windsurfing
- Other Activity

Sleeping
- Sleeping
- Camping

Eating
- ❌ Eating

Drinking & Nightlife
- Drinking & Nightlife
- Cafe

Entertainment
- 🌟 Entertainment

Shopping
- 🅰 Shopping

Transport
- Airport
- Border crossing
- Bus
- Cable car/Funicular
- Cycling
- Ferry
- Metro station
- Monorail
- Ⓟ Parking
- Petrol station
- S-Bahn/Subway station
- Taxi
- T-bane/Tunnelbana station
- Train station/Railway
- Tram
- Tube station
- U-Bahn station
- Other Transport

Information
- Bank
- Embassy/Consulate
- Hospital/Medical
- @ Internet
- Police
- Post Office
- Telephone
- Toilet
- Tourist Information
- Other Information

Geographic
- Beach
- Lighthouse
- Lookout
- ▲ Mountain/Volcano
- Oasis
- Park
-)(Pass
- Picnic Area
- Waterfall

Population
- Capital (National)
- ◉ Capital (State/Province)
- City/Large Town
- Town/Village

Boundaries
- International
- State/Province
- Disputed
- Regional/Suburb
- Marine Park
- Cliff; Wall

Routes
- Tollway
- Freeway
- Primary
- Secondary
- Tertiary
- Lane
- Unsealed road
- Plaza/Mall
- Steps
- Tunnel
- Pedestrian overpass
- Walking Tour
- Walking Tour detour
- Path/Walking Trail

Hydrography
- River, Creek
- Intermittent River
- Canal
- Water
- Dry/Salt Lake
- Reef

Areas
- Airport/Runway
- Beach/Desert
- Cemetery (Christian)
- Cemetery (Other)
- Glacier
- Mudflat
- Park/Forest
- Sight (Building)
- Sportsground
- Swamp

Our Story

A beat-up old car, a few dollars in the pocket and a sense of adventure. In 1972 that's all Tony and Maureen Wheeler needed for the trip of a lifetime – across Europe and Asia overland to Australia. It took several months, and at the end – broke but inspired – they sat at their kitchen table writing and stapling together their first travel guide, *Across Asia on the Cheap*. Within a week they'd sold 1500 copies. Lonely Planet was born.

Today, Lonely Planet has offices in Melbourne, London and Oakland, with more than 600 staff and writers. We share Tony's belief that 'a great guidebook should do three things: inform, educate and amuse'.

Our Writers

Regis St Louis

Coordinating Author, La Rambla & Barri Gòtic, Barceloneta & the Waterfront, Camp Nou & La Zona Alta Regis first fell in love with Barcelona and Catalonia on a grand journey across Iberia in the late 1990s. Since then he has returned frequently, learning Spanish and a smattering of Catalan, and delving into the rich cultural history of this endlessly fascinating city. Favourite memories from his most recent trip include earning a few scars at a wild *correfoc* in Gràcia, watching brave *castellers* build human towers at the Santa Eulàlia fest and feasting on *navallas* (razor clams), *pop á feira* (Galician-style octopus) and *carxofes* (artichokes) all across town. Regis is also the author of Lonely Planet's *Barcelona* guidebook, and he has contributed to *Spain*, *Portugal* and dozens of other Lonely Planet titles. He lives in Brooklyn, New York.

Sally Davies

El Raval; La Ribera; La Sagrada Família & L'Eixample; Gràcia; Park Güell; Montjuïc, Poble Sec & Sant Antoni Sally landed in Seville in 1992 with a handful of *pesetas* and five words of Spanish and, despite a complete inability to communicate, promptly snared a lucrative number handing out leaflets at Expo '92. In 2001 she settled in Barcelona, where she is still incredulous that her daily grind involves researching fine restaurants, wandering around museums and finding ways to convey the beauty of this spectacular city. Sally also wrote the Shopping chapter and cowrote the Sleeping section.

Andy Symington

Day Trips Andy hails from Australia but has been living in Spain for over a decade where, to shatter a couple of stereotypes of the country, he can frequently be found huddled in subzero temperatures watching the tragically poor local football team. He has authored and coauthored many Lonely Planet guidebooks and other publications on Spain and elsewhere; in his spare time he walks in the mountains, embarks on epic tapas trails, and co-bosses a rock bar.

Published by Lonely Plane
ABN 36 005 607 983
3rd edition – January 2015
ISBN 978 1 74321 404 6
© Lonely Planet 2015   Photographs
10 9 8 7 6 5 4 3
Printed in China

and Lonely Planet have taken all reason-
g this book, we make no warranty about
pleteness of its content and, to the maxi-
ed, disclaim all liability arising from its use.